PERSONAL BRANDING FOR ENTREPRENEURIAL JOURNALISTS AND CREATIVE PROFESSIONALS

Personal Branding for Entrepreneurial Journalists and Creative Professionals outlines and describes the complete process of building and growing a successful personal brand. Focused on the independent journalist or creative professional in the new digital marketplace, Sara Kelly gives readers the ability to create the sort of personal brand that not only stands out, but remains relevant for years to come. Features such as exercises and worksheets will guide readers in creating the various components of their personal brand, and case studies of real-world branding scenarios will allow readers to analyze the practical aspects of implementing a personal brand. Covering theory and practice, this text is a powerful resource for modern journalists, multimedia storytellers, and content creators hoping to ply their talents online and beyond.

Sara Kelly, EdD, is chair of the Department of Journalism, Film and Entertainment Arts at National University in San Diego, where she serves as lead faculty for the BA in Digital Journalism. Kelly also holds an MBA and an MFA. While at NU, she has helmed programs in journalism and strategic communications, as well as the integrated marketing communication specialization of the MBA. Previously, Kelly served as the long-time executive editor of the *Philadelphia Weekly* and the editor of *In Pittsburgh Newsweekly*. Her professional publications include *Salon*, *Mother Jones*, the *New York Times Book Review*, *Men's Health*, *Town and Country*, and *Utne Reader*.

PERSONAL BRANDING FOR ENTREPRENEURIAL JOURNALISTS AND CREATIVE PROFESSIONALS

Sara Kelly

Routledge
Taylor & Francis Group

NEW YORK AND LONDON

First published 2017
by Routledge
711 Third Avenue, New York, NY 10017

and by Routledge
2 Park Square, Milton Park, Abingdon, Oxon, OX14 4RN

Routledge is an imprint of the Taylor & Francis Group, an informa business

© 2017 Taylor & Francis

Library of Congress Cataloging-in-Publication Data
A catalog record for this book has been requested

ISBN: 9781138218468 (hbk)
ISBN: 9781138218475 (pbk)
ISBN: 9781315437576 (ebk)

Typeset in Bembo
by Apex CoVantage, LLC

CONTENTS

PREFACE

Most of us would agree the Internet has affected our lives in largely positive ways, bringing us together as a global society and making our lives easier. The Internet has also opened countless doors and broken down barriers to access, allowing regular people to connect and share ideas with others around the world. For journalists and other creatives, the Internet has fundamentally changed the way work is done. Now that everyone with a computer or a mobile device and high-speed Internet access can publish and promote themselves online, journalists and creatives must find new ways to stand out in an increasingly crowded global marketplace. Personal branding is a must.

We live in an on-demand culture. We watch movies and TV shows when we want to and on any number of devices. We find dates and jobs, buy and sell, and monitor our messages, homes, and finances around the clock using apps on our mobile devices. And many of us now, whether we work for ourselves or others, must produce and deliver goods, services, and content of all kinds exactly when and how our customers, clients, and employers would like them. This requires us to be extremely flexible and responsive to others' needs, but it also requires us to anticipate and prepare for future demands. This is challenging enough, but it isn't even the hard part. For most of us who serve others in an increasingly on-demand world, the biggest challenge lies in identifying and reaching our core audiences with relevant messages that are different from the countless other messages they are bombarded with every day. This is what personal branding is all about.

Branding is about differentiation, defining what makes you and your business unique, and building a community of loyal followers based on your particular story and ability to provide relevant, useful information, items, or services. The good news is that as a creative, you are likely quite accustomed to doing your own thing and telling your own story. You probably already have a personal brand that works for you. That's great, but it doesn't mean your work is over. In fact, it's only just begun.

Much of this book is dedicated to strategies for promoting your personal brand in the most efficient way possible. That means maximizing the impact and reach of your branding campaigns so that you can spend less time trying to reach and engage clients and customers, and more time doing your creative work. This requires an entrepreneurial mindset, some basic business skills, and a strong understanding of yourself and the stories that lie at the heart of what you do.

Creativity and branding are terms not often paired. For many in the creative fields, branding is a business term, and many creatives made career and life choices in part to avoid what they consider business. But the truth of the matter is that today's economy—particularly in the creative fields—is becoming increasingly entrepreneurial, and entrepreneurship is business. For many creatives, including journalists, being an entrepreneur is preferable to working for someone else. But being a successful entrepreneur requires some business knowledge. You don't have to go to work on Wall Street. You don't even need to wear a suit. But you do need to know how to represent yourself and what you do, expand your reach, and work on building your community every day.

Regardless of whether you have a well-developed brand or hadn't thought about branding before you picked up this book, the following chapters will provide you with all you need to know to establish your personal brand, and introduce you to tools and strategies that, through ongoing practice and refinement, will help you develop your personal brand into an enterprise that will support your creative endeavors for years to come.

In much the same way the Internet has made our lives easier, a strong personal brand and a flexible, responsive strategy for promoting it will make your creative life easier. Consider the concepts, tools, and tips in this book a starting point. Not everything you read here will apply to your particular business or brand, but the main concepts should. Whenever possible, try to apply examples from another field or occupation to your own. For example, Chapter 7 includes a Q&A with Realtor Steve Matsumoto. Real estate sales may not seem to fit the definition of a creative field. But when you read Steve's interview, you'll see that he utilizes many of the same personal branding strategies those in more obviously creative fields employ. He publishes a regular newsletter for his clients and community that includes stories about his family. He shares videos he produces with his children. This is all part of his campaign to build trust and loyalty across the community of followers and fans he has built. You are likely engaged in similar kinds of storytelling efforts to promote your own brand across social media and other channels.

Creative people can bring creativity to any job. Regardless of whether you're a journalist, a visual artist, a filmmaker, a teacher, a real estate agent, or anything else, building your personal brand will allow you to do exactly the kind of work you want to for as long as you want, without worrying about how technology or changes to the global employment marketplace might impact your ability to survive. There has never been a better time to blaze your own career path. Prepare yourself well, never stop learning, and the future is yours.

1

THE CHANGING EMPLOYMENT MARKETPLACE

In the first years of the 21st century, after the dot-com boom and bust and then the terror attacks of 2001, journalists, thinkers, and economists were hard at work trying to determine how the economic exuberance of the 1990s had so quickly devolved into the economic insecurities of the aughts. In truth, the economic slump that became so widely apparent in late 2001 had been years in the making. A general rule with economic trends is that by the time you notice them, it is too late to do much about them. They are already in full force.

Although the Internet was in common use by the turn of the 21st century, its full impact was yet to be felt. Even the best economic minds at the time could not fully grasp the effects this new technology would have on global economic markets. In fact, we do not yet know the extent to which the Internet will ultimately change human life.

Despite their inability to predict the future with complete accuracy, *The Rise of the Creative Class* (2002) author Richard Florida and *The World Is Flat* (2005) author Thomas Friedman, among others, did understand that the Internet's effects, whatever shape they would ultimately take, would be significant. The Internet would globalize—or flatten—the world, and an infinitely connected and accessible world would bring new importance to the geographic locations where people lived and work was done.

Friedman focused on economic factors such as outsourcing, offshoring, and insourcing. He explored how new possibilities in these areas would, through the natural forces of capitalism, create class divisions among workers as work that could now be done anywhere, thanks to the Internet, would move to wherever it could be done most inexpensively and efficiently. Aside from service workers such as nurses, home health care aides, restaurant servers, gardeners, farmers, and laborers, all of whom needed to be in a particular physical location to do their

FIGURE 1.1 The "gig economy" supports increasing numbers of freelance workers.
Credit: Shutterstock ID #331645418

jobs, employment would become increasingly virtual, more work would be done outside of offices, and geographic location would gain new significance. Florida examined the issue through a cultural lens, focusing not on how widespread Internet use would change where work was done, but rather, how the mobility of labor markets would heighten the importance of geography—particularly cities.

Although we will not embark on a complete economic analysis here, both authors, from their own quite different perspectives at the time, described the early days of a massive global economic shift that continues to this day, and pondered its future consequences. Although both books are now old, looking back at them can help us to better understand current conditions and remember where all of this started.

It is a gross oversimplification to suggest that the Internet transformed the world economy. Of course there are multiple other significant factors that have helped shape the current economy and labor markets. Yet Friedman's and Florida's ideas endure. Both researchers, from their different perspectives, understood technology's power to transform economies and cultures. And both rang the alarm over global trends they thought could bring economic and social devastation. Some of their predictions have since manifested in ways that could not have been anticipated even 10 years ago.

No one could have predicted how far the "gig economy" would have come by 2016, when the term "uberization" (a reference to Uber, the technology company that manages an elaborate network of freelance cabbies while owning no cars and employing no drivers) was applied to everything from higher education and banking to healthcare and trucking. In a late 2015 report from the Brookings Institution nonpartisan think tank, Jerry Davis, a professor at the University of Michigan's Ross School of Business, argued that "the death of the career and the rise of the gig economy are directly connected to changes in the shape of the American corporation."[1]

The proliferation of the Internet and the accelerated globalization it has brought has dramatically increased the flexibility of world markets and employment marketplaces. It has expedited an existing move toward freelance work, an arrangement that brings increasing numbers of independent contractors more freedom and flexibility while depriving them of the benefits in-house workers often receive—not just health insurance and pensions (or 401(k)s), but also a sense of community and loyalty to the corporate or work family.

That more work can now be done remotely, virtually, and flexibly, in distributed locations at every hour of the day, has certainly increased business efficiency, allowing companies to operate more nimbly, more quickly, and with lower overhead costs and a decreased commitment to employees. These changes have allowed companies like Airbnb (which connects property owners to guests willing to pay to stay in those properties for one or more nights) and Uber to flourish.

Employees are expensive, healthcare and insurance costs are always rising, and organizations—including many in the media and creative industries, and across higher education—are increasingly turning to independent contractors to do the same work once done by traditional full-time employees. Historically, these workers, who were often well compensated by companies that were actually invested in their welfare, even when they were not at work, enjoyed a sense of community and an attachment to both their fellow employees and the company itself. You may recall stories of longtime employees receiving gold watches at their retirement, along with generous pensions that would sustain them for the rest of their living years. Those stories are rare today.

Younger workers and workers new to the employment marketplace may not recall the era of company loyalties and corporate community. You yourself may have spent all of your working life in the era of the gig economy. Yet freelance, casual, or gig workers, as they age, and more advanced workers who remember the old days will notice that the shift to contract work requires a different and more diverse skill set than they may have once needed.

Regardless of how you may feel about it, the reality is that the entire global economy is moving toward a casual workforce, or flexible, temporary, or part-time workers who adjust their hours to accommodate employers' needs, and who receive no benefits or health insurance, and must pay their own taxes and expenses. There is a good chance this describes you.

The morality or appropriateness of this arrangement is something best left to our political leaders to sort out. Your job is to make the most of the current employment marketplace, and to find ways to work within it. Of course there are many attractive aspects to contingent or casual work. Among the better-known perks of the new employment paradigm are flexible schedules and the ability to work from home.

While office work fosters a sense of community those who work from home sometimes miss, few workers complain about being able to stay home and spend more time with family and friends. Compared to traditional nine-to-five desk jobs, flexible work has real appeal. The arrangement can improve work-life balance; however, it can also lead to isolation or even longer work hours, as work life bleeds into home life in ways not possible when both lives were physically separate.

Like it or not, we are living in a gig economy. With decreasing support from governments, industries, and employers (as even large legacy corporations downsize their full-time workforces to become more nimble and efficient), we are increasingly on our own to create, build, and maintain our own careers. Even those who work traditional jobs for established companies no longer enjoy the guarantees their predecessors might have taken for granted. None of us can afford to assume that a good job will sustain us until retirement. Many, both creatives and those employed in more easily defined industries and positions, now find themselves having to think about things they may have never given much thought to before, and in ways they may have never previously imagined. Essentially, they have had to think like businesspeople, marketing, shaping, and selling their skills and themselves just to maintain a distinct identity in an increasingly crowded field. It is a challenge for most, and personal branding lies at its heart.

Whether you work in a traditional environment or you are carving out an independent career for yourself, you need to conceive, develop, and grow your personal brand. This alone can seem like a full-time job if you are not organized and strategic about it. That is why this book exists.

A Glance at the Official Picture

In the United States, the Bureau of Labor Statistics (BLS) tracks employment trends by occupation, employment sector, geography, and other characteristics. BLS statistics are robust, offering in-depth insights into all aspects of the job market, identifying trends, and providing a big-picture view of the economy. However, BLS data does not account for entrepreneurial and freelance activity. That is largely because, although the trend is toward freelance and entrepreneurial work, most of the workers the government knows about are employed by companies and other people.

BLS data do track some creative jobs and industries you may want to learn more about. After all, most people preparing to graduate from college and begin

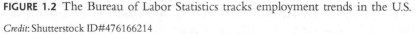

FIGURE 1.2 The Bureau of Labor Statistics tracks employment trends in the U.S.
Credit: Shutterstock ID#476166214

new careers still plan to take jobs rather than launching an entrepreneurial venture right away. Yet it is important to keep in mind that entrepreneurship, or working for yourself, is a viable and growing possibility—if not now, then perhaps in a later phase of your career. Most of us know of entrepreneurs who have done pretty well for themselves. (Perhaps you've heard of Bill Gates or Sir Richard Branson? More on them later.)

The vast majority of entrepreneurs work incredibly hard—usually more hours than those who labor in traditional offices—and lacking the safety net that an employer provides, the work often never really ends. An entrepreneur is on the clock around the clock. That said, many believe the tradeoffs are well worth the extra work. How often do you hear people complain about their jobs or their employers? You've probably done this yourself. By contrast, how often have you heard people declare a desire to work for themselves or to be their own boss?

Case rested.

According the BLS, the fastest growing occupations through 2024 are in the service sector. These are jobs that, by and large, cannot be outsourced to other countries. The list includes no inherently creative or entrepreneurial occupations; however, many positions that may have once been firm-based (such as consulting and sales positions) can now be done independently.

The BLS does track the growth of some creative professions. Following are highlights of a few. Keep in mind that the numbers don't tell the whole story.

The Bureau of Labor Statistics tracks employment numbers as they relate to the U.S. economy. That means jobs as the government defines them. The listings that follow undercount jobs that are not easily tracked by the government because they do not fit into the BLS description or because they have changed, fragmenting, recombining, or merging with parts of other jobs.

Many of the occupations the BLS tracks in the fast-changing areas of media and communication are disappearing, painting a misleadingly negative picture of the occupation group. Further, many of the occupations we focus on throughout this book are too new or diffuse to yet be reflected in BLS data. That's good news for you, showing that the traditional labor market still offers plenty of opportunities. The occupations listed on the following pages may provide you with options or ideas as you consider or work to build an entrepreneurial career.

Bureau of Labor Statistics Employment Projections

Occupation Group: Art and Design

Although in-house art and design jobs are expected to grow more slowly than the job market overall, expect more freelance and contract-based opportunities in this area. According to the BLS, the biggest projected growth in this group will be due to increasing demand for animation and visual effects in video games, movies, television, and smartphones. "As companies continue to increase their

FIGURE 1.3 Many artists and designers are self-employed.

Credit: Shutterstock ID#168161747

digital presence, more art and design workers will be needed to help create visually appealing and effective layouts of websites and other media platforms."[2]

Art Directors

BLS job description: Responsible for the visual style and images in magazines, newspapers, product packaging, and movie and television productions. They create the overall design of a project and direct others who develop artwork and layouts.
Job growth through 2024: 2% (slower than average)
Median pay: $89,760 yearly
Self-employed: around 50%

Craft and Fine Artists

BLS job description: Use a variety of materials and techniques for sale and exhibition. Craft artists create handmade objects such as pottery, glassware, textiles, and other objects designed to be functional. Fine artists, including painters, sculptors and illustrators, create original works of art for their aesthetic value, rather than for a functional one.
Job growth through 2024: 2% (slower than average)
Median pay: $45,080 yearly
Self-employed: around 50%

Graphic Designers

BLS job description: Create visual concepts, using computer software or by hand, to communicate ideas that inspire, inform, and captivate consumers. They develop the overall layout and production design for various applications such as advertisements, brochures, magazines, and corporate reports.
Job growth through 2024: 1% (little or no change)
Median pay: $46,900 yearly
Self-employed: around 20% in 2014

Industrial Designers

BLS job description: Develop the concepts for manufactured products such as cars, home appliances, and toys. They combine art, business, and engineering to make products that people use every day. Industrial designers consider the function, aesthetics, production costs, and usability of products when developing new product concepts.
Job growth through 2024: 2% (slower than average)

Median pay: $67,130 yearly
Self-employed: None known. These tend to be office jobs. Watch for some of these positions to move outside the company to freelance or consultant status.

Multimedia Artists and Animators

BLS job description: Create animation and visual effects for television, movies, video games, and other forms of media.
Job growth through 2024: 6% (as fast as average)
Median pay: $63,970 yearly
Self-employed: more than 50%

Occupation Group: Media and Communication

This occupation group is projected to grow more quickly than the art and design group (4% compared to 2%), and its average incomes are higher. While median average wage for art and design professionals in the United States in 2015 was $43,950, the median for media and communication professionals was $53,530.

Editors

BLS job description: Plan, review, and revise content for publication.
Job growth through 2024: -5% (decline)
Median pay: $56,010 yearly

FIGURE 1.4 Journalists now need several skill sets.
Credit: Shutterstock ID#287665082

Self-employed: Unknown, although the BLS notes that editors increasingly work from home (and these positions may not be reflected in the official numbers).

Photographers

BLS job description: Use their technical expertise, creativity, and composition skills to produce and preserve images that tell a story or record an event.
Job growth through 2024: 3% (slower than average)
Median pay: $31,710 yearly
Self-employed: Not stated.

Public Relations Specialists

BLS job description: Create and maintain favorable public image for the organization they represent. They design media releases to shape public perception of their organization and to increase awareness of its work and goals.
Job growth through 2024: 6% (as fast as average)
Median pay: $56,770 yearly
Self-employed: Traditionally, public relations has been an in-house position. Increasingly, as the field changes and embraces new media, work is done on a freelance or consultancy basis.

Reporters, Correspondents, and Broadcast News Analysts

BLS job description: Inform the public about news and events happening internationally, nationally, and locally. They report the news for newspapers, magazines, websites, television, and radio.
Job growth through 2024: -9% (decline)
Median pay: $37,720 yearly
Self-employed: Unknown, but increasing as these roles change to embrace new technology.

Technical Writers

BLS job description: Prepare instruction manuals, how-to guides, journal articles, and other supporting documents to communicate complex and technical information more easily. They also develop, gather, and disseminate technical information through an organization's communication channels.
Job growth through 2024: 10% (faster than average)
Median pay: $70,240 yearly
Self-employed: According to the BLS, "most technical writers work full-time in offices,"[3] yet that is changing with media and technology. It is likely that this occupation will move out of offices and become more freelance and consultancy based in the years to come.

Writers and Authors

BLS job description: Develop written content for advertisements, books, magazines, movie and television scripts, songs, blogs, or other types of media.
Job growth through 2024: 2% (slower than average)
Median pay: $60,250 yearly
Self-employed: Most writers and authors are self-employed.

Social Media Career Paths

Now that we have explored the official status of the creative fields, an obvious next step is to consider the kind of business or career path one might pursue entrepreneurially. These can range from basic entrepreneurial journalism to more traditional businesses. The reality is there are limitless career pathways and ways of running a creative business. We now consider a few that are closely tied to media.

Because many of these job descriptions are fairly new, and some terms are used interchangeably, it is important to keep in mind that none of the following are intended to be limited, and there is much overlap among them.

FIGURE 1.5 Entrepreneurs must often be their own social media managers.
Credit: Shutterstock ID#411450487

Social Media Manager

A social media manager may work for a specific employer or may be a free agent with multiple clients. Either way, people who occupy this position ensure that whoever they work for is as well represented as possible across social media. That could translate to a number of duties, from creating original content to managing social media posts that people make about the company or client. As social media grows less exotic in the workplace and new workers who are more comfortable with technology begin to replace older workers who are not digital natives, the position is quickly becoming demystified.

In the first decade of widespread social media use, older workers and entire companies often dismissed social media—or tried to—at their own peril. Now management at most every company understands that social media cannot be ignored. Even if the company itself chose to forgo a social media presence (which is generally a bad idea), if any fraction of its customers use social media, the company must use it too. However, as social media becomes a reality in almost every aspect of our lives, the role of the social media manager becomes more diffuse.

According to *Forbes*, social media manager "isn't even a job at all anymore." Arguably, social media is now every employee's job. Amy Crow of the job search site Indeed, told *Forbes*, "We are seeing an increased demand in social savvy candidates across the business—from human resources to product to customer service. In addition, we're seeing this demand span many levels, from executive assistants to senior vice presidents."[4]

Forbes identified essential skills for social media managers in 2015. That list has since grown. The essentials, in 2015, included graphics production, writing skills, a customer service orientation, SEO skills, and an understanding of advertising on social media.[5]

This was a tall order in 2015, and the job has become only more challenging since then, now including basic video production skills. The good news is that over time, the more technical skills (including graphic design, photography, basic photo manipulation, search engine optimization, and now video production) have become more commonplace as most active social media users become accustomed to them. Not too many years ago, simply posting attractive images on Instagram may have seemed challenging to a large share of users. Now Instagram users are used to seeing video posts, and can easily post their own video directly from their smartphones.

Automation is another reason why the social media manager role is changing. There are now several robust Web-based tools available to those who would like to save time and money by automating content across social media and on websites. (Read more about them in Chapter 8.) Despite this game-changing fact, it is important to keep in mind that like with other tasks that have been automated over the years, the need for human involvement and oversight in this role has not been eliminated completely. In some ways, as the consuming public has grown savvier about social media and can differentiate among human-generated and automated content, demand for nuanced authentic content created by human beings (not just a scheduled posting bot) for a specific time and platform has also grown. This may point to an increased demand for human involvement in content creation in the future.

Hootsuite is among the best known companies to offer content automation. The company offers plans that allow large organizations and individuals to build, strategize, schedule, and measure their social media presence across multiple platforms. Even so, in early 2016, the Hootsuite blog published a post underscoring the need for the social media manager role titled "Six Essential Skills You Need in a Social Media Manager Job Description." The post began with a definition of the role, as defined by the job search site Monster.com: "Social media managers are responsible for developing and implementing marketing strategies for a business' social media sites. This might include blogging, creating social media profiles, managing regular posts, and responding to followers."[6]

The skills Hootsuite identified as essential for social media managers aligned closely with the *Forbes* list. Hootsuite included visual and writing skills, as well as an understanding of SEO and how social media work, as well as a customer service mindset. In the "visual intelligence" section, Hootsuite mentioned live streaming via platforms like Vine and Periscope.[7]

In another blog post titled "Skills Social Media Managers Will Need in 2016," Hootsuite analyzed trends affecting the social media manager role that year. These trends affect social media in all aspects of our lives. You are likely familiar with most of them. Hootsuite advised those who conduct business on social media to pay close attention to how each platform has evolved and will continue to evolve, as well as how the addition of new functionality and services has brought more similarity across platforms. For example, many platforms now accommodate video. Those who publish video content are no longer limited to YouTube. They can publish on Vimeo, LinkedIn, Facebook, and Instagram, among others. They can stream live video on periscope, Facebook, and YouTube too.

Despite the increasing similarity of social media platforms, Hootsuite cautioned, there are still enough differences across them to require social media managers to individualize content for each. Sometimes the differences are small (such as recommended image sizes and aspect ratios), but sometimes they are significant (including file size limits, video length limits, specifications for desktop vs. mobile content, whether content can be streamed, and how long content remains accessible).

Several large companies employ social media managers to respond to customer complaints and queries. Regardless of whether this is a formal part of the role at a particular company, all social media managers and anyone who represents a company or enterprise on social media (even unofficially) must demonstrate strong customer service skills. This means that even those whose job duties do not include a social media role must represent the values of the company online and on social media if their profiles even informally connect them to their employer. As we are all becoming increasingly aware, there are no secrets online. Anyone who works for or represents others online or on social media, and even those who merely want to maintain a professional reputation must exhibit a customer service orientation at all times. The Internet has a very long memory. We all need to play nice.

Social media manager is a broad term. The position may be modified or emphasize certain tasks or skill sets to create some variation. It is important to pay close attention to job descriptions because different employers or clients may have either slightly or vastly different understandings of the job descriptions for various titles and roles. When you see a position listing that looks like social media manager, it may be the same as or quite similar to the role described above. It could also be quite different. When in doubt, make sure to ask questions. Remember that this entire job family has not existed for long, and position names can be deceptive.

Other names you may see that may to a greater or lesser extent describe the social media manager role include: social media brand manager, social media marketing manager, reputation manager, social media account manager, social media community manager, social media specialist, and countless other variations on these terms. While there is likely to be much overlap across these positions, some (social media marketing manager, reputation manager, social media specialist) may focus more on internal concerns. Others (social media account manager, social media community manager) may be externally oriented.

The marketing software company Hubspot, like other companies that sell services to help automate the process of finding, reaching, and converting potential customers online, also produces its own content to establish credibility and do for itself what it exists to do for customers: publish useful content to generate leads, lists, and sales. On its website, Hubspot offers several sample job descriptions within what the company describes as the marketing field. While those who come to social media management from the business side will not be surprised to see the field described as marketing, those who approach it from a communications, media, or journalism background may not immediately see the connection.

The truth is that while writing, editing, media, and professional communication of all kinds were once firmly editorial fields, free from the demands and compromises of sales and marketing, now media and communication professionals, along with independent filmmakers and even artists, would be wise to accept the fact that they are now also in the marketing business. Now that the industry gatekeepers are gone and content creators have access to the tools they need to brand and market themselves, creatives must be businesspeople too. The Internet has required all of us to learn how to sell ourselves. This fact may be discomfiting, but it is true. The good news is that whether you realize it or not, you are probably already doing much to market yourself online and through social media.

According to the Social Media Marketing 2015 Industry Report, more than 90% of companies are focusing on social media as a primary means of engaging with their audience.[8] Although this report, like most reports on media and technology, was outdated almost as soon as it was published, its projections for the future (now) are worth examining. The report's highlights include the growing importance of video in social media marketing efforts and, more unexpectedly, the growing influence of podcasting in developing and engaging audiences and communities. We are clearly seeing both trends play out today.

There is little doubt social media, whatever it may look like in the future, is central to branding and marketing efforts for both individuals and companies. What follows is Hubspot's sample responsibilities and requirements for the Social Media/Community Manager job.[9]

Social Media/Community Manager Responsibilities and Requirements

Responsibilities:

- Build and manage the company's social media profiles and presence, including Facebook, Twitter, LinkedIn, and appropriate channels that may be deemed relevant.
- Create sharable content appropriate for specific networks to spread both our brand and our content.
- Monitor and engage in relevant social discussions about our company, competitors, and/or industry, both from existing leads and customers as well as from brand new audiences.
- Run regular social promotions and campaigns, and track their success (e.g., Twitter chats, LinkedIn discussions, etc.).
- Work alongside other marketers and content marketers to help distribute content that educates and entertains our audience and supports marketing goals.
- Drive consistent, relevant traffic and leads from our social network presence.
- Explore new ways to engage and identify new social networks to reach our target buyers.
- Track, measure, and analyze all initiatives to report on social media ROI (return on investment).

Requirements:

- BA/BS degree or equivalent work experience.
- Active and well-rounded personal presence in social media, with a command of each network and their best practices.
- Excellent communicator and creative thinker with an ability to use both data and intuition to inform decisions.
- Proficiency in using social media software to monitor social media conversations. You will be our ear to the ground to route the appropriate marketer, sales rep, and/or support rep to social conversations.
- Bonus experience and skills include Adobe Creative Suite, demand generation, inbound marketing, and blogging.

FIGURE 1.6 Bloggers and content creators can work from almost anywhere.
Credit: Shutterstock ID#442889473

Blogger, Blog Manager, or Content Creator

Most people who use social media are online content creators. Some people are fortunate enough (through a mixture of talent and hard work) to create and disseminate content professionally. Most of us would consider these people fortunate because humans are, by nature, creative. Creating content of all kinds, whether written words, images or video, is a natural human urge. If we can make a living following that urge, we are fortunate indeed.

Keep in mind that online content creation now takes many forms. While we may have once considered blogging the key content generating activity, it is now only a relatively small part of the job. Not too many years ago, media companies routinely hired full-time bloggers. Blogging was their exclusive role, and they held an esteemed position for their ability to do it.

While once a rare and exotic position, professional bloggers are fairly common now, and for most, their jobs have expanded. Because in most organizations there are now many people capable of and willing to create online content, the position has lost some of its cachet. Corporate blogs now often have many authors from across an organization, along with freelance contributors. Blog entries can be short, and they can take many forms of media.

In the early days of blogging, as readers and editors transitioned from the idea that content needed to resemble a newspaper story, blog posts were long and writerly. They were almost always exclusively text. Now they tend to be shorter, and they often include a mix of media. They may not even be called blogs anymore, and the term has broadened almost to the point of meaninglessness. There are still blogging jobs available, but like many jobs in media now, they are likely to be part-time and external (not in-house), and offer little job security. In other words, working as a blogger may be one aspect of your career, but it will probably not be enough to sustain an entire career.

Despite this, the marketing company Hubspot emphasizes the importance of business blogging. Particularly large companies with huge marketing budgets may hire blog managers, which, depending on the employer, likely entails more than just blogging. What follows are Hubspot's sample responsibilities and requirements for a blog manager.[10]

Blog Manager Responsibilities and Requirements

Responsibilities:

- Writing various types of articles on a wide range of topics for our blog.
- Providing feedback to other contributors, and editing other writers' content.
- Optimizing content for search engines and lead generation.
- Contributing to long-form content projects such as e-books.
- Conducting analytical projects to improve blog strategies/tactics.
- Growing blog subscribers, converting visitors into leads, and expanding our blog's overall reach.

Requirements:

- A passion and strong understanding of the industry and our business' mission.
- Exceptional writing and editing skills, as well as the ability to adopt the style, tone, and voice of our business' various types of content.
- An analytical mind and interest in using data to optimize/scale blog marketing strategies and tactics.
- Excellent organizational skills to work independently and manage projects with many moving parts.
- Two to three years of marketing and content creation experience.

Content Marketing Manager

A similar and related position companies may hire is a content marketing manager. Although there is much variation among what these and similar positions are called in various companies and how each role is defined, what follows is Hubspot's sample responsibilities and requirements for the job.[11]

Content Marketing Manager Responsibilities and Requirements

Responsibilities:

- Create one to two free resources each month to drive leads, subscribers, awareness and/or other important metrics (examples include e-books, whitepapers, infographics, guides, templates, etc.)
- Blog on an ongoing basis to support and promote your offers and to attract site visitors through search, social media, and email subscribers.
- Grow our subscriber base by providing them with regular, helpful content that is aligned with their needs and interests.
- Collaborate with designers, product marketers, sales professionals, and external influencers and industry experts to produce relevant content that meets the needs of both key stakeholders and our audience.
- Convince others that your creative ideas are worth investing time and effort in. This role is at the core of the marketing team, and others will rely on your work every single day.

Requirements:

- BA/BS degree or equivalent working experience.
- Past experience producing content for the Web specifically, as well as channel-specific knowledge (blog, SlideShare, Facebook, Twitter, etc.).
- A dual-minded approach: You are highly creative and an excellent writer but can also be process-driven, think scale, and rely on data to make decisions.
- Proficiency with Adobe Creative Suite (particularly Photoshop and InDesign).

FIGURE 1.7 Every entrepreneur and creative now needs market research skills.

Credit: Shutterstock ID#432009058

Marketing Consultant or Educator

Working as a social media consultant requires a general background in marketing. That does not mean you need an MBA or a business degree. It simply means you need to do your homework. The good news is that all the information you need to succeed at consulting is available online. The challenge comes in sifting through and interpreting the massive amount of information available, then packaging it for a client or customer.

Consultants, like other media entrepreneurs, must regularly produce content that goes beyond simple branding images and social media posts. To establish their expertise and their value to a potential client or company, they must be prepared to do some work for free, then make it available on their website (like Hootsuite and others do) or through other channels. In addition to blog posts and short videos, they may consider publishing e-books, whitepapers, and original research of likely interest to their audience.

Useful content now goes far beyond click bait. Whether you work for yourself or for a firm, the pressure to produce and distribute useful content can be high. And for content to have value to your audience and key stakeholders, a certain amount of research is required. The task may be particularly challenging if you are working for yourself or with one or two other people. Large and even medium-sized firms may employ teams of a dozen or more to plan and create an editorial calendar, research and produce media content, and then distribute it through the appropriate networks.

The degree of research required differs depending on your audience and their needs. For example, an audience seeking design inspiration has much different expectations than an audience seeking to build a social media marketing consultancy. A growing number of professionals who are expert at social media marketing now make a living consulting and teaching others to do what they do. These people (you may be one of them) may make a career out of guiding others through processes they themselves have just learned.

Some Terms to Know

Audience is the group of people you expect to be key users of your product or services, or particularly interested in your brand.

Community is an audience that is established, developed, maintained, and grown in order to develop brand loyalty that may result in conversions (i.e., sales, or increased reach or influence).

Convergence describes how ideas, practices, professions, and disciplines have come together since widespread adoption of the Internet. Now once clearly defined and separate fields such as business and media share skill sets and roles.

E-book is an electronic book, often distributed for free online.

Inbound marketing is a form of content marketing designed to use various media channels, including social media, to attract potential clients, customers, and followers with the goal of conversion (i.e., a sale or a signup).

Influencers, discussed at length elsewhere in this volume, are people who command an audience online, on social media or even in person. You are likely an influencer. Influencers with large audiences and many followers are coveted by those who manage brands. Influencers' opinions matter to others, so their endorsement of your brand can bring more leads, which can then convert to sales or other positive outcomes.

Leads are potential clients, customers, or users.

Presence is a company's or individual's online footprint. Presence refers to how and the degree to which one (or a company) is known through various channels.

Return on investment (ROI) is a marketing term that compares the resources invested in an initiative to the resources generated by the investment. In almost all cases (the likely exception being when you are in the early stages of building a brand), you want your ROI to be a positive number.

White papers are authoritative research reports on topics of interest to a particular audience. While they are well known in the government sector, in business, white papers may present research supporting a particular initiative, explaining a trend, or promoting a point of view.

Notes

1 "Capital Markets and Job Creation in the 21st Century." 2016. *Brookings*. Accessed October 2, 2016. https://www.brookings.edu/research/capital-markets-and-job-creation-in-the-21st-century/.

2 "Arts and Design Occupations: Occupational Outlook Handbook: U.S. Bureau of Labor Statistics." 2016. *Bls.gov*. Accessed September 25, 2016. http://www.bls.gov/ooh/arts-and-design/home.htm.

3 "Technical Writers: Occupational Outlook Handbook: U.S. Bureau of Labor Statistics." 2016. *Bls.gov*. Accessed September 25, 2016. http://www.bls.gov/ooh/media-and-communication/technical-writers.htm.

4 "Forbes Welcome." 2016. *Forbes.com*. Accessed September 21, 2016. http://www.forbes.com/sites/jaysondemers/2015/06/08/5-skills-your-social-media-manager-must-have/#2147addc73f4.

5 Ibid.

6 Ibid.

7 Ibid.

8 *Socialmediaexaminer.com*. 2016. Accessed September 21, 2016. https://www.social mediaexaminer.com/SocialMediaMarketingIndustryReport2015.pdf.

9 Fleishman, Hannah. 2016. "12 Marketing Job Descriptions to Recruit and Hire an All-Star Team." *Blog.Hubspot.com*. Accessed September 21, 2016. http://blog.hubspot.com/blog/tabid/6307/bid/34029/8-Ready-Made-Job-Descriptions-to-Recruit-an-All-Star-Marketing-Team.aspx#sm.00001kf6wxk1pnfnuquzjd989bmnk.

10 Ibid.

11 Ibid.

2

WHAT IS CREATIVITY?

Creativity is what makes us human. Creating things is a natural impulse for most people, whether they express their creativity by designing clothing, cooking, or decorating, or as part of their career path. Our jobs—and most of what we do, in fact—involve some degree of creativity. It may be expressed in something as simple as problem solving or finding creative solutions to management problems. Even if you do not consider your job creative, there is a good chance that at least some of your responsibilities are creative.

In Chapter 7, you will read about Steve Matsumoto, a school teacher turned Realtor. (Realtor is a trademark, by the way. That's why it is capitalized. You will read more about trademarks in Chapter 6.) While you may not at first think of a sales profession as creative, Matsumoto's branding campaign for his business (which carries his name) is every bit as creative as those of bloggers or visual artists. The point is that even if your job or business is not inherently creative, there are likely many ways you can enhance it and bolster your own success through creative channels.

Some people are able to do creative work most of the time. And most of us would find them fortunate. We may ask ourselves why we consider these people fortunate. What is it about their jobs that we covet or envy? Is it that they get to employ their own judgment in what they do every day and how they get the job done? Is it because they do not have a supervisor directly monitoring their work from minute to minute? Is it because they have something to directly show for their efforts?

It may be all of these things. Or maybe none of them apply, although there are some commonalities across creative professions. Given the option to work for others, on their supervisors' schedule, or to work for themselves, accomplishing tasks that they deem important on their own schedule, most people would

FIGURE 2.1 Creative work still happens in offices.

Credit: Shutterstock ID#377075614

opt for the latter. The main reasons are clear. They often include: autonomy, self-direction, self-expression, and satisfaction.

Increasingly across the developed world, even occupations that have not traditionally been characterized by these terms are incorporating more creativity. Although most would say this is a positive trend, the reasons behind it may not be quite so positive. In recent years, across most professions, shrinking budgets and the push for greater workforce efficiency has created leaner workforces with fewer layers of administration.

In many cases this has meant that administrative professionals who once had fairly limited job descriptions that did not involve much creativity or choice over the way work was done are now, by necessity, charged with making decisions and solving problems on their own. This may be a result of cost-cutting measures, and it may mean longer hours and greater responsibility for administrative workers. Regardless, their increased responsibility has made their jobs more creative, and likely more fun.

The good news is that most of us—even those of us not privileged to work in an explicitly creative field or occupation—probably enjoy more autonomy and creativity in our everyday lives as the economy gravitates from shift work to project-based work, and as telecommuting and flexible schedules become more common. The news is even better for those engaged in explicitly creative work. These are people employed as writers, reporters, video producers, podcasters, filmmakers, graphic designers, as well as entrepreneurs of all kinds. If you are reading this book, there is a good chance you are one.

If you are younger or early in your career, you may have never worked a traditional nine-to-five desk job. You may have begun your career as an entrepreneur. If you are older—mid-career or later—setting out on your own, or becoming an entrepreneur, may mark a break from the security and stability of an office job. Entrepreneurship may still seem scary or uncertain to you. You may still be getting used to budgeting for a variable paycheck. This is one area in which younger or less experienced workers have an advantage. It is much more difficult to adjust to the variability of entrepreneurship than to begin your career as your own boss.

It's common to hear people who work in a more traditional field, in an office or in a more conventional environment, express longing about working for themselves, wishing that they did not have to work according to someone else's schedule, or to simply be self-guided when it comes to work. The appeal of entrepreneurship is easy to understand. There is little wonder why so many people want to work for themselves, creating a living by their own rules. However, creative and entrepreneurial work is not without its challenges and downsides. After all, if there were no downsides, many more of us would have struck out on our own long ago.

One of the main reasons why more people are not entrepreneurs is that it is difficult to be 100% responsible for yourself, without the help of an employer or office full of other workers ready to support you. Of course our conventional office jobs can be every bit as challenging, but the difficulties associated with these jobs tend to be much more predictable. We may know, for instance, that the boss is often cranky on Monday mornings, or that she routinely expects her employees to contribute more hours or effort to their projects than we think is reasonable. We may have little tolerance for long meetings or some of our co-workers.

Despite all this, at the end of the week (or two weeks, or month), we know we will receive a paycheck, and we know exactly how much money we will receive. We can count on this money to pay bills or to qualify for a mortgage or auto loan. We may have benefits such as 401(k)s or pension plans, health insurance, maybe a gym membership. Knowing exactly what to expect in this area can be essential—especially for those with limited resources, high bills or dependents to support.

As an entrepreneur or an independent contractor, you often do not know how much money you will (or will not) make during any particular time period. Making matters even more difficult, there are likely expenses related to the creation, maintenance, and promotion of your business. You will probably have to spend money to get the word out about the goods and services you offer. Nearly all businesses have these expenses, but as a salaried or hourly employee, you likely never have to consider them.

FIGURE 2.2 Entrepreneurs often find themselves playing multiple roles.

Credit: Shutterstock ID#324738974

It is also important to consider that those who work for themselves often work more than 40 hours a week. In many ways, the work of an entrepreneur is never finished. There is always something more that can be done to build the business. Many in the traditional workforce can mentally "turn off" work once the workday is over. Their weekends, holidays, and even paid vacations are relatively carefree. Entrepreneurs, on the other hand, are always on the clock. Granted, it is their own clock and they are accountable mostly to themselves, but that may come as little solace to family members and friends who wish their entrepreneurial loved ones could more fully enjoy down time. Although the longer hours tend to be more tolerable for those who work for themselves, overwork and burnout are real possibilities as the stress of starting, maintaining, and growing a business build up.

Before launching your own business enterprise, you need to honestly answer a few basic questions. No matter how creative, talented or business-minded you may consider yourself, entrepreneurship is not for everyone.

Are You Ready for Entrepreneurship?

There is no way to know for sure whether entrepreneurship is right for you. But there are a few questions you can ask yourself to help gauge your readiness to start your own business venture. The following should be just the beginning of the conversation.

Ask yourself:

1. Do I need to make a certain amount of money on a regular basis to meet my financial obligations?
2. Do others count on me for financial support?
3. Do I have the time to devote to developing, maintaining, and growing an entrepreneurial venture?
4. Do I have the temperament to strike out on my own, without a steady, reliable paycheck, and likely having to dedicate much more than 40 hours a week to the enterprise?

This last question—No. 4—is something you may not have considered. While the other questions are more straightforward, this question attempts to determine personality traits and native talents that are impossible to measure with complete accuracy. In any case, you owe it to yourself to at least try to honestly answer this question before investing too much time or money in an entrepreneurial venture that may ultimately lead to burnout or worse.

What Is the Entrepreneurial Temperament?

Again, there is no strict science to this designation, but many have created lists, tips, and tools to measure entrepreneurial aptitude. There is significant overlap among most lists, mostly because they draw from the same research studies. Here are highlights from a few:

FROM *FORBES*

5 Personality Traits of an Entrepreneur[1]

1. Passion: Entrepreneurship is difficult. Unless your heart is in the venture 100%, it is probably not worth the time, dedication, and expense.
2. Resilience: Most business ventures fail. Successful entrepreneurs are able to dust themselves off after a failure, and go on to try something new.
3. Strong sense of self: You need to believe in yourself. It sounds like a cliché (and it is), but if you do not have complete faith in your ability to succeed, it is unlikely you will.
4. Flexibility: True entrepreneurs continuously monitor the world around them for environmental changes. The world never stops, and the needs and demands of your customers are always in flux. To succeed with a business venture, you must pay attention to changes in trends, technology, politics, legislation, and anything else that may affect demand for your product or how you deliver it.

5. Vision: You cannot plan a business venture if you have no future vision for it. If you do not know what you would like your business to be in a year, in five years, in 10 years or whatever time span, there is no chance your venture will get there.

FROM *ENTREPRENEUR*

The 7 Traits of Successful Entrepreneurs[2]

1. Tenacity
2. Passion
3. Tolerance of ambiguity
4. Vision
5. Self-belief
6. Flexibility
7. Rule-breaking

Entrepreneur's list is quite similar to *Forbes'* list, with the exception of No. 7. This one should really jump out at a potential entrepreneur. According to *Entrepreneur*, the very act of entrepreneurship breaks the rules. Instead of following the expected path by going to work for someone else, venturing out on your own is a way of breaking the rules. Entrepreneurs are accountable to no one (or almost no one) but themselves. And only they can save themselves if things go wrong. If you are not comfortable identifying and solving your own problems, and working without a safety net, entrepreneurship may not be for you.

Following is a final list with some overlap.

FROM *BUSINESS INSIDER*

10 Personality Traits Every Successful Entrepreneur Has[3]

1. Passionate
2. Resilient
3. Self-Possessed
4. Decisive
5. Fearless
6. Financially prepared
7. Flexible
8. Zoom lens-equipped
9. Able to sell
10. Balanced

This is a particularly comprehensive list. While 1 through 3 and 7 are repeats from the other two lists, this one introduces a few new concepts—some of which may be uncomfortable to those outside of traditional business. Even so, it is useful for creatives to understand what makes all kinds of entrepreneurs tick. While creative entrepreneurs may not be under the same kind of split-second time pressures that strictly business-oriented entrepreneurs often find themselves in, the concept of "opportunity costs" remains valid for both groups. Creative entrepreneurs are more likely to undervalue their time. Although the old business cliché "time is money" does not have quite the same resonance with creatives, it is important for even artists to appreciate the fact that anything they spend time doing takes time away from something else they could be doing. This is the definition of an opportunity cost.

Although the time pressures they face tend to be ongoing and deadline-oriented, creative entrepreneurs need to put a premium on their time, all the time. If you have not asked yourself already, ask yourself now: Which of your tasks or activities are most important for you to do yourself? Which might others do just as well or better? How much time would assigning these tasks to someone else save you? How much money would assigning them to someone else cost you? It's a fairly straightforward calculation.

For example, you manage a company that consults and manages social media campaigns for various clients. The business is growing quickly, and you are becoming increasingly concerned that you will soon have to start turning away clients. After all, there are only so many hours in the day to send out tweets and post updates on Facebook and Instagram. The question you should be asking yourself at this point is whether your time is best spent tweeting and posting updates on social media.

Ask yourself: (1) Can these tasks be taken on by an assistant or other employee? And more important (2) What are the opportunity costs of my spending time doing these tasks? Asked another way: Are you missing an opportunity to grow your business by not delegating work to other people so you can focus on what you do best (on what is the greatest value to the company)?

As you grow your business, pay close attention to the way you spend your time. If you find yourself spending too much of your limited time doing less skilled tasks like ordering materials, packing orders or tweaking your website, consider hiring someone to do that work so you can focus on delivering your most valuable contributions to the business.

Being fearless, one of *Business Insider's* listed characteristics of successful entrepreneurs, may also have a somewhat different meaning for creatives than for businesspeople. Launching any new venture is a risk, and a certain amount of fear is to be expected when taking a risk. However, the startup costs of a creative business are likely much smaller than those Elon Musk faced when building his Tesla electric car company. You may have to spend a few hundred dollars to build and host a website, buy stationery, take a few people to lunch, or whatever, but you probably won't need to spend millions of dollars just to launch your business.

"Financially prepared" may also mean something different to creative professionals, but the concept is important to consider. For creatives, this basically means "don't quit your day job" (unless you are financially prepared to do so). This is a no-brainer for creatives, most of whom don't expect to get rich quick through a fabulous new business venture. Creatives are patient and willing to invest the time and energy required to succeed without cutting corners. This is why they are creatives, not businesspeople first and foremost.

"Zoom lens-equipped" is an interesting quality. This basically means that you can "zoom" back and forth between the big picture and the details. All too often individuals working on a business venture alone or with limited resources tend to get myopic. They become so focused on small details (like tweaking their website's SEO) that they lose sight of the big picture (like whether they understand their audience). A successful entrepreneur needs to focus on both big and small.

"Able to sell" is a concept likely to make most creatives squirm. Many of us believe we entered creative fields precisely to avoid having to sell. We believe in ourselves, our products, and what we do, but the idea of sales can be a real turnoff. If this describes you, try to surrender any preconceived notions you may have about sales. The good news here is that even though you may have negative associations with the concept of sales, if you are a good entrepreneur or creative professional, it is likely that you actually are good at sales—because you are doing it already. To succeed at your own venture, you are perpetually selling yourself and your business. It just may not seem like sales in the classic sense because you believe so strongly in your product and yourself, and because the vision you are selling is your own.

FIGURE 2.3 One key to successful entrepreneurship is balance.

Credit: Shutterstock ID#418781818

"Balanced" is an important trait for entrepreneurial success, and one that you, as a creative person, may have already mastered. If you have yet to master it, there is a good chance you at least understand the importance of living a balanced life. This is one area where creatives have a distinct advantage over strictly business-oriented entrepreneurs whose perhaps single-minded focus on making money may blind them to other important aspects of the business. You probably already know that entrepreneurial success is impossible if other parts of your life are not successful. If your mental or physical health declines, if you are unable to sleep, if you are paralyzed by existential fear, you will not succeed as an entrepreneur.

What Is Entrepreneurship?

Entrepreneurship is about working for yourself, crafting a career path for yourself and possibly others. Historically, entrepreneurship has meant building your own business or maintaining an existing business. Small family-run businesses embodied the old model of entrepreneurship. That model still exists. But entrepreneurship is so much more now. It embraces not just traditional business ownership but also relatively small but rapidly increasing numbers of independent contractors who, instead of owning hardware stores or corner bakeries, offer goods and services on a small scale, often virtually, via the Web or through mobile devices. While economic turbulence and declining job security have driven some to

FIGURE 2.4 Entrepreneurship is about more than running the family business.

Credit: Shutterstock ID#327831641

entrepreneurship, technological advances that have made entrepreneurship easier, lowering costs and other entry barriers, have convinced ever greater numbers of individuals to go to work for themselves.

Less than a generation ago, most college students prepared to enter the workforce with ambitions of securing long-term jobs with stable, established companies that offered great benefits packages and often pensions at retirement. Now those kinds of jobs are rare. Few workers receive pensions, and no one expects companies to survive forever. Failures of a number of prominent financial companies, insurance companies, and other companies that may have once been considered "too big to fail," along with global economic contractions in the wake of financial slumps in 2001 and 2008, taught many young or new workers that the economy was constantly in flux, and that the key to economic survival lie in nimbleness, flexibility, and a willingness to constantly reassess and retrain.

While members of past generations may have been caught off-guard when the companies they worked for failed, potential failure is a known risk today. Journalists, in particular, have witnessed the transformation of their industry. And we now know other industries are not immune from existential threats. After all, if banking giant Lehman Brothers, which was founded in 1850, more than a decade before the U.S. Civil War, could be brought down by 2008's subprime mortgage crisis, no business or industry is 100% reliable or safe. Fortunately, most workers have long since accepted that reality. This has allowed some to consider exciting new ideas they may not have felt comfortable pursuing a decade or more before.

FIGURE 2.5 High-profile bank failures stoked global economic insecurity.

Credit: Shutterstock ID#426112249

Entrepreneurship in Journalism

Entrepreneurial journalism, like entrepreneurship in general, can mean a number of things, and the meaning is forever in flux. One of the nice things about entrepreneurship is that you don't have to wait to graduate before you get to work. There are no formal barriers to entrepreneurship. All you need is an idea, the time (it need not be full-time), and commitment. Naturally, you will need some upfront investment in time and money, but you can manage those with the help of a solid business plan that takes into account your resources, and provides a realistic projection for growth.

Because the freelance model has long been popular in journalism, entrepreneurship is a natural fit for journalists. For some people entrepreneurship has felt like more of an extension of what they have always done. This has meant less adjustment for those who did not enter the job market with the expectation of long-term work for a single stable employer. For many, especially younger people and those just starting out, entrepreneurial work is the first option, not a last resort.

An Explosion of Ideas

Journalism and other creative fields have been swiftly moving toward individualism in recent decades. The rise of the Internet and proliferation of social media has expedited the fragmentation of mass media and marketplaces, as the old gatekeepers (editors, bosses, buyers, etc.) slowly disappeared, leaving almost limitless opportunities for those with good ideas, talent, strong and diverse skill sets, and the willingness to work hard.

Just as journalists and creative workers are no longer reliant on full-time employment with large organizations with access to printing presses or factories to publish their work or manufacture their products, consumers are no longer reliant on mass media for their news and information, advertising and marketing firms to create their promotional materials, or legacy department stores to furnish their household and personal goods. Customization, personalization, and the increasing availability of goods and services on demand has empowered both consumers and producers. The result is an excellent climate for entrepreneurship.

Is Your Environment Right for Entrepreneurship?

At a glance, the outlook is good. In many ways there has never been a better time to start a new business or sideline than now. But keep in mind that you are far from alone. Odds are high that around the world, countless other people likely have ideas that may be quite similar to your own. Because you will no doubt face significant competition from the very start of your venture, as you compete for attention with every other brand with an Internet presence, you need to thoroughly and honestly assess the environment so you can determine the likelihood of your ultimate success.

Be careful to prevent your eagerness to launch from pushing you toward overly sunny conclusions. If conditions are not right for your venture, it is much better to understand that before you waste time and money—while risking exhaustion or worse—pursuing a project that will not ultimately succeed. At the very least, do a quick SWOT analysis. This is a simple snapshot of current market conditions and the relative strength of your position within them. SWOT stands for "strengths," "weaknesses," "opportunities," and "threats." Draw your own SWOT template or find one online. Then populate it with internal factors (your own strengths and weaknesses) as well as external factors (opportunities and threats in the marketplace).

Consider Your Business Structure

Should you create a legal business? Your answer to that question depends on how large you expect your company to grow, how involved you plan to be in the company's operations, and how comfortable you feel being exposed to the company's potential risks and gains. For many entrepreneurs starting out, pressure to start a business stems from liability or tax concerns. The first thing forming a legal business entity does is separate you, the individual, to some degree from your business.

Following are common types of business structure in the United States. Similar structures exist in Great Britain and other countries, although they may go by different names. Before you form any legal entity, make sure to check with local and state offices to ensure you are compliant on all levels. Consulting a lawyer, if that's in your budget, is always a good idea.

Although state and federal laws usually agree, the occasional disagreement can lead to legal gray areas—and potential trouble for both your business and yourself. An oft-cited example of conflicting state and federal laws regards the operation of marijuana dispensaries. Although laws are quickly evolving in this area, disagreements among state, federal, and even municipal code still occur, and are known risk factors in certain industries. Such disagreements have led to significant complications and financial losses for companies like the Los Angeles-based marijuana dispensary Farmacy, which was an officially registered, tax-paying business in California for more than a decade, and yet was raided by federal Drug Enforcement Administration (DEA) agents in 2014.[4]

Let us consider the most common business models in the United States. They include the following.

A *sole proprietorship* is the simplest business structure. In this model, the owner shares legal status with the business, assuming all its risks and responsibilities. The owner collects all profits and pays all debts. Perhaps most significantly, the owner is personally liable for any losses, including those resulting from lawsuits or legal actions. In most locations, you don't need to do anything special to qualify as a sole proprietor. If you are already working yourself, you are most likely already a sole proprietor. In most areas, the way you file and pay taxes is the only way a sole proprietorship is different from working for an employer who deducts taxes directly from your paycheck. In the absence of automatic deductions, you need to pay self-employment tax (for social security and Medicare) and estimated taxes quarterly. Sole proprietors essentially are their business. If you are a sole proprietor and your business gets sued, you want to make sure you have protected your personal assets.

If you operate under a business name that is different from your own, you should register your "doing business as" (or DBA) name with your state. Filing a DBA allows you to cash checks and file other paperwork under a business name (instead of your own), but it does not offer any legal protections. If you are concerned about your home, your car or other personal assets that could be seized in a lawsuit, ask your insurance agent about buying an umbrella policy. Although specific coverages differ across companies, GEICO insurance company's umbrella policies cover typical homeowners' claims (such as bodily injury and property damage), but extend to liabilities beyond the home, including slander, libel, false arrest or imprisonment, and mental anguish, among other broadly defined damages.[5]

A *limited liability company* (or LLC, also a "limited company" in England and other countries) offers somewhat more protection to business owners, who are defined as "members" of the company. In an LLC, members are like partners. They report profits and losses on their personal tax returns. LLC structure is a popular middle ground between the sole proprietorship and more restrictive kinds of ownership. They ensure less liability than a sole proprietorship and lower taxes than a corporation. Taxation differs from state to state and location to location, but in general, an LLC's profits and losses are realized by members alone. The exact tax form that is used differs depending on how the LLC's members want to identify the company on their tax forms.

The steps involved in creating an LLC differ from state to state and from nation to nation. In the United States, the process is fairly simple and requires little time to process. First, you select and register your business name with your state (your "doing business as" or DBA registration, which can often be done almost instantly online). Then you file the "articles of organization" for your business. This includes basic information such as the business name and address, as well as the principals' names. File for any required licenses or permits, then advertise the formation of the LLC. Unless your business plans to broadcast radio or television programming (which would require Federal Communications Commission, or FCC, licensing in the United States), you should not need any special operating licenses from the federal government. Other licenses may be needed on the state or municipal level. Check with your state and local offices or with your Small Business Administration (SBA) chapter to ensure you have not overlooked any important filings.

Alternatively, entrepreneurial journalists and creatives may want to form partnerships or cooperatives for their business ventures. A cooperative would be a tricky business structure for a media endeavor. Cooperatives have members that apply for membership and then contribute to the organization. Bylaws are created and a board is elected. This business form is far more common for informal businesses such as health food or farmer's markets. Partnerships are like sole proprietorships except two people instead of one share all profits and losses. And limited partnerships are much like LLCs that involve more than one person.

Although it is not common to start a business as a corporation (and you will probably not be forming a corporation for your entrepreneurial venture anytime soon), this business structure must also be mentioned. A corporation is its own entity, legally separate from its principals. When Republican U.S. presidential candidate Mitt Romney said, "Corporations are people, my friend" on the campaign trail in 2011, he was factually correct, although emphasizing this technicality did not endear him to the electorate.[6]

The big advantage to a corporation is protection from liability. Major downsides include higher expenses and double taxation. This is because both the company and its shareholders pay taxes on realized profits. Corporations exist to maximize profits for shareholders—which is why it may be an uncomfortable structure for a journalism or media business, or for any small business that plans to act ethically. Incorporation is unusual for small companies. Even many large companies (Dell, Toys "R" Us, Hearst, SC Johnson and Son, Bloomberg, among others) have opted to retain control of the company, remaining private instead of filing an independent public offering (IPO) and selling ownership shares to the public. The bottom line is that corporations have high costs and overhead. Company founders may lose their controlling interest, and bureaucracy or internal politics can kill their interest in running it. Besides this, many IPOs fail, as initial stock offerings sink below projections, disappointing investors and tainting the company's future prospects.

The Business Plan

There is no shortage of business models and plans readily available to entrepreneurs across industries. Regardless of the kind of business startup you have in mind, the Small Business Administration (SBA) is an excellent resource for the planning stages and beyond. The SBA provides basic information that applies to all small businesses. Start with their Business Plan Tool, which you can access for free at http://www.sba.gov/tools/business-plan/1. (You need to register to access the Tool.) Although you do not need a detailed plan to start a new venture, drafting a plan (if only for your own use) can go a long way toward helping you understand the challenges you may face as a new entrepreneur, and to avoid some of the hiccups new business owners often face. Not only can the act of building a plan help you get off to a more promising start, but it also shows potential investors or loan officers that you have done your homework, you are serious, and your business is more likely to succeed.

FIGURE 2.6 Entrepreneurs who plan well are more likely to succeed.

Credit: Shutterstock ID#416135350

Although business plans differ, the basic sections the SBA recommends include, in order: executive summary, company description, market analysis, organization and management, service or product line, marketing and sales, funding, and financial projections. One small note to potential entrepreneurs: If you do not like working with numbers, hire or partner with someone who does. Even the most innovative startup will likely fail without solid financial projections and a real understanding of the costs of establishing and maintaining the business.

Executive Summary

Leave the executive summary for last. This is where you summarize the other sections of the business plan. Key to a successful executive summary is brevity. Use bullet points whenever possible to make it easy for your audience to scan. Readers (potential partners or investors) may set aside only a few minutes to review your business plan. The easier you make it for them to glean the plan's highlights, the more likely they will be to read past the executive summary. Keep it to a single page.

Company Description

The SBA calls the company description "an extended elevator pitch,"[7] a succinct paragraph or two that allows stakeholders and potential investors to quickly understand the business and how it will serve an unmet need. Writing a clear, concise company description is good practice for honing your elevator pitch. Your pitch should immediately get to the point and closely focus on the needs and interests of your audience. Anticipate any questions they will likely have in advance, and answer them here.

Market Analysis

This is just what it sounds like: analysis of the competition's relative health, its potential threats to your planned business, and any weaknesses you may be able to exploit. Make sure there is at least one weakness or area in which the competition falls short. Ask yourself how you can serve needs that are not already being met by others. Keep in mind that you may have a great product ready to bring to market, but if there is no demand or if the need is already being met by another company, your enterprise will likely fail. Consider Google Video Player, which the company launched in late 2005, then discontinued in 2007, 10 months after Google acquired YouTube. By all accounts Google Video Player was a fine product, but so was YouTube. Those already using YouTube did not need another video player, so Google's version could not compete.[8]

Also know that your struggle to gain market share may be more difficult than you anticipated. This is part of the value of a business plan. If your plan shows little chance of your business finding a niche, meeting a need, or creating competitive advantage, it is always better to abandon it before dedicating time and money to its launch.

Company Organization and Management Structure

For many entrepreneurs just starting out, and likely you, this may be the simplest part of your business plan. If you are the sole owner and manager of your company, summarize your relevant credentials, and include your plans for expanding your workforce as the venture grows.

Product Description

This should be your most extensive section because it describes what you actually plan to do. Include as much detail as possible about exactly what you will provide and to whom, along with your goals and measures of success. Inclusion of a mission statement and strategic plan will help. Even if you do not share your mission statement with others, the act of creating and fine-tuning it can help you better understand your plan and how best to pitch it to others. While there is no universal format for mission statements, yours should include: (1) what you provide; (2) to whom you provide your services; and (3) how your services are different from what anyone else can provide. Entrepreneur.com suggests studying other companies' mission statements for ideas.[9]

FIGURE 2.7 People who know where they're going are more likely to get there.

Credit: Shutterstock ID#359155502

Vision Statement

Your vision statement is about the future of the organization—where you would like it to go or what you would like it to look like in the future. It is a simple description of your company at some point in the future. Here's an old vision statement from the software company Microsoft: "A personal computer in every home running Microsoft software."[10] Here's a current vision statement from the greeting card company Hallmark: "We will be the company that creates a more emotionally connected world by making a genuine difference in every life, every day."[11]

Marketing Strategy

You have likely put a lot of thought into your marketing strategy already. If not, this book should help you consider approaches. Keep in mind that there will probably be some overlap among your marketing strategy, company description, and market analysis. Among the questions you want to consider when conceiving your marketing strategy are:

- Who is your target market? OR: Who are your target markets?
- How will you reach your targets and with what messages?
- How will you convert targets to followers, subscribers, or buyers?
- What are your goals for one year out? For three years out? For five?
- How will you measure your progress toward (or achievement of) those goals?

Funding Request

If you are not ready to make a funding request, you can skip this section. But if you are soliciting potential investors, you will want to create a budget for launch along with a monthly (or quarterly) operations budget. Because potential funders will want to know where their investment is going, you should provide as much detail here as possible to avoid unpleasant surprises down the road. Make sure to avoid vague language that could worry or deter potential investors. Remember, investors are businesspeople first. No matter how much they like you or your business idea, if the numbers look shaky or your pitch sends up red flags, they may not be inclined to support your venture.

Financial Projections

Financial projections for startups are largely a matter of speculation. Unless the business already has a financial record, it will be difficult to project the future financial picture. However, you should include general industry information such as marketplace trends in your financial projections section. Conduct consumer research on the media. The Pew Research Center publishes an annual report titled "State of the News Media."[12] The report includes some of the most current data available on trends in technology, media ownership, and news reporting. Pew's searchable "Media and News Indicators Database"[13] includes more than enough specific trend data to build a solid report. For general news and trends based on search habits, visit Google Trends (https://www.google.com/trends/).

Strategic Plan

Your strategic plan and business plans should work together. While the business plan may ultimately be used to attract investor support, the strategic plan provides guidance for the first few years. Make sure to revisit both your business plan and strategic plan on a regular basis, updating sections as your enterprise evolves, environmental conditions change, and your outlook matures. Remember you don't need to wait until the term defined by your last strategic plan (one year, three years, five years, or more) is over before updating or replacing it. Market conditions change quickly, particularly in media and technology, and your plan must change with them.

Let Your Core Values Guide You

So far we have discussed SWOT analysis, mission and vision statements, and business and strategic plans. At the heart of all of these ways of considering a business venture are your core values. Your values determine what you stand for and how you do business. The core values of some businesses are quite well known because they've done a good job publicizing them. The retailer Target, for instance, became known for volunteerism by promoting the fact that it donates 5 percent of its profits to local charities and encourages its employees to volunteer. The famous Maine clothier L. L. Bean developed a core values statement as straightforward as its sturdy, mostly utilitarian products: "Sell good products at a reasonable profit, treat your customers like human beings, and they will always come back for more." That it is a quote from company founder Leon Leonwood Bean only reinforces the company's reputation for authenticity. Build-a-Bear Workshop has a more challenging core values statement that manages to capture the company's tone: "Reach, Learn, Di-bear-sity, Colla-bear-ate, Give, Cele-bear-ate."[14]

Whatever core values you choose, and regardless of whether you make them public, an effective values statement can help you differentiate your brand and maintain consistency in the face of future challenges or pressures to make shortsighted changes or modifications in pursuit of short-term returns.

Notes

1 "Forbes Welcome." 2016. *Forbes.Com.* Accessed July 10, 2016. http://www.forbes.com/sites/johnrampton/2014/04/14/5-personality-traits-of-an-entrepreneur/#3f4075fa22f6.
2 Robinson, Joe. 2014. "The 7 Traits of Successful Entrepreneurs." *Entrepreneur.* Accessed July 10, 2016. https://www.entrepreneur.com/article/230350.
3 "10 Personality Traits Every Successful Entrepreneur Has." 2016. *Business Insider.* Accessed July 11, 2016. http://www.businessinsider.com/traits-of-successful-entrepreneurs-2013-2.
4 "DEA Raids Two Los Angeles Medical Marijuana Dispensaries." 2014. *The Huffington Post.* Accessed September 29, 2016. http://www.huffingtonpost.com/2014/10/24/dea-raid-medical-marijuana-los-angeles_n_6038926.html.
5 "About Umbrella Insurance." 2016. *Geico.com.* Accessed September 29, 2016. https://www.geico.com/information/aboutinsurance/umbrella/.
6 Rucker, Philip. 2016. "Mitt Romney Says 'Corporations Are People.'" *Washington Post.* Accessed September 29, 2016. https://www.washingtonpost.com/politics/mitt-romney-says-corporations-are-people/2011/08/11/gIQABwZ38I_story.html.
7 "Company Description." *SBA.gov.* Accessed August 20, 2016.
8 "5 Google Products that Failed and What Startups Can Learn from It." 2016. Accessed September 29, 2016. https://blog.kissmetrics.com/google-products-that-failed/.
9 "How to Write Your Mission Statement." (October 30, 2003) *Entrepreneur.com.* Accessed July 7, 2016. https://www.entrepreneur.com/article/65230.
10 Bly, Robert. 2015. "Vision Statements: Why You Need One and How to Create One." *Entrepreneur.* Accessed October 2, 2016. https://www.entrepreneur.com/article/251682.
11 "Hallmark Corporate Information: Hallmark Vision Statement." 2016. *Corporate.hallmark.com.* Accessed October 2, 2016. http://corporate.hallmark.com/OurCulture/Our-Vision.
12 "State of the News Media." (June 16, 2016) *Pew Research Center's Journalism Project.* Accessed September 16, 2016. http://www.pewresearch.org/topics/state-of-the-news-media/.
13 "Media & News Indicators Database." 2014. *Pew Research Center's Journalism Project.* Accessed September 29, 2016. http://www.journalism.org/media-indicator-tags/.
14 Rossi, Holly. 2015. "7 Core Values Statements that Inspire". *Fortune.* Accessed September 29, 2016. http://fortune.com/2015/03/13/company-slogans/.

3

HOW BRANDS BEGAN

Brands, as we know them today, have existed only since the 19th century, when mass production changed the way people shopped for and bought things. Gone were the days when people would buy undifferentiated commodities direct from individuals they knew. Through the 19th century, as formerly rural populations began moving to the cities in great numbers, companies could target large customer bases for the first time. And for the first time, customers had choices about what they bought.

That customers had choices also meant that producers had to find ways to successfully compete against other producers, which were now available to customers in the same markets. No longer was it sufficient to simply produce products and wait for customers to buy. Companies had to find ways to make their items stand out. They had to differentiate their product. Without differentiation, their products would not be noticed among so many other similar products. This was the birth of branding.

Branding's Early Days

The earliest brands served fairly broad customer bases. Before the explosion of brands in the 20th century, competition was still fairly small, and customers were not highly differentiated. The first companies to serve large swaths of the American public in the early 19th century, before large-scale manufacturing, and when the United States was still a farm-based economy, were mail-order concerns like Montgomery Ward and Sears. These companies aimed their marketing messages at the vast middle swath of the American public. They were themselves brands, but not in the way we know brands today. Over time, their business models and the large number of products they carried made it difficult for them to sustain a strong brand long term.

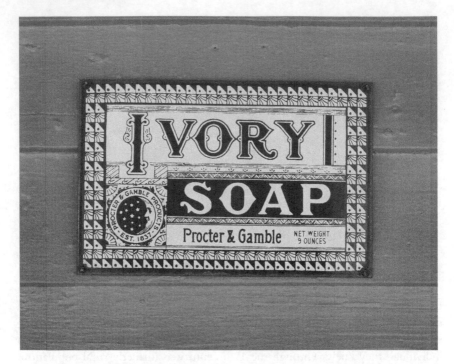

FIGURE 3.1 Ivory soap was one of the first ubiquitous brands.

Credit: Shutterstock ID#241774027

In his seminal 1990 book *New and Improved: The Story of Mass Marketing in America*, Richard S. Tedlow examined the evolution of large companies like Procter and Gamble that did not become household names for decades after their founding. For Procter and Gamble, success was a long time coming. The company was founded in 1837, but it was not until 1879 that Ivory soap made Procter and Gamble one of the world's best-known companies.[1]

The Biggest Brands Ever

Ivory soap was one of the world's first universally known brands, and it remains a known name to this day. As a brand more than a century old, Ivory has household recognition, yet its age and its product category (it is soap, after all) prevent it from generating much excitement among consumers. However, it is a stable and tremendously successful brand.

To fully understand the significance and meaning of the Ivory brand, it is useful to compare it to other branded products in the same category. You might, for instance, think of Zest (a Procter and Gamble product) or Irish Spring (a Colgate-Palmolive product), both successful brands in the heyday of mass marketing. Both once-iconic brands have lost some of their luster in recent years, as the masses in mass marketing have become more savvy and demanding, and new companies—like Tom's of Maine, Burt's Bees, and countless others—have diversified the consumer products marketplace and trained consumers to demand features—like all-natural ingredients or special formulations for specific skin types—that most did not even know existed decades ago.

Faced with new competition from higher-quality or more specifically targeted products (like soap for dry, normal, or oily skin), legacy brands like Zest needed to refine their branding for a more sophisticated consumer marketplace. In a similar sense, you, as an entrepreneurial journalist, creative, or content creator, are a product of the post-mass marketing era, competing in a world of Tom's of Maine and Burt's Bees, not Zest and Irish Spring.

Strange as it may seem, many of the same forces that brought seismic changes to mass marketing brought similar changes to mass media. These changes have roots in economic and social shifts that transformed the developed world, but mostly in the major technological advances at the end of the 20th century. These changes rendered the old ways obsolete for content creators from Madison Avenue to you.

Consumers in the developed world have steadily grown in sophistication since the early days of radio and television, when advertising messages were straightforward affairs that often simply directed consumers to buy. For the last several decades, companies have been moving toward a less direct approach, swapping their straightforward sales appeals for more nuanced tactics—specifically branding campaigns. This approach matched the growing sophistication of consumers whose increasing exposure to media allowed them to more thoughtfully scrutinize the advertising messages they saw.

As consumers grew more discriminating, subtlety became increasingly important. Moving past a transactional approach to marketing that stressed sales, successful branding campaigns began to create feelings around products and companies. While not specific and not easily described, these campaigns ultimately proved more powerful than their predecessors by extending the reach of a company or product's message far beyond a mere sales interaction to an overarching way of thinking about a product. This is the strength and importance of branding.

Successful branding is pervasive. It extends far beyond the products themselves, tapping into human psychology to create intense associations with and loyalties for specific brand names. The world's most iconic brands have reached that status because of successful, strong, consistent marketing campaigns. As an independent creative, you want to create similar associations for your target audiences (potential clients or customers) and forge similarly strong loyalties.

Of course you are not a bar of soap, and personal branding does not mean that you have to think of yourself as one. Instead, you do want to think of your product—what you can deliver to potential clients, customers, and employers—as a branded item that resonates and has meaning beyond the product itself. Like the most successful brand names, your personal brand means something to those who have connected with it. The question, then, is how to get people to connect to your brand message in the first place. To better understand this problem, we will look at some branding basics, and consider how they might apply to you.

Consider Your Brand

In building your personal brand, you will have similar considerations to those faced by large companies that sell consumer products. With some exceptions, you will want to consider the following:

- Your name or brand's name, and whether they are the same
- Your product or pitch in one or two sentences
- The ideal target audience (or audiences) you hope to reach
- The need or demand your product fulfills
- The look and feel of your brand
- Logos and imagery
- Strategy for establishing your brand with your potential customers, clients, or employers
- Strategy for maintaining and building your brand with your core audiences

Contemplate these considerations as you consider the following basic branding rules.

Successful Branding Is Consistent

In addition to the specific elements of a strong brand, brand managers (and you) must always keep in mind how these elements work together. Even the strongest brand element will likely fail if it does not fit well with the brand's other elements.

This may seem simple and straightforward. However, even the most successful brand managers must sometimes make difficult or unintuitive decisions when faced with the prospect of brand inconsistency. This means that you, as an individual, should choose your brand well, making ample time for research before you commit. Once you have established your brand, you will not want to change it or have to modify it constantly to maintain consistency.

For instance, as your own personal brand manager, you regularly create and publish content on your blog and through various social media channels. You do this to keep your brand in front of your audience and top of mind for them. When you consider what kind of content you should produce and publish, you need to keep in mind not just the content of your social media entries, but also their look and the mood they create at a glance. (Often a glance is all it takes for a potential client to decide whether they want to buy into or join your team.)

Let's say you have established your brand as a mommy blogger and a resource for other moms. You test and review products, blog about childcare trends, and respond to reader questions about the challenges of being a new mom. You resist the temptation to blog about the environment or workplace politics (if you can't connect them to motherhood) because those issues are not related to your brand. Other audiences may be interested in these topics. Your audience may even be interested in these topics, but they would be more likely to seek out their discussion or analysis in *The New York Times* or on a website with a reputation for delivering news and expert opinion. In other words, people will not consult a mommy blog for global warming news. People seek out different brands for different things. Trying to be all things to everyone will dilute, and ultimately destroy, your brand. Specializing keeps your brand consistent and helps maintain your credibility.

Keep in mind that brand dilution and confusion can happen in smaller ways too. These are not always quite as intuitive, and although they may seem small, their impact can become significant over time. For example, you have carefully crafted a brand that is all about the outdoors, conservation, and sustainability. Maybe you are an environmental writer, or a graphic designer or filmmaker who focuses on environmental subjects.

Your website design and images are consistently in earth tones—mostly brown and forest green. You want your online identity to suggest a lush natural environment: tall green redwoods, woodstove-lit log cabins, dense underbrush, tame deer. At a glance, your Instagram posts suggest woodsy warmth. At least they did until last week, when you took a tropical vacation and could not resist posting updates from your sunny island retreat. Now when potential clients or customers glance at your Instagram feed, they see dozens of woodsy images abruptly interrupted by bright images of palm trees and blue skies. What does this say about your brand?

No matter how beautiful these images may be, they will, at best, confuse your audience, and at worst, alienate them completely. The reason is simple: You have deviated from your brand. Your brand is your calling card, and inconsistency shows a lack of commitment to it.

Successful Branding Is Strategic

Launching a brand is not as simple as coming up with a good idea and unleashing it upon the world. For a successful launch and a long-term future for your brand, you need to think strategically. Strategic thinking is different in that it takes the long view. Instead of tactical thinking, which focuses on immediate tasks at hand, strategic thinking requires one to consider the entire planning process from beginning to end. It differs from tactical thinking in that it is proactive instead of reactive. From the very beginning, the planning process should be undertaken with the end goal in mind.

A well-planned strategy will consider all steps toward the goal. It will also include measureable outcomes. Taking sufficient time to develop the plan at this stage will yield huge dividends as it will make brand management an automatic process instead of requiring continuous reinvention. A strategy includes outcomes or milestones along the way toward achieving your goals. These allow you to determine how close you are to achieving those goals, and how much further you still need to go.

Another important benefit of strategic planning is the ability to assess your progress and make any necessary changes to your plan based on comparing your actual accomplishments to your expectations. A well-laid strategic plan allows for assessment and adjustment based on outcomes. A comprehensive plan accounts for all stages of an enterprise's life-cycle—from idea, to development, to growth, to assessment, and, if necessary, to change or termination.

At this point it may be instructive to look more closely at tactical versus strategic planning. Most of us are familiar with tactics. We employ tactics regularly in response to everyday challenges. For instance, while searching for city parking, we may employ the tactic of circling a city block until we see someone back a car out of a coveted spot. While this approach may help us find a place to park the car, it is short-range and not particularly useful in achieving our ultimate goals. This is because tactics are immediate and limited to a fairly specific problem, while strategies consider the big picture.

Much of the current scholarship on tactics and strategies are from the military sphere, where examples of both concepts are plentiful. Let's look at a few examples.

Tactic: Escaping an enemy ambush.
Strategy: Winning the war.
Tactic: Avoiding starvation.
Strategy: Creating a plan for sustainable agriculture.
Tactic: Getting an A on an exam.
Strategy: Getting a good job after graduation.

Now consider some of the tactics you have employed or are employing on the way toward fulfilling your larger career strategy. It may help to create a simple worksheet like the example following to differentiate your tactics from your strategies.

Career Tactics and Strategies

For each tactic you list, determine the broader strategy into which it fits. Keep in mind that several tactics may be part of the same strategic plan.

Tactic	Strategy

Some Ubiquitous Brands, and What You Can Learn From Them

Coca-Cola

Coca-Cola provides what may be the most extreme example of proprietary branding on the planet. The company has long been known to be fiercely protective of its intellectual property, just as it is famously protective of its iconic beverage's formula.

The company has developed a huge, sprawling infrastructure around the maintenance and protection of its story and marketing strategy, even going so far as to establish an Atlanta, Georgia, museum dedicated to the company and its iconic product. Asked for a brief interview about the company's approach to branding, Tommica of Industry and Consumer Affairs at Coca-Cola, responded quickly (even on a Sunday), only to explain that no representative of the company would be available to talk, and further, that "information regarding our marketing strategy is considered to be proprietary."[2]

In addition to its size, Coca-Cola remains an excellent branding case study for the duration of its product, if nothing else. The first Coca-Cola was poured in 1886, more than 100 years ago. Few companies of its age remain in existence today. The company would not have been nearly so successful had it not fiercely protected its brand almost since the beginning. That said, in recent years, the Internet and social media have to some degree transformed not only the way the company is perceived, but also how it must function to remain successful.

FIGURE 3.2 The Coca-Cola logo decorates a wooden boat in Cambodia.

Credit: Shutterstock ID#394241830

The now-ubiquitous Coca-Cola logo was among the first recognized brand images in the world, although at the time, the company's founders were more concerned with protecting their secret formula than the product's name. The formula was patented in 1869, and the Coca-Cola logo was patented in 1893, two dozen years later.[3]

Although the company was slow to realize the significance and power of its logo and brand message, it was among the first to develop a coherent message that went beyond the use of a brand name to sell products, creating an entire branded environment that was reinforced by iconic illustrations— mostly on metal trays, but also on signs, postcards, and even sheet music—that depict, among other eager Coca-Cola drinkers, women in Victorian dress or in flapper attire, and white-clad nurses during World War II. In a 2006 *Observer* article, British reporter Phil Hogan recounted his tour of the World of Coca-Cola museum in Atlanta, Georgia, the soft drink's birthplace and the company's home to this day. He quoted his tour guide's description: "'See how they used one image across a range of things just to get the message out there.' Here now are the Coke calendars, the Coke barometers, lampshades and tea sets."[4]

More than a century ago, Coca-Cola understood the importance of making strong associations with its brand, making those associations ubiquitous, and considering them an investment in future sales if not as a tactic that would directly lead to sales. This was a new idea at the time. Although the world's consumers have grown more sophisticated over the last several decades, Coca-Cola still has much to teach independent creatives who, to compete in the current economy, must adopt a similarly strategic approach to branding.

The Lesson: Be strategic; be consistent. Protect your brand image because building an iconic one can take decades.

Apple

The name "Apple" invokes strong reactions from most. Love it or hate it, Apple Inc. has become one of the world's most prominent brands in the last couple decades, particularly since it introduced the world's first smartphone, the iPhone, in 2007. For users of Apple products (who often buy into the entire product line), loyalty to the brand is akin to religion. Critics have described Apple customers' relationship to the brand as "cult like."[5]

In fact, researchers have conducted studies into the religious nature of faithful product users' interactions with the products themselves. In 2008, *Advertising Age* fleshed out the religious comparison by describing successful brand elements in religious terms. Among the categories discussed by writer Martin Lindstrom were: grandeur, evangelism, and symbolism. Apple has strong entries in each of these categories, with its sleek silver, white, and clear Apple stores serving as the brand's cathedrals.[6]

FIGURE 3.3 The Apple store on Fifth Avenue in New York is a modern-day cathedral.
Credit: Shutterstock ID#115231372

This is no accident, and it is anything but negative. The degree to which Apple products have come to dominate loyal users' business and personal interactions illustrates the company's successful approach to branding. However, no amount of savvy branding could have inspired this degree of loyalty had the products not delivered exactly what their customers wanted.

At its root, no enterprise—whether a company or an individual—can build a successful brand without delivering a quality product for which there is demand. However, the inverse is not true. It is, in other words, possible for a high-quality product that is in demand to never find its audience in the absence of a strong marketing campaign. In recent years Apple has faced competition from several smartphone makers with their own loyal followings. Despite sometimes unfavorable comparisons to other company's products, the iPhone remains synonymous with "smartphone" and among the world's most recognized technology devices.

The Lesson: Brand loyalty is more about emotions and feelings than about logic or reality.

Google

Google has so successfully branded itself that it has become a verb. Like Band-Aid and Xerox before it, Google the advertising company may be ubiquitous, but it is perhaps not as well known as the concept of "googling." Although Xerox, a company best known for its photocopiers, has issued reminders and warnings about the use of its trademarked name to refer to any kind of copying, by any device, Google has not publicly complained. The company hasn't had to complain. Not only does it play an increasing role in our daily lives, through its search engine but also through e-mail, hangouts, and its video platform You-Tube, but it faces no close competition.

Since its founding in 1998, Google has created dozens of tools and apps designed to make our online lives easier. As an early entrant into the consumer Web technology field, Google did not have to work too hard to cultivate a distinctive brand. Although its initial official mission statement was "to organize the world's information and make it universally accessible and useful," its unofficial mission, "Don't be evil," was better known.[7]

While most of us will never step foot on Google's famous main campus, the Googleplex, we probably know a little bit about it. It is likely we've heard tales of such lavish workplace perks as onsite gyms and lap pools, video games, free food, haircuts, and dry cleaning, and lots more things that supposedly make Google a great place to work. Stories about these perks helped Google cement its brand as a great, progressive employer.

From a distance, we outsiders admired and mythologized the company's eagerness to please and keep employees, along with the extreme intelligence and purpose we assumed its dedicated employees to have. In an employment marketplace in which part-time, freelance, and home-based jobs become ever more common, the once-lauded Google lifestyle seems more and more of an anachronism. Google's

FIGURE 3.4 Employees use bikes painted in the company's colors to get around the Googleplex.

Credit: Shutterstock ID#302746334

image has evolved over the last decade or so, moving to embrace more millennial-generation values such as quality of life and free time. (A 2016 study by Fidelity Investments found that "millennials would take an average pay cut of $7,600 if they could improve their career development, find more purposeful work, better work-life balance or a better company culture."[8]) Like Facebook and other technology companies, Google now offers generous maternity and paternity leave, along with other pro-family perks.

The Lesson: Like its departure from policies that may have discouraged work-life balance, Google has abandoned dozens of its less successful products over the years, including the news aggregator iGoogle, the real-time collaboration tool Google Wave, and the photo organizing and editing app Picasa, among others. Take a lesson from Google if you want to keep your brand fresh and functional. Facilitate constructive evolution by casting off parts of your brand or image that no longer work for you or make sense in the current environment.

A Fragmented World Means Faster Evolution

Just as widespread adoption of the Internet changed the media forever, globalizing communication campaigns and introducing the world to ideas and products that had previously been limited to local audiences, the Internet also transformed the world into a vast global marketplace, allowing companies and their brands to compete with others around the world. This meant more options for consumers, and more competition for the companies that owned brands.

Now, when we go to a grocery store, where we may have once seen only one, two, or three major brand competitors, now we most likely encounter a large number of choices in each product type. What was a great development for consumers became a turning point for brands and the companies that owned them. The large companies that owned once-ubiquitous brands, perhaps for the first time ever had to consider how they would position their brand and the products it represented. As consumers gained options, brands could no longer sell themselves.

Much like how big trailblazing mass market companies like Coca-Cola and Procter and Gamble had to rethink their branding strategy as competitors began to flood the marketplace, independent contractors like you need to rethink—or perhaps consider for the first time—how you will differentiate yourself through your personal brand. Companies that did not adequately differentiate and refine their brands as new competitors arose disappeared eventually. Take a lesson from them if you want to build an enduring brand. Reading this book should help.

Notes

1 Tedlow, Richard S. *New and Improved: The Story of Mass Marketing in America* (New York: Basic Books, 1990), 14.
2 Personal communication.

3 Petty, Ross D. "Coca-Cola Brand Protection before World War II. It's the Real Thing!" *Journal of Historical Research in Marketing* 4, no. 2 (2012): 224–244. http://dx.doi.org/10.1108/17557501211224430.

4 Hogan, Phil. 2006. "Soft Drink Hard Sell: For Coca-Cola, the Fiasco of New Coke and 'Pure' Dasani Tap Water Were Mere Hiccups on the Road to Global Domination. Now, with a $2bn-a-year Spend on Marketing, the World's Biggest Brand Is Zeroing in on Its New Target Customer. Phil Hogan Heads for Coke HQ in Atlanta as It Prepares to Serve Up 'Bloke Coke'." *The Observer,* July 9.

5 "Apple's Emotional Branding." 2014. *Financial Express*, September 9.

6 Lindstrom, Martin. "How Apple, Others have Cultivated Religious Followings." *Advertising Age* 79, no. 45 (2008): 16–17.

7 Roberts, Daniel. 2015. "Alphabet Drops Google's Famous 'Don't Be Evil' Motto." *Fortune.* Accessed September 29, 2016. http://fortune.com/2015/10/05/alphabet-google-evil/.

8 Chew, Jonathan. 2016. "Why Millennials Would Take a $7,600 Pay Cut for a New Job." *Fortune.* Accessed September 29, 2016. http://fortune.com/2016/04/08/fidelity-millennial-study-career/.

4

BRAND YOU

In earlier chapters, we explored the origins and meaning of branding—what it is and where it came from. In this chapter, we explore the question of why we do it and how we personalize it. Branding may make perfect sense when we're talking about dish soap or cereal. But how does it apply to people? And how can we talk about branding people without turning them into objects?

These are all good questions that lie at the heart of this book. To many, the idea of branding human beings rankles. It can sound a bit dehumanizing. Perhaps someone—a teacher, a boss, a career counselor—advised you to launch a personal branding campaign as a career strategy. Why? Isn't it good enough to have a solid resume, great skills, and a good start at experience?

In some fields, that may be the case. But today, especially if you plan to work in the creative industries—including media, art, design, and consulting, and some parts of the service sector (in real estate sales or financial or personal counseling, for example, or as a hairdresser, esthetician or anyone else who may rely on personal marketing for financial survival)—branding is essential. Without a brand, we may find ourselves without a business or a means to support ourselves.

Personal branding for professionals is a fairly new concept. It's unlikely your parents or their parents had to concern themselves much with forging and promoting a personal brand. The reason for this is simple: The economy has changed. And more of us—particularly in the creative fields—are now working for ourselves. Even if you work for a big firm with a huge, well regarded name today, the nature of today's economy suggests you probably can't count on being with that firm forever. According to the U.S. Bureau of Labor Statistics, the average length of time someone stays in a job is now 4.6 years.[1] That number may have surprised previous generations.

FIGURE 4.1 You are more than a brand.

Credit: Shutterstock ID#203978866

FIGURE 4.2 U.S. workers stay in their jobs for less than five years on average.

Credit: Shutterstock ID#447401257

No longer directly connected to the huge, well-recognized brands that employed their predecessors, today's creative professionals must create and even *be* their own brands. And it is no easy task. For writers, it may be as clear a problem as no longer having a *New York Times* or *Washington Post* business card with their name printed on it to earn them access and establish credibility. Instead, they may have to introduce themselves with a simple card that bears the occupation "writer." Without significant name recognition, a business card emblazoned "writer" may not get someone very far. This is another reason why personal branding is important.

Perhaps the most significant reason why personal branding is important for creative professionals is that there is now so much more competition, and with that has come a greater need to stand out from the crowd. Because there are now so many independent creatives jockeying for attention in an increasingly crowded field, brands are under more pressure than ever to distinguish themselves. While simple talent, a good work ethic, and excellent interviewing skills may have once allowed writers and other creatives to get good jobs and advance in their careers, these things alone are not enough in a world where countless other creatives with similar talents and skill sets are competing for the same jobs and opportunities online.

Even if you have not yet settled on the specifics of your brand, at least you are now actively thinking about it. You don't need to concern yourself with putting it into words or a plan just yet. Simply focus it in your mind. This will make it easier to define or clarify your brand later on. Because you are so close to it personally, building a brand requires some degree of reflection. That takes some time, and it may not come naturally.

Journalists in particular have been trained to report on stories without becoming part of the story. Since the rise of Web-based journalism and the new competition it has brought, journalists, like other creatives, face increasing pressure to make a personal impression, to risk becoming part of the story. The days of journalists as neutral, objective interpreters of the facts are over. Readers, viewers, and listeners now want to know who is telling the story (and this applies to every creative field) before they determine whether the story is worth their investment in time.

Although the unique nature of every creative's work requires a subtlety and nuanced approach to brand crafting, there are a few basic requirements to be considered by every brand crafter. Here are a few of them:

- Skill sets and specializations. Explain that you can do everything required of your profession, but also show you have a special skill or characteristic that sets you apart. This is the value added of your brand. That could be your edge, the reason your CV or proposal is selected among dozens from other well-qualified candidates.
- Flexibility and open-mindedness. The economy and creative industries change quickly. Demonstrate your understanding of the world beyond your

own, and show that you are preparing to serve the future needs and demands of your field.

- Client/customer-centeredness. Show that you are eager and prepared to solve people's problems. Although your resume, CV, or online portfolio is about your work and career, the actual focus should be on its reader or viewer.

Learn From Examples

As we discuss throughout this volume, successful branding campaigns create immediate familiarity and strong positive associations. Well-conceived brands are recognizable at a glance and memorable over the long term. However, unlike Coca-Cola or Target, your brand is most likely relatively new, and it is almost certainly not as well known. The good news is, your brand will never need to be as big and successful as these huge household names. You merely need to get your brand message across to those you are closely targeting.

To better understand the power of strong branding, research the brand campaigns of those most closely competing for the same share of the marketplace in your field. You will probably see fairly quickly which campaigns hit their mark and which just miss. It may be more difficult at first to determine exactly why a campaign you can immediately identify as successful actually is. You should have a better idea of what to look for by the time you finish this book.

Do Your Homework

How do you even start planning your brand? This is a daunting question. A logical first step is to explore. Hit the Web, and search for sites that represent brands similar to your own. Find a few sites you find particularly appealing or compelling, and take note of why you noticed them. Sites that represent strong brands will stand out immediately, although you may not yet know why. If you have to stop and consider whether a particular site is successful, you can rule that one out.

Finding sites that provide appropriate points of reference for your brand is good practice for choosing keywords for your own brand. Pay close attention to not just the sites themselves, but also to the search terms that brought them up. Ask yourself if these are the search words you plan to use for yourself, and if so, consider how your own brand might fit in (or not) among the results. Choosing keywords is not an exact science. However, Google, which hosts around three-quarters of all Web searches,[2] is itself the best resource for decision-making about keywords—whether for search engine optimization (SEO) or simple searches to help you assess your potential competition.

Examining how others in your field have branded themselves can be a big help. But how do you know what to look for? And before you look anywhere, you have to know where to look. Before you can even begin to conceive a branding campaign, you need to clarify two key questions: (1) Who is your audience or target market?; (2) Where can you find them?

Research Google Trends

If you don't already use it, familiarize yourself with Google Trends (https:// www.google.com/trends/). Searching Google Trends is the most direct way to research what people around the world are googling. The Google Trends home-page lists 200-plus of the most popular searches currently trending on Google. Click on any one of them, and you will find a graph of search interest in the topic over the span of a few days. You will see which geographical areas were home to the most searches. You will see the actual words people typed into Google to access information on the topic. And you will be presented with related topics that you can click on for the same information.

Use Google Trends to optimize the way people find your content through Web searches. (Search engine optimization, or SEO, is discussed at length later in this volume.) This is one of several essential research tools Google provides users. Others include Google Analytics, Google Ad Words, and Search Console. These three products help drive traffic to your website and help you learn more about improving your site based on information about the behavior of visitors to your site.

FIGURE 4.3 Creatives should know how to read basic analytics data.

Credit: Shutterstock ID#487846861

Google Analytics provides you with much more than just the number of visitors to your site, but also provides insights on important things like where visitors to your site are located, where on your website they first arrive, how long they stay on your site, how many pages they view, and any referring site that led them there. Of course none of this will help you much until you determine who you are, what goods or services you offer, and how you will brand yourself online. That said, having a sense of the online landscape in your field should help inform the way you build your brand online. We return to a more complete discussion of Google Analytics in Chapter 10. There, we consider how you can use analytics data to tweak or fine-tune your online content. For now, though, a basic understanding of how to build awareness of your brand online should be enough.

Let's assume you are new to branding. If you are a journalist or artist accustomed to working alone, the thought of branding may not at first sit well with you, but you know you have to do it. Your professional success may depend on it. You may be open-minded and willing to learn, but you are not yet sure where to start. You are not sure what makes you unique or what might make you identifiable as a brand. How do you even begin to conceive your brand?

Before you can begin to craft your brand, you need to know what kinds of goods or services you will provide to your target market. In other words, what value will you provide others? What is your business? Is it to inform and enlighten? To entertain? Something different?

For the moment, let's assume you are in the services business. At its most basic level, branding is the same for those offering products (which can include art or handmade items) as it is for those offering services (which can be anything from journalism and social media management to marketing and sales). The kind of business you are in should help determine the nature of your relationship to your brand. Are you your brand? Do you represent branded products? Does your personal brand differ at all from your professional brand? Answering these questions will help you determine your brand's positioning.

Position Your Brand

In business school, one of the core concepts taught in the marketing and entrepreneurship classes is product positioning. In short, product positioning is about knowing who your customer is and what they are looking for. It is not being all things to all potential customers. Rather, it is about determining the best way to present your product (or yourself) to the customer, and single-mindedly pursuing that approach.

This is important because not focusing on a specific approach based on the profile of your client or customer will likely result in failure. For instance, if your enterprise differentiates itself on the basis of high-quality products or exceptional customer service, marketing messages that promote low prices or deep discounts can confuse the message. And that undermines your brand.

You can see this at work in the marketing of personal injury attorneys on TV, radio, and the Web. Coming on strong with money-focused messages will naturally lead viewers to assume that the services offered by the law firm are shoddy and possibly corrupt. It will be difficult for an attorney who has presented his or her services in this light to win the trust of clients who are looking for excellent ethical representation. That is not to say that a brand's reputation cannot change or evolve. But a brand should stick to one positioning strategy at a time.

Among the main choices you will want to make when positioning your product or service is whether you will compete on the basis of quality or cost. In other words, will your ideal customer be more interested in a great deal or in high quality? If you are your own product, selling your own services, you most likely want to position yourself as a quality choice (unless you are a personal injury attorney).

For the vast majority of one-person businesses, whether they sell products or services (such as writing, editing, photography, videography, graphic design, etc.), competing on the basis of cost is not a good idea. When you are an individual going up against large companies, your innate advantage is the personal touch. That is the main differentiator between you and a large advertising company or copywriter or marketing firm.

You will eventually need to choose a strategy. You cannot compete both on cost and quality because each branding position cancels the other out. To

FIGURE 4.4 Most creatives choose quality over cost.

Credit: Shutterstock ID#297677570

determine which way to go, you want to, as always, try to envision your real or ideal customer base. Consider what they may be looking for when they visit your business. If you are a maker of unique handmade soaps, dolls, or jewelry, distributing too many branding messages focused on low cost or discounts would likely backfire by diminishing the association with quality for your audience and leading them to question the value of your goods or services.

This applies to pricing too. Remember that the price charged for an item or a service conveys to the customer its degree of quality. Pricing something too low may suggest to potential customers or clients that the product or service is low quality or, quite literally, cheap. There are countless anecdotes about businesses selling unique, handmade, or otherwise high-quality items that actually increase their business volume after raising prices. Take this as a lesson that, counterintuitive as it may seem, lower prices are not always what customers are seeking.

Unless you plan to be a cost leader (basing your business on offering the deepest discounts and the lowest prices), quality and customer service are most likely where you want to position your brand. Besides, it is a rare small business or new entrepreneurial venture that is either able to or would be smart to compete on cost.

Like with almost every concept in this book, there are no hard and fast rules regarding positioning your brand. But there are guidelines that you should consider. Determining whether you will position your brand to compete in the quality or cost realm is only the start, and it's likely an easy decision. There is much more to positioning a brand. As On the Mark marketing consultants explain it, product positioning is about three things: differentiating yourself from the competition; addressing the needs of your customer, client, or audience; and articulating (showing) how you are uniquely able to meet those needs.[3]

On the Mark suggests that those looking to determine or refine the positioning of their brand consider the following: positioning yourself against or away from a competitor (thereby differentiating yourself), any specific benefits you offer to the potential client or customer, what is unique about your brand or business, how (if at all) your brand crosses product lines (i.e., marketing for creatives), any specific uses or conditions in which your product or service would be particularly relevant, and any differentiating aspects of your target audience or community.

You may have noticed a common theme emerge here: Your brand is unlike any other brand, provides value no other brand does, and serves a dedicated, highly specialized client. This means, as we discuss elsewhere in this book, that delivering a high-quality product or service itself is not enough in a crowded consumer marketplace. The key to success as an entrepreneur is to deliver high quality differently in some way, to find your specific niche. Especially these days, when most people claim to suffer from information overload, the more you can do to quickly communicate the unique advantages of your product or service, the more likely you will be to stand out and succeed.

Be a Generalist *and* a Specialist

One of the most challenging quandaries creative professionals face today is balancing generalization with specialization. Being a generalist or a specialist today is not enough. Successful creatives are both.

Thanks to the Internet, there are now so many others available who have all the important qualifications for a job in any field that no one can afford to come up short in any relevant area. Rather, creatives need a number of basic skills and at least a working knowledge of everything. They *also* need a well-developed specialty that sets them apart from all the others. Quite simply, they need to be the whole package. This wasn't necessary in days when labor markets were more localized.

Recent developments in the field of journalism have made this abundantly clear. In rare instances these days are entry-level journalists hired to simply write. It is widely expected that any freshly minted journalist also has basic Web-building skills, the ability to create competent short videos, social media savvy, and some editing experience. On top of that, they are also expected to bring something special to the table. Otherwise, how could they distinguish themselves from the dozens (or hundreds, or even thousands) of other candidates out there with similar foundational skills?

Distinguishing factors are likely skills, but they can also be backgrounds or experiences. Perhaps a writer can distinguish herself because she holds an advanced

FIGURE 4.5 Creatives need to do a bit of everything—and also specialize.

Credit: Shutterstock ID#422883451

degree in astrophysics, or because she is recovering from a drug addiction or was once homeless, or because she speaks three languages. These specializations can give people a unique perspective or special access to communities their peers may never get.

But how do you know what you need to know in a particular field? There is no exact answer because the tools change continuously, and not all employers or clients have the same demands. That said, there are a few essentials.

All entrepreneurial creatives should have basic facility with the following skill sets:

- Professional writing and editing
- Basics of photography and photo editing
- Graphic design
- Web development skills
- Video and audio recording and editing

Of course they now also need basic entrepreneurial skills, and skills that aren't directly related to their work. These include:

- Marketing and promotion, including advertising fundamentals
- Budgeting and accounting
- Navigating tax law
- Personal finance

Now comes the specialty or background that sets someone apart from potentially thousands of other job applicants or bidders for a job. Yes, this is something that is needed *in addition to* all of the above skills, talents, and abilities.

If this seems like a tall order—particularly for one just entering the employment marketplace—it is. Just because the old gatekeepers are gone, and all of us can now publish to a worldwide forum for free does not mean that a creative, journalism, or media job these days is any easier than it once was. In fact, in many ways it is probably more difficult. However, it is now much easier to break into fields that once required the help of an employer or corporate sponsor.

You may be starting to wonder what all of this has to do with branding. In truth, your unique skill set, specialty or background *is* your brand. It's what sets you apart and makes you special. Branding is all about differentiation, so it is the differences, not the similarities, that should serve as the basis of your brand.

If you do not yet know what sets you apart or makes you special, you may struggle to build a solid, distinct brand. You need to know what you are promoting before you promote it. Let's say you have all the required skill sets for your field, but you are not quite sure what sets you apart. Sure, you may have many potential characteristics that could qualify as a differentiator, but how do you know which one will work best? This will require some research and reflection.

The following exercise will help you explore possible branding differentiators. Of course, if you have not yet mastered one or more of the required skill sets above, you will want to work on building up those basic skills before moving on to your specialization.

To explore potential avenues for personal branding, answer the questions in the following table. Then follow the steps listed below.

Topic area	List any special abilities, experience or background
Family or life experience (access to special communities, experience living in other countries, exposure to or knowledge of unusual environments)	
Additional languages	
Specialized technical skills	
Unique or highly developed talents	

1. For each of the items you identified in the table above, consider which might be interesting to a potential employer or client. Ask your friends, teachers or others with knowledge of current marketplace conditions and demands to help you rank each specialized skill, talent, ability, or background in order or importance or significance. Try to come up with a list of three to five items.
2. For each item (or branding position), identify 5 to 10 keywords that one may search for when identifying possible job candidates or researching your field.
3. Enter the keywords for each item you identified above into a search engine such as Google, one at a time. Note how many results each search yields, how closely they match this potential personal specialization, and how many of the results would qualify as direct competition if you were competing from this brand position.
4. Note those results that are similar to your own potential branding message.
5. Follow numbers 3 and 4, above, for each additional potential branding position.
6. Compare the results for each, determining which positions may be saturated (where the needs you would fulfill are already more than sufficiently served by other people or companies) and which may indicate an unmet need or demand that you could fill.

You should now have a good start on developing a unique branding position—something that could make you particularly valuable to potential employers, customers, and clients. If, even after this exercise, your unique branding position is not obvious to you or if you have too many potential unique branding positions (this is a good problem to have), ask friends and family members to help identify your unique characteristics, and to help you pick the best one. Often we do not have enough perspective on ourselves to be able to clearly discern our strengths and weaknesses, or our competitive advantages.

Consider Your Resume, CV, or Portfolio a Work in Progress

Regardless of what you do across social media to build and reinforce your brand, keep in mind you still also need a static page or site to house your digital resume or CV, and provide links and contact information. You may also want to use this space to house samples of your work, client testimonials, informational downloads, or your blog. The point is to clearly spell out what you do, and make it easy for potential clients, customers, and employers to find you.

Although there are a number of sites and platforms now available for creating and sharing employment information and enabling connections (LinkedIn is the best known), you just can't beat having complete control of your own site. Particularly if you are an artist, photographer, designer, or if you do other work in a visual field, a busy, business-oriented platform like LinkedIn may undermine your brand identity. A visual person needs a visual site.

Regardless of what tool you use to build your online resume, there are a few basic items you want to make sure to include. In addition to resume basics such

FIGURE 4.6 Creatives need to represent themselves well online.

Credit: Shutterstock ID#411934717

as contact information, education, and job history, you may also want to include a simple head-and-shoulders photo. It doesn't need to be a professional studio shot, but it should reinforce your brand. For instance, if you are a nature photographer, your photo might show you in the woods or holding a camera. Also plan to include a short personal video in which you introduce yourself to potential employers or clients. This will help build trust with those who need reassurance that you are who you say you are, and that you will make good on your promises.

Here are a few things to keep in mind as you create your online resume or home page:

- Reinforce your brand. Your online resume, CV, or portfolio should not just be aligned with your brand. It should also reinforce your brand. Include a brief bio, video, and images that play up what makes you different or special.
- Sell your skills. Although your primary motivation may be to find work, focus on what you can do for others.
- Link like crazy. Link to your professional websites, social media accounts, and professional organizations (that align with your brand) with which you are affiliated. Link to your personal (but professional) blog if you have one. If you don't, consider starting one. A blog on your professional website or portfolio doesn't carry the same expectations as a stand-alone blog. You don't need to post every day to a blog you use to supplement your professional site. After all, the purpose of this kind of blog is specifically to establish your credibility and help you get work. Chances are low that general readers will want to check in each day to read the latest posts on your career site (unless you are a career counselor). That said, if you create content that may help inform others and you make it searchable through thoughtfully selected keywords or tags, people who are searching for information may wind up on your site. If they like what they read, they may even hire you.
- Solicit and share testimonials. Ask for former and current bosses and supervisors to write short testimonials about your work. Ask if you can feature the testimonials on your website.
- Share samples of work, including presentations and papers. Highlight content that may be relevant or of interest to your readers. Include downloadable resources. Providing a short list of useful information, or worksheets to help readers solve problems is your best opportunity to make a lasting impression.

Once you have created your brand and an online landing page to show it off, remember to revisit both from time to time to ensure they stay current. Employment conditions and technology are in constant flux. A line or term in a CV can quickly look outdated. While changing careers is now common, it is particularly so in the creative fields, where job descriptions can be vague, overlap or change entirely. As a creative, you will likely find opportunities you hadn't considered before if you are open to considering new ways of applying your skills. The uncertainty and flexibility of today's global job market is a good reminder of the need to not only keep your job skills current (and updated on your resume, bio, and online profiles) but to also maintain your contacts, create a strong professional brand, and keep your eyes open.

One tip for every professional looking for new opportunities and planning for the future is to keep a key eye on job openings and larger marketplace trends. Follow the news, and consider its implications for you and your field. (How will a change in Instagram's algorithms effect your social media strategy? The aging boomer population has brought surging demand for technical writers in the medical field.) Also make a habit of reading job postings—even if you are not actively looking for work. Paying close attention to the kinds of jobs that are being offered and the requirements for each will provide clear insights into the real labor market while helping you prepare for your own future. For example, if you see an increasing number of job postings in your field that list among their requirements a library science degree or grant writing experience, you may want to consider going back to school or taking a grant writing workshop.

As you continuously prepare for the labor market of tomorrow, resist the temptation to be all things to all people. Among the insights you glean from job postings, consider which ones are a good fit for your particular strengths, interests, and skill sets, and above all, which ones align with your brand.

Make It Mobile

Don't forget to think beyond the website—particularly if your key audience is young or in the developing world, where more people connect via mobile devices than desktop—or even laptop—computers. According to Deloitte Global, as of Spring 2016, 85 percent of younger millennials in 13 developed countries had access to a desktop or laptop computer, while 89 percent had access to a smartphone.[4] In the developing world, smartphone use, which once lagged far behind use in the developed world, is now nearly as widespread, according to Pew Research.[5] And everywhere, mobile devices are dominating—particularly for eCommerce and social media. In the United States, consumption of digital media on mobile devices eclipsed that on desktop and laptop computers all the way back in 2014, according to a comScore report that opened with the compelling line, "The days of desktop dominance are over."[6]

As smartphone use has become more widespread, people have grown more comfortable with using their phones and mobile devices for tasks they may not have imagined using them for previously, including making purchases and, most significantly, using social media. This simple fact should significantly inform your approach to personal branding. It will no doubt complicate your branding strategy, but it will also help focus your efforts and yield better results.

FIGURE 4.7 Millennials use smartphones more than they use computers.

Credit: Shutterstock ID#431964640

How much you need to vary your branding campaign on various platforms will depend on the diversity of your target audience, market, or client base. The narrower and more specific your ideal client or target market, the easier it will be for you to maintain consistent brand messaging. And when it comes to branding, consistency is key.

Practice Your Pitch

Elevator pitches are called what they are for a reason. They force you to focus your personal pitch to the mere 30 seconds or so a typical elevator ride takes. The term is old, but the concept remains relevant. Whether you are ever actually asked to make a 30-second pitch, being able to clearly and succinctly present yourself, your brand, and what you can do for your audience, followers, or community is a highly useful skill. It will become even more useful in the future, as people face ever more distractions and demands for their time. Honing your elevator pitch, even without the opportunity to deliver it, is great practice. If you cannot quickly summarize your brand and what it delivers, you need to dedicate more thought to exactly what your competitive advantage may be.

As you consider your elevator pitch, keep in mind two basic questions:

- Who is the audience, and what are their needs?
- Why am I uniquely qualified to satisfy those needs?

FIGURE 4.8 Elevator pitches aren't just for elevators.

Credit: Shutterstock ID#357640448

Practicing elevator pitches (even reciting and wordsmithing them in your head when you get a free moment) will ensure that when the time comes, your delivery will be smooth and confident. Hurrying through the pitch or merely reciting memorized lines will make the listener uncomfortable, as if they are fielding a sales pitch. Even if you *are* selling something (and you are—yourself) and you think you can offer something the listener needs, no one wants to hear a hard sell. The aim of an elevator pitch is to pique the listener's interest enough to want to hear more.

What to pitch is up to you. It depends on what you can offer. In business, elevator pitches are often about specific ideas such as requests for startup investment. Your pitch will likely be a bit more nuanced, but keep it as simple as possible. Limit the purpose of your pitch to explaining what you can do for the listener, and why you're the person to do it. Also make it memorable. Leave the listener with a distinct impression—ideally, that you are exactly the person to solve their problem. Have business cards on hand so they can easily follow up if they want to.

Decide What You Will—and Won't—Do

Although you may be hesitant to turn down work, especially in the early days of establishing your business, keep in mind that the kind of work you do—and the clients you take on—helps define your brand. In other words, your work represents you. As a rule, don't take on clients or jobs that could undermine, interfere with, or diminish your brand. Even if you believe you are not in a position to say no, consider that even one bad client or job could make it more difficult to get the kind of work you want later.

When considering whether to accept a client or a job, ask yourself whether you would be proud to display the product on your website or share the association through social media. Also ask yourself whether it is consistent with the other clients, jobs, products, or images that you have chosen to represent your brand. Keep in mind that you do not have to have a strong objection to a particular client, company, or job to respectfully decline an opportunity to represent it.

You may, for instance, opt not to take on a graphic design job for a gun shop. You may not take a personal, political, or moral position on guns. Perhaps you decline the opportunity because it conflicts with your brand or could create brand confusion for your target audience. Maybe you specialize in wedding invitations or your signature style tends heavily toward pastels and elaborate script. If this is the look of your brand (as well as your website and social media accounts), a dark design for a gun shop, featuring heavy black and gray text and straight lines, will clash with your established brand in a way that could damage your business. This is common sense.

Grow and Protect Your Reputation

Your success as an independent contractor, journalist, or creative entrepreneur depends on building and growing a positive reputation. Whether you are a journalist, artist, photographer, social media manager or any other kind of creative, the only way to establish yourself and your brand is to get your work—your name, your brand—out there. That means you need to not only develop a coherent brand identity, but you also need to create content that influencers and others will see, consume, and—you hope—help spread.

Put yourself everywhere it makes sense for your brand to be online—definitely on social media, but also on the Web. Write and produce content regularly, and share it liberally. Keep it simple, consistent, and recognizable. Develop a look, a style, or a signature that is exclusively yours. Protect and monitor your brand at all times. Perhaps most important, keep your personal and professional online lives separate—except when details of your personal life can reinforce your brand. For example, if your business is social media management for a charity that supports breast cancer research, posting photos of yourself running a half-marathon to raise money for cancer research makes perfect sense. Posting photos of your dog does not.

You don't need to delete your personal online accounts, although you may want to edit them, deleting any content (not just photographs, but posts too) that does not align with your brand. As a rule, you should not post anything

FIGURE 4.9 Don't be surprised by what you find when googling yourself.

Credit: Shutterstock ID#357697235

online anywhere that you would not like a potential employer to see, even on accounts on which you have restricted your privacy settings. Remember that privacy settings change frequently, and often without notice. You may learn too late that a compromising photo or post (even on someone's else's account) has compromised your brand. When in doubt about what information about or photos of you may be available online, google yourself. Do this once a month or so. You may be surprised at what you find. Just make sure you find it before potential clients, customers, or employers do.

BASIC BRANDING ELEMENTS

Keep in mind that strong branding images and words in themselves are not enough. To succeed, they must be coherent and consistent. What follows is a preview of some branding basics to help prepare you for a more in-depth exploration of these elements in later chapters.

Logos

We discuss logos at length in Chapter 9. For now, think about personal branding logos as somewhat subtler versions of corporate logos. In fact, personal branding logos may not seem like logos at all. They are often as simple as artful type. They may be your name or the name of your business. They serve a few purposes, including to:

- Provide a quick visual cue that identifies your brand and unifies whatever it appears on.
- Lend a professional appearance to your Web pages, business cards, and documents.
- Telegraph your style, creating a mood to help people quickly understand your work and how it might benefit them.

Taglines

Branding taglines, or slogans, are often associated with slick marketing campaigns, and are not as commonly used as they once were. Taglines sometimes appear as part of corporate logos. That said, it may not be a bad idea to consider a catchy tagline or slogan as it can make your brand more memorable. Of course taglines tend to convey a strong tone, so they may not be right for your business. Taglines, if you use them, should be short and to the point. Used well, they can quickly establish tone or demonstrate what differentiates your brand.

Tagline examples:

- Think different. (Apple)
- Just do it. (Nike)
- I'm lovin' it. (McDonald's)
- Got milk? (California Milk Processor Board)

Headlines

Much like a newspaper headline, branding headlines (on your website, on your blog, on your social media profiles) should, in a few words, preview the kind of work you do or establish how you can satisfy a need. Unlike taglines, which apply to an entire organization, company or product, headlines are specific, and they change. They also tend to be a bit longer than taglines because they are more detailed and specific. Use a headline on your resume, CV, or professional bio.

Headline examples:

- Committed to creating personal branding solutions
- Expert in social media messaging
- Ready for the next big idea in educational technology
- Finding communication solutions for you

Images and Other Graphics

Images and other graphics on your site and profiles should reinforce your brand. Consistent imagery consists of similarities in color palette, aspect ratio, quality, framing, type treatment, and subject matter among other factors.

Background and Layout

Make sure to also consider subtle things like background images or design and your site (or app) layout. If you lack the resources needed to hire someone to design your own site from scratch, choose a website theme that matches your brand and the kind of work you do. Some considerations to keep in mind as you select a theme include what function the theme was designed for. There are countless themes now available to highlight text blogs or photography, video, and portfolio showcases, among other specialties.

Color Schemes

Color schemes go hand in hand with background and layout. Like your website theme, they should be consistent. If you have not yet chosen a dominant color or colors for your site, you will want to choose one or two to stick with. If you chose complimentary shades of green for your headline and logo, you do not want to suddenly switch to red or blue. The bottom line, as always, is consistency.

Notes

1 2016. *Bls.gov.* Accessed May 27, 2016. http://www.bls.gov/news.release/archives/tenure_09182014.pdf.
2 "Search Engine Market Share." 2016. *Netmarketshare.com.* Accessed October 2, 2016. https://www.netmarketshare.com/search-engine-market-share.aspx?qprid=4&qpcustomd=0.
3 *Otmmarketing.com.* 2016. Accessed July 31, 2016. http://www.otmmarketing.com/Portals/42226/docs/product_positioning.pdf.
4 "Younger Millennials: The Pro-PC Generation—Deloitte CIO—WSJ." 2016. *Deloitte.wsj.com.* Accessed June 1, 2016. http://deloitte.wsj.com/cio/2016/04/21/younger-millennials-the-pro-pc-generation/.
5 Poushter, Jacob. 2016. "Smartphone Ownership and Internet Usage Continues to Climb in Emerging Economies." *Pew Research Center's Global Attitudes Project.* Accessed June 1, 2016. http://www.pewglobal.org/2016/02/22/smartphone-ownership-and-internet-usage-continues-to-climb-in-emerging-economies/.
6 "The U.S. Mobile App Report." 2016. *Comscore, Inc.* Accessed June 1, 2016. http://www.comscore.com/Insights/Presentations-and-Whitepapers/2014/The-US-Mobile-App-Report?cs_edgescape_cc=US.

5

WHAT'S YOUR STORY?

How do you distinguish yourself from all the others out there, so many of them just as talented—or even more so? How do you begin to conceive a personal brand? Like with most creative or journalistic projects, you start with a story. Although it may seem silly to those accustomed to thinking in strict business terms, storytelling is the essence of every successful business and individual. And if you are selling a service, it is in fact your story you are selling.

Of course we all have any number of stories we tell about ourselves. Not all are appropriate for establishing your personal brand. Keep in mind the story that defines your brand can be compiled from parts of several different personal stories. Just make sure that whatever you put out to your audiences is consistent, and that it tells a consistent story. Most important, make sure your branding story makes your products or services appealing to your target audiences, customers, or clients.

Before you choose a story, you may need to access thoughts, memories, and ideas you may not have considered in years. This may not be easy, but below are a few prompts that may help. To get the memories and ideas flowing, ask yourself some or all of the following questions:

- The guiding principle of my life is:
- I learned most from:
- My influences include:
- I believe:
- I am unique because:
- Friends would describe me as:
- I was drawn to my career because:
- My future life goals include:

- My strongest childhood memory is:
- My moral and ethical framework was informed by:
- The most significant experiences in my life include:
- The most important day of my life was:
- My most unusual life experience so far was:
- The highlight of my life so far was:

Once you start asking yourself these questions, you will likely find they lead to other questions, launching you on a journey of self-discovery that should help you to better understand why you chose your career path, what you have to offer others, and how your story informs who you are and makes you unique.

As you explore these topics, adding your responses, take copious notes or record your conversation with yourself. Do not censor yourself. Let your mind wander. There is no need to share your stories, memories, or ideas with anyone else. Simply consider this exercise a kind of brainstorming for your brand.

This initial process may take an hour, or it could take days or more. It does not need to be structured, although you do want to have something to show for it. Determining a quick take-away is important so you remember the main points and highlights in the moment, before the ideas fade as you return to the present. The ideas you come up with in this brainstorming session may be like dreams that fade too quickly as you wake to the morning light.

If you took copious notes during your brainstorming, go back through them quickly and highlight or underline the key points. If you recorded your thoughts, isolate the most relevant parts. Then put your notes aside overnight, allowing yourself to casually contemplate them before returning to them in a day or two. As you take this mental break from your initial thoughts, without advance planning, share the most compelling details with someone else or with yourself (either aloud or in your head).

Pay close attention to the details you end up focusing on as these are probably the aspects of your story others will find most compelling. It is easy to see why, if these were the thoughts that stood out most to you, they will also be the thoughts that stand out most to others. As soon as possible after sharing your thoughts, write them down or record the most interesting or relevant parts. These will likely become the core of your story.

Storytelling Isn't Just for Storytellers

Most journalists understand the value of story. If you want to make an idea, a concept, or even a person relatable (and you do), tell it as a story. This applies to every field and profession. It applies to life. We understand the world through stories. The more you can frame the world for others through story, the more others will enjoy hearing your stories.

FIGURE 5.1 Video helps humanize you to online audiences.

Credit: Shutterstock ID#411674473

This doesn't mean you have to write news or feature stories about people or yourself to make a point, and you shouldn't attempt to tell the entire story at one time. Even mini-stories (including photo stories, audio stories, and video stories) are compelling. Leaving your audiences wanting more is the goal, and it is a highly marketable skill.

Keep in mind that no matter how small or inconsequential they may seem, stories are everywhere. You just need to look out for them. Of course the most compelling story you will ever tell should be your own. Your story provides the context for your brand. It answers the what, where, why, and how of your brand. But it is not an ego exercise. As we discuss throughout this book, your personal brand is not really about you. Rather, it is about how you are uniquely qualified to serve your clients', customers', employers', or patrons' needs. Establishing trust among these audiences requires some context.

Before they go into business with you or associate themselves with you, people need to know, both figuratively and literally, where you are coming from, and whether they can trust you. This probably doesn't mean they want to know everything about you, but it does mean they do want to know enough to understand your motivations. Regardless of whether they consciously realize it, these stakeholders are looking for common ground. They can be superficial commonalities. Maybe you share a hometown or attended the same college. But often these connections go deeper. People want to feel good about the people with whom they work. Just as they may check out an insurance company or a bank before signing on with them, or read the Yelp reviews before trying out a new restaurant, your potential clients and customers want to know you share some experience or goals, and that you are worth their investment of time, money, or both.

This brings us back to the question: "What is your story?" Like most people, you likely have many stories you can tell. These are all part of the same story; they differ according to your perspective. Which you choose to tell depends on your reading of the audience's needs. Your approach to storytelling is unconscious and intuitive. For example, talking with a mother of small children, you may choose to talk about your own children or childhood. When talking with struggling students you tutor, you may choose to talk about your own struggles in school. Most of us do this automatically. It is a large part of how we relate to others. Thinking of what may seem like anecdotes as actual stories should help us keep the larger story in focus and consistent with our personal brand.

Apply Narrative Techniques to Your Story

When considering how to present your story, regardless of the medium or form, remember to make it as relevant and relatable as possible. Basic narrative techniques can help. What follows are a few you should consider.

Start Strong

As journalists well know, you should lead with your strongest point. Lead with whatever part of your story is most likely to interest the listener, viewer or reader. While this may not be what interests *you* most, remember that *you* are not your audience.

Stay on Message

Stick to the highlights, and your story will seem like poetry. Remember it is always better to leave the audience wanting more than to turn them off with too much or irrelevant information. Keep your main point in mind as you talk or write. Don't allow yourself to get sidetracked—unless the listener seems to want to take the conversation in a different direction. As a rule, you want to stay on message, but don't close your mind off to verbal or physical cues suggesting your message is somehow not the right one for the audience, situation, or time.

Be a Great Listener and Observer

As an entrepreneur in any field, you are customer-focused. Their needs—not yours—come first. That means you have to listen and observe. If you are too busy thinking about how you will deliver your pitch or make your case, you could miss something big, making yourself seem thoughtless or worse. An entre-preneur with poor listening or observing skills won't stay in business for long. If you hope to build a community of followers and fans (and you should), you need to know who these people are and what motivates them. Learn their stories.

As journalists and writers know, good stories come from good interviews. Creatives should routinely interview their constituencies, not necessarily in a formal way. If you are not used to interviewing people, you will be pleasantly surprised by how many of them relish any opportunity to talk about themselves. You'll learn this pretty quickly if you just start asking questions. Once they determine that you are actually listening, most will go on for as long as time allows. Listen closely, making mental notes to memorize key points (names are most important) and ask focused follow-up questions that show you were listening. Also make sure not to think so hard about the process that you forget to listen.

The best interviews are conducted in-person. For the interviewer or listener, they provide ample opportunities to learn about a person beyond what can be gleaned only through language. If you can, try to meet with people in their offices or homes. Their physical environment and behavior on their own home turf can be revealing. Does she have her framed degrees on the wall? Does he snap at his assistant? Does she interrupt your conversation to check text messages? Does he leave the room to take a call? Pay attention to these seemingly irrelevant things. They can provide helpful clues about a person's story, as well as their attitudes, and problems, and allow you to more effectively meet their needs.

FIGURE 5.2 You may be surprised by how much you hear when you listen.

Credit: Shutterstock ID#83465158

Revered sales trainer and author Dale Carnegie, in his famous 1936 volume *How to Win Friends and Influence People*, included listening skills as one of the six ways to make people like you. Of course, entrepreneurship isn't about being liked. However, it is difficult to succeed as an entrepreneur if people don't like and trust you. This fact does not just apply to sales. As Al Tompkins, senior faculty for broadcast and online at the Poynter Institute for Media Studies in St. Petersburg, Florida, and a veteran journalist, declared, "Listening is the essence of journalism."[1] It is also the essence of being a thoughtful, engaged human being. Don't take it lightly.

Think Cinematically

English, writing, and journalism teachers are fond of saying, "Show, don't tell." This is important advice for anyone. Particularly these days, when you have few words to make a strong impression, you can't afford to waste them on dull description. That said, most of our communication consists of summary—simple past-tense retellings of events and descriptions of feelings. It's unlikely anyone but close friends and family will be engaged by this kind of writing or speech. To leave your audience with lasting impressions, think cinematically. Describe a scene as if it were in a movie. Use action verbs to create a mental picture for your audience. Instead of summarizing an abstract idea in hundreds of words, drop your audience right into the action with just a few words. Make them the stars of their own movie. Showing (not telling) comes more naturally with video and photography, but you should practice it in writing too. Look at the following examples, then consider which approach is more effective at engaging the reader, listener, or viewer.

FIGURE 5.3 The best stories are cinematic.

Credit: Shutterstock ID#354487061

- Summary

I felt terrible about what happened. He was just in the wrong place at the wrong time. It wasn't his fault.

- Scene

As he crossed the street to the corner store, a bullet ripped through his back. He fell to the sidewalk, blood pooling around his naked torso.

End Strong

We know that stories, like the rhythms of life, have beginnings, middles, and ends. As a rule, middles are most easily forgotten. That's where you should put boilerplate facts and information. Making a strong impression requires a strong beginning and end. While a strong beginning gets the listener's or reader's attention, a strong ending ensures the message is retained. So end with a bang.

Include a Call to Action

Every tale worth telling has a point. You work hard to capture and keep your audience's attention. Why squander that by neglecting to "close"? In sales, closing means closing the deal. Although sales is not the direct objective of brand-building, you should have some goal in mind for every interaction. When you pitch your story on your website or through social media, consider what you want your readers or viewers to do with the information you've given them. Do you want them to remember your name and keep you in mind for future projects or collaborations? Do you want them to sign up for your e-newsletter? Do you want them to like your Facebook page or attend your pancake breakfast? Leave them with a call to action or something they can actually do aside from simply enjoying your story or video.

Move Effortlessly From Story to Brand

So you have your story, and you're well on your way to telling it. It is now your job to translate that story into a coherent branding message. Although you may quite literally choose to share your story on your website's "About" page, your story need not actually appear anywhere. It may merely be the narrative you maintain in your head as you contemplate your personal branding decisions. Having a clear, coherent story—even if you never express it directly to anyone else—will keep you grounded in the ideas behind your brand, and makes it easy to determine what will work and what won't work for your brand.

The idea may sound more complicated than it really is. The concept is actually quite simple. For example, your personal story is about growing up on a farm in Kentucky, surrounded by lush green fields, and defined by demanding but wholesome farm work. Your brand is about promoting natural, organic products, and sustainable business practices. Even if that information is not directly communicated anywhere on your website, it may guide your decision to restrict the site's background colors to neutral shades of green, yellow, and brown. You may personally love the color pink, but you know it just won't work on a site that projects the peaceful calm of the Bluegrass State.

Maybe your story—or part of it—is compelling enough to attract and keep potential customers. If your story is highly integrated into your brand, it is definitely worth telling. In this case, a compelling story will lend credibility to your brand.

Much has been written on branding stories in entrepreneurial literature. We covered some famous brand stories in Chapter 3, where we discussed ubiquitous corporate brands like Coca-Cola and Google. Of course, corporate brands are often a mix of truth and embellishment. Most corporate branding stories are grounded in fact, but quickly move beyond fact to legend and kitsch. To today's savvy (and often cynical) consumers, these stories can seem manufactured and inauthentic. That is not to say these stories do not work. In some of the most successful cases, buying into these stories is simply part of the brand experience.

For example, most visitors to Disneyland or Disney World (who are more than about 15 years old) understand that the magic of the experience of visiting one of the company's theme parks is not magic at all, but rather a carefully orchestrated visitor experience. The degree of theater involved in delivering the Disney experience is only underscored by the notorious secrecy park employees are sworn to on the subject of the conditions of their employment.

Beyond the veil of secrecy, Disney is known for requiring park employees to be well groomed, with no visible tattoos, jewelry, nail polish, or elaborate facial hair. Regardless of their role (this includes even the janitorial staff), they are expected to remain in character while on the job, and all are regarded as "cast members" acting out the company's brand like accomplished thespians. Because Disney staffers are not allowed to discuss the terms of their employment, the rules they work by cannot be verified, although there are many corroborating stories online.

Most companies' branding efforts are not as comprehensive as Disney's, although customers are often just as eager to go along with branding narratives they know are false—or at least highly exaggerated. Take, for example, the Ruby's chain of retro diners, or 1950s-style diners in general. Customers understand that Ruby's and most of its peers are contemporary attempts to capture the look and feel of an era and mythology in American culture a decreasing number of Americans and others can even remember. Most retro diner customers have

FIGURE 5.4 All Disney employees—not just costumed characters—are considered cast members.

Credit: Shutterstock ID#111541730

come to anticipate eating hamburgers and fries, and drinking milkshakes alongside images of Elvis, James Dean, and Marilyn Monroe (and maybe a few of those retro metal Coca-Cola trays), even though, in reality, there's no connection at all between these late celebrities and casual dining.

Of course, you are not a company, and your brand story will differ greatly from the depersonalized and corporatized stories of Disneyland and Ruby's diner. Your story will be more personally relevant to your clients and customers. That's what makes it important. If you don't immediately see why your potential clients and customers would care about your story, consider the stories of a few individuals whose personal stories have eclipsed those of their companies. You may have heard of the following folks.

Sir Richard Branson, Founder, Virgin Group

Virgin Group founder Richard Branson is an institution in himself. So powerful is his personal brand that it almost doesn't matter what kind of business he attaches his name to. Whatever Branson touches seems to turn to gold. From record labels to airlines, cellular phone companies, and even space flight ventures, Branson's story remains front and center for his followers and the media. Indeed, Branson's ventures come and go, but the world will not easily forget the charming blond sexagenarian who is always ready with a smile and never seems to take himself too seriously, regardless of his billions.

By all accounts, Branson is a family man. He has two adult children by a wife with who has been his partner for more than four decades. Yet he is frequently photographed surrounded by beautiful—and sometimes naked—young women, hanging out of airplanes, waterskiing, skydiving. These images are all about his brand, even if the story they tell may not be particularly accurate. Because Branson is so likeable—always smiling, always having fun—most of us are willing to support whatever he does, regardless of its success or lack thereof.

FIGURE 5.5 Sir Richard Branson.

Credit: Shutterstock ID#171314414

Since 1966, Branson has launched more than 100 companies. Many of them failed, including Virgin cola, Virgin vodka, a bridal business, a cosmetics and toiletries business, a clothing line, a car company, a lingerie company, a flower retailer, an iPod competitor, a discount airline, a charter airline, and a Facebook competitor targeted at students, among other forgettable ventures.[2] Although most of us have forgotten these failures (and likely never heard of most or any of them in the first place), most of us still know the man behind all of them—because we like his story, regardless of its veracity.

Bill Gates, Founder, Microsoft

Microsoft founder Bill Gates is at least as well known as Richard Branson, although his personal story and brand could not be more different from Branson's. Unlike his British counterpart, Gates seems an introvert and a humble figure. Regardless of its accuracy, the Gates story is, for most of us, a romanticized version of a now-familiar trope: Computer geek makes good. That there are countless movies on a variation of this theme shows it resonates on some level with many of us. In some ways, the story we construct for Gates is an American story, lending support to the American myth that anyone with reasonable intelligence who works hard can succeed.

FIGURE 5.6 Bill Gates.

Credit: Shutterstock ID#155863793

Interestingly, the Richard Branson story, as told by Americans, is one of humble origins, the clichéd rags-to-riches story. Ever hopeful about their own social mobility, Americans like to emphasize the struggles Branson faced—dyslexia, difficulty in school—while overlooking the fact that Branson grew up privileged. His father was a barrister, and he attended elite prep schools before dropping out of school altogether at 16 to launch his first venture, a magazine called *The Student*.

Gates' story is more relatable, at least by American standards. While few of us could imagine being the charismatic Richard Branson, Gates' life seems almost ordinary. We admire Gates for his success, and most of us have positive associations with the man who lent his name to an international foundation committed to curing disease and alleviating the problems wrought by poverty in the developing world. Yet Gates' personal story is not as interesting to us for at least a couple reasons.

First, Gates himself has done next to nothing to promote his story or his personal brand, and second, Gates does not seem to care much about branding his company, and seems even less interested in branding himself. After all, this is the man who, while delivering a 2009 TED Talk about curbing the spread of malaria in the developing world (a noble cause, we can all agree), released a jar of mosquitoes into the audience, saying, "Not only poor people should experience this."[3]

It was a brave symbolic move, but it did not endear people to Gates, who struck people as clueless or mean-spirited for the stunt. The good news for Microsoft is that it's big enough to pick and choose which parts of its founder's story to promote. No need to focus on a mosquito stunt when Gates, through the Bill and Melinda Gates Foundation, the world's largest private foundation, has put $28 billion of his own money toward humanitarian causes.[4]

Ben Cohen and Jerry Greenfield, Co-Founders, Ben and Jerry's Homemade, Inc.

You are probably at least somewhat familiar with the corporate story of Ben and Jerry the gourmet ice cream pioneers. Perhaps you learned somewhere that the two friends started making ice cream in the late 1970s after taking a $5 correspondence course in ice cream making offered by Penn State. You may have heard that they wanted to make bagels at first, but they could not afford the equipment.[5]

It's a cute story. Ben and Jerry are definitely relatable, and they make the company relatable too. After all, with elaborate combinations of ingredients and playful names for their flavors (including the old classics Cherry Garcia, Chunky Monkey, and Chubby Hubby), the company seems approachable and friendly. And by all reports, its founders live up to their reputation.

FIGURE 5.7 Ben and Jerry's remains an approachable brand, despite its purchase by Unilever.

Credit: Shutterstock ID#106243091

The Ben and Jerry's story, as promoted on company literature and ice cream cartons, is about two ex-hippies who thought it would be fun to make ice cream, and wanted to do it ethically. Even though Ben and Jerry sold the company to the multinational conglomerate Unilever in 2000, the company still promotes its founders' friendly hippie vibe through colorful packaging replete with illustrated images of fluffy clouds floating in blue skies and friendly black-and-white dairy cows. Unilever was smart to protect its ice cream subsidiary from its own faceless behemoth reputation, and the company's founders' personal stories and aesthetic remain the most valuable aspect of the Ben and Jerry's brand.

Your story may not become as iconic as Richard Branson's or Bill Gates'. But unless you expect to become the next celebrated billionaire entrepreneur, that doesn't really matter. What does matter is that you have a story that is compelling and that reinforces your brand. Although on a smaller scale (for now), your story helps build your brand's credibility through relationships and trust.

Many of the most successful attempts at personal branding on a smaller scale are in the personal care or cosmetics industries. Because consumers have intensely personal relationships with the products they use on their faces and bodies, it is important for them to trust and like the people who developed these products and brought them to market. It is little wonder why so many entrepreneurs in these fields have been able to generate such fierce loyalty among their fans and followers, while not being particularly well known outside their companies.

Here are two you may or may not have heard about.

Paula Begoun, Founder, Paula's Choice Skin Care

Paula's story is important for a few important reasons. First, it gives her credibility and humanity. People are more likely to risk trying a new product if they know there is a person behind it instead of a huge faceless corporation. Second, Paula's story is relatable. As a young person, Paula suffered from acne and eczema, according to the profile on her company's website.[6]

Paula's struggles prompted her to research skin care solutions and treatments that ultimately became her products. Her story and success also led to several books and countless media appearances. In 1995, after writing 20 books on skin care, she launched her own product line, Paula's Choice. Not only does the Paula's Choice website feature Paula's story, but it features the company's story, profiles of the company's research team, and even customer stories. It also offers definitions and explanations of products and conditions, and advice on everything from skin care to hair care.

The site projects a sense of community that is difficult to forge in an online environment. Paula's Choice rarely runs sales or offers discounts, but sends each new customer a mini-booklet explaining Paula's philosophy and debunking some common skin care myths. After visiting the Paula's Choice website, reading her books or reviewing her literature, a customer may feel as though they know Paula. While this is highly important to the company in creating and maintaining a strong brand, it is not necessary that the world outside of Begoun's likely customer base knows anything about her story.

Kate Somerville, Founder, Kate Somerville Skin Health Experts

Like Begoun, Kate Somerville has an eponymous skin care line that brands itself as health-conscious and progressive. Like the Paula's Choice site, the Kate Somerville site offers photos and a bio of the company's founder, her story, and her philosophy. Although Kate came to prominence as the proprietor of a skin care clinic in Los Angeles (rather than a sufferer of skin problems), her story is just as important to her customers and fans as Paula's is to hers. While Begoun's story has attracted loyal followers through her books, media appearances (including on Dr. Oz), and frank commentary on beauty products and skin care gurus, Somerville's presence is more reserved. After all, she came to prominence treating the skin of Hollywood's elite, and she is not about to risk her reputation by making controversial statements or possibly offending her key customers by speaking too freely about them.

So, you might be wondering, what does all of this beauty talk have to do with branding? Everything, actually. Both Paula Begoun and Kate Somerville are celebrated, highly successful entrepreneurs in the skin care business, and their names are their brands. Both have dedicated followers, fans, and customers. By all accounts, both sell high-quality products at moderate to high prices that make them inaccessible to some (although Paula's Choice offers a 10% student discount).

Both women have personal stories and brands that are at least as big as their companies. But their brands are quite different. While the differences are certainly more noticeable to each brand's current and potential customers, they are real and significant. Somerville has branded herself as an esthetician to the elite, and joining her team will (at least psychologically) put you in the ranks of the Hollywood insiders who quietly (we assume) use her products. Begoun, meanwhile, brands herself as an approachable straight talker. As a self-proclaimed cosmetics cop who routinely reviews competitors' products and calls out ingredients and practices she finds problematic, she told *New York* magazine, "Don't encourage the [skin care] industry to be assholes."[7]

Before signing on to either team, potential customers might ask themselves: "Am I more of a Real Housewives of Beverly Hills sort of woman or an Oprah sort of woman?" This question is likely more important to customers than the actual quality of either line's products. Story (and the image it creates) matters.

One media entrepreneur who has translated his personal story into a successful brand is Dominic Gill. In the following pages he discusses his own journey to personal branding and how he helps his clients define, redefine, or reinforce their own brands.

Q&A: DOMINIC GILL, CO-OWNER, ENCOMPASS FILMS

Describe your business

In 2011, my wife and I set up a small production company called Encompass Films. We came out of the world of adventure travel. That's what I did for a few years, that's how I cut my teeth for filming, and it's an area in which we still specialize. I'm director of the company and creatively a director, cinematographer, and editor. What I do depends on the size of the job we have. The bigger it is, the more directorial I get, and the more we hire out the other jobs. But if it's a small job, which the majority of our jobs are, I do the directing and cinematography, and sometimes the editing. And Nadia, my wife, is the producer. Producing is an absolute nightmare, so I'm pleased I'm not doing that.

How did you get started?

The first television documentary I ever made, *Take a Seat*, was about a long-distance tandem bicycle journey from Alaska to Argentina, where I picked up strangers to get on the back of the bicycle and tell their story on the

FIGURE 5.8 Dominic Gill.

way. When we set up this company, anyone who knew us—if anyone knew us—knew us because of that journey.

When we were trying to get our first client, we focused on tradeshows. We went to outdoor retailer trade shows and bike expos. At a bike expo we came across a brand that had been around since the 1960s. They were a big bicycle accessories brand. They were going through a slump. That slump was the result of having lost the respect of the core of the cycling community when they started manufacturing in China. They wanted to find a medium with which to regrow the trust they had lost with their customers and distributors.

You can start making great products again, but no one will buy them if they think they're the same crappy products you made five years ago. You need marketing. The way they decided to do that was through what's commonly known now as ambassador programs. They hired us to curate, with their help, a program whereby they would pick real people and tell real stories that happened to have some of the company's gear in them. It fits under the arena of branded content for sure, but what they wanted to do was profit from the storytelling of the everyman. Suddenly someone who's not a bike nerd, somebody who's not a specialist or a superhero is going on an adventure that inspires the vast majority. That itself is a powerful message, and if you can attach it very loosely to your company, it's an excellent starting point for rebuilding trust for your product.

What sets your brand apart?

In our industry, there is a lot of amazing cinematography, but the bottleneck will forever be storytelling. Storytelling that is applicable to everyone. This world is getting full of hairy-chested, very exclusive stories: "I can do this, but you should never dare do this. It's very extreme, very dangerous."

What we try and do is stand out by moving in the opposite way, and say, "This is exciting. It's hair-raising. It is life-affirming. But we're not that special, and we want to communicate that in a way that makes you believe that you can also do it." So rather than feeding off this derring-do, we try and feed off a more inclusive kind of inspiration, which is difficult because it goes against the commercial know-how of the industry as a whole, but I do honestly believe that it's growing. People want to feel like you're talking to them as if they could do something as opposed to talking to them as a theatrical piece.

Do you actively work to ensure the projects you take on fit your brand?

On the whole we're very, very lucky. I guess because of where we come from, we rarely get projects on the table that we do not want to participate in.

Any given month our willingness to participate in a project depends on how much we need some work, and that will then affect how much the project inspires us. Only once or twice have we done something we are not willing to put in our portfolio, and our portfolio is something we are proud to have represent us. Generally, companies gravitate toward us for the same reasons we want them to. They might not be as interesting or as inspired a project as we would want, but they're enough in the same vein for us to want to be associated with it.

A lot of it comes down to the quality with which you've become accustomed to living. If you need to bring in $80,000 a month because of choices you've made, then the chances of you doing the work that you want to do is slim—unless you're Tarantino. Unless you're at the top of your game.

What I attribute any modest success to is that when I was a biologist and decided to have a change of career, I didn't have a pair of golden handcuffs. My salary was so low that I probably could've worked at McDonald's and made the same amount of money. I think a lot of people fall into the trap of: "I need to make this money," and those jobs are the ones we don't put in our portfolios. I would rather take a job I agree with that doesn't pay us very much and hopefully win the respect of that brand sufficiently to get more money for the future or to be able to help them grow and have a bigger part of the creative process to make it worth our while emotionally.

One of our first projects was a season of television based on the tandem bicycle idea, and it went out on Universal Sports, which was a very small network, not a network that would garner you much respect in the industry. But it was on rabbit ears. Everyone could see it. I got more emails about that television series than anything ever, from vets, from people living on the bread line, from people who are heavily disabled, saying how much it inspired them or saying how in some small way it got them to think differently or changed their life. I still get caught up in that emotional perk of wanting to be on HBO or Netflix, but actually, I think I'll look back at my career and realize that that was one of the most valuable things we've done and we ever will do.

What if Walmart came calling?

If Walmart came to us and wanted to make a publicity campaign about their new look at sustainability or their look at providing all the power they need for their manufacturing process or distribution process, I'd be excited about that. I think a lot of artists cut off their nose to spite their face when it comes to taking the moral high ground, only working on things that no one sees and that perhaps only affect people that already have all their morals intact. I'm a big believer in putting things out on networks that the vast majority see and need to see, as opposed to, at the other end of the spectrum, the film festival circuit, where no one needs to be inspired, or no one needs to learn. They're already supposedly enlightened.

Do you have advice for other creatives?

If you're trying to craft yourself in a way that you think you should craft yourself as opposed to the way you feel you should craft yourself, you're less likely to succeed. Most people, especially in this world of instant gratification, fall into the trap of seeing a person and thinking they ought to behave like that person. But I think you're much more likely to succeed if you follow your heart. It's difficult to do, but I'm still optimistic that the money will follow.

Notes

1 Tompkins, Al. 2011. *Aim for the Heart: Write, Shoot, Report and Produce for TV and Multimedia, 2nd edition* (Washington, DC: CQ Press).
2 Russell, Mallory. 2016. "Richard Branson's Fails: 14 Virgin Companies That Went Bust." *Business Insider.* Accessed June 27, 2016. http://www.businessinsider.com/richard-branson-fails-virgin-companies-that-went-bust-2012-4.
3 Davidson, James. 2009. "Bill Gates Releases Mosquitoes into Audience." *Msnbc.com.* Accessed June 27, 2016. http://www.nbcnews.com/id/29022220/ns/health-infectious_diseases/t/bill-gates-releases-mosquitoes-audience/#.V3DGoZMrIdU.

4 "Bill Gates Retakes World's Richest Title from Carlos Slim." 2016. *Bloomberg.com*. Accessed June 27, 2016. https://www.bloomberg.com/news/articles/2013-05-16/bill-gates-retakes-world-s-richest-title-from-carlos-slim.

5 "Ben Cohen & Jerry Greenfield." 2008. *Entrepreneur*. Accessed June 27, 2016. https://www.entrepreneur.com/article/197626.

6 "About Paula Begoun, The Cosmetics Cop." 2016. *Paulaschoice.com*. Accessed June 28, 2016. http://www.paulaschoice.com/who-we-are/about-paula/.

7 "Meet the Beauty Guru Calling Foul on the Industry." 2015. *The Cut*. Accessed June 28, 2016. http://nymag.com/thecut/2015/01/beauty-guru-calling-foul-on-the-industry.html.

6

NAMING RITES

One of the most enjoyable tasks when it comes to starting a business is choosing a name for the venture. Yet the task is not without risk. You had better like what you call yourself or your business because if the name catches on and becomes an integral part of your brand, it may be difficult to change or move away from. You will almost certainly lose much—if not all—of the name recognition you worked so hard to build.

Especially in these days of ubiquitous media, names must compete with countless other names for recognition. To succeed in introducing and representing a brand, a name must be memorable, simple, and easy to spell and pronounce. It should not pose a challenge to potential clients and customers by utilizing complicated spelling conventions or making obscure references. It should not be exclusive or intimidating. On the other hand, a name worth branding should be unique. Names that are too generic or broad, which can seem straightforward once remembered, often fail to make an impression. (Names like The Communication Experts, The Social Media Company, or Content Unlimited are simple and straightforward, but they are too broad and generic to engender strong brand recognition.)

Your brand name should be both simple and distinctive. Finding the right combination of both can be challenging. Artist Morgan Phillips who goes by "The Sucklord" professionally, advises those looking for brand names to avoid words already in use. (See his interview at the end of this chapter.) When a fellow artist launching her brand asked him for feedback on the name "Ad Hoc Art," he told her to google "ad hoc." "That's already a word," he said. "How many pages of Google will people have to go through to find you? It's better to have a name that no one else has."[1]

FIGURE 6.1 Choosing a brand name should be fun.

Credit: Shutterstock ID#187406165

Choosing a name that is easy to remember and find in a simple search is key, and Phillips' advice is good. Once you have a short list of names to choose from, google each to see what search results they bring up. If there is significant competition and you will face an uphill battle to be seen among so many similar names and words, move on to the next option.

There are a few other steps you want to take before you ultimately settle on a name. If you anticipate the brand growing (which you should) and your using the name professionally for years to come, you also want to check to see if the name or variations of the name are registered domains. After all, you don't want to choose a brand name only to later find that someone else owns a URL with that name. If that URL is not in use, its owner may sell it to you at a premium, but the price may be prohibitive. Cybersquatters, who speculate on and buy potentially desirable domain names in the hope that they can sell them to people like you when you need them, may want more money for the URL than you can afford. If the URL is in use and you can't acquire it, the likely brand confusion is obvious.

If a Web search doesn't bring up a site bearing your potential brand name, you can determine whether similar URLs are owned or in use through a search at Whois.net. If you can't acquire the most obvious URLs for your brand name (if the ".com" variation is taken), move on to the next name on the list. Even if the ".com" URL for your potential name is available, you may also want to do a U.S. trademark search. While registering a trademark may seem unnecessary when you are just launching your brand, ensuring that your selected name is not already a registered trademark can save you much future grief.

Should You Register a Trademark?

Conducting a trademark search is easy. The United States Patent and Trademark Office maintains the Trademark Electronic Search System (TESS) database of current and expired trademarks at:

http://tmsearch.uspto.gov/bin/gate.exe?f=tess&state=4801:pma00y.1.1

It's not a very catchy URL. For background and more information on the search process, go to:

http://www.uspto.gov/trademarks-application-process/search-trademark-database

Clearly, given the complicated URLs, the U.S. Patent and Trademark Office is not particularly concerned with branding itself as an easy-to-use source of public information. After all, these are government sites. There are no competing sites for people who need the information they provide.

Once you have determined that the business or brand name you want to use is not already trademarked, you may want to register it yourself. Registering a trademark costs money and may not even be necessary. Make sure you need to register your trademark before taking the next step.

FIGURE 6.2 Should you register a trademark?

Credit: Shutterstock ID#342232103

According to the U.S. Patent and Trademark Office (USPTO), trademarks "protect brand names used on goods and services."[2] Filing a trademark prevents other people from using your name and potentially creating confusion with your brand. Some U.S. states may require additional filings to exercise your trademark rights within their borders.

There are several reasons both for and against registering a trademark. A trademark offers two kinds of protection: protection from others who may want to infringe on or take advantage of your brand, and liability protection against anyone who accuses you of infringing on their brand. Avoiding either kind of infringement before it occurs can save you the trouble and hardship of having to rebrand yourself later. It can even help you avoid a lawsuit. If a court finds that you profited from association with a brand name that had been trademarked by someone else, you may have to relinquish the money you earned under that name to the registered trademark owner.[3]

There are also reasons to not file a trademark. Trademark attorney Peter Sloane offered the following cautions in a post on the American Express OPEN Forum:[4]

- Filing a trademark application may bring unwanted attention to yourself. Because trademark filings are public record, filing could give potential competitors advance warning about your business plans. That said, unless you are rolling out a brand new invention or an innovation that will fundamentally transform your industry, this may not be among your concerns.
- The name is too descriptive or broad. The USPTO will reject filings for names that are overly broad, descriptive, or in common use. "Quality Branding" or "Popular Media," for example, may not be eligible for trademark.
- The brand's lifespan is short. It takes at least six months to register a trademark. If you don't anticipate using a phrase or image over the long term, it may not be worth registering.
- You own a similar trademark. If you own a trademark for one part of your business, you don't need to register a variation of that trademark for another part. For example, if you own a social media marketing service with a trademarked name, you need not also register a trademark for your new Web development sideline.

What's in a Name?

When it comes to selecting a name for your brand, one of the first questions you will want to ask yourself is how closely you want to align your personal identity with your brand. In other words, do you want to use a variation of your own name as your brand name, or do you want to select a name that ensures your brand is separate from your personal identity?

A large proportion of lifestyle and women's brands take the names of their founders or owners. The advantage of this approach is that it builds legitimacy and authenticity by connecting the brand to an actual person. Particularly when it comes to highly personal subjects such as cosmetics, fitness, or fashion, connecting a brand to an individual encourages trust. Paula Begoun is the face of Paula's Choice, and sharing a name with her company shows pride and a willingness to stand by her product. Paula also uses her personal story to promote her brand. You can read more about her in Chapter 5.

If you want to establish a brand identity that is larger than life, using your own name as a brand may not make much sense. Further, if your personal brand lacks a clear connection to your business, ego may be the only reason to name your company after yourself. This may explain why Rashmi Sinha, who founded the Web-based presentation sharing platform SlideShare, did not name the business after herself. Media and technology products just don't benefit from a personal connection in quite the same way beauty products do. Similarly, networking company Cisco Systems co-founder Sandra Lerner was wise to not name that business after herself. When Lerner left Cisco in 1990, she went on to found the cosmetics company Urban Decay.[5] It would have made more sense for her to put her own name on that product, but brand confusion may have resulted if customers learned of her previous high-profile technology career. This is the risk of association with more than one separate brand.

In high-profile fields and professions in which the individual himself represents both the brand and the product, it may make sense for him to rebrand himself entirely, creating an alter ego that is larger than life. These branding campaigns tend to be particularly memorable because their creators, by the very nature of their brand identity, become the stars of their own created universe. Done well, this kind of branding can quickly take off and enjoy great success. (After all, no regular person could ever be as charismatic or fascinating as a deliberately crafted identity.) Yet that success comes with a huge potential downside. A highly successful personal brand that creates an image of its owner that is not completely authentic may be difficult to evolve out of or retire as that brand image loses its currency or relevance.

Two great examples of creatives who have crafted larger than life brands for themselves are the Los Angeles-based celebrity blogger Perez Hilton (real name: Mario Lavandeira) and the New York-based artist Sucklord (real name: Morgan Phillips). Both address their branding successes and challenges over the following pages. As you will read, Lavandeira occasionally addresses Perez Hilton in the third person, while Phillips tries hard to embody his brand, careful not to distance himself too much from The Sucklord. The former interview was conducted with a person, while the latter was conducted, intermittently, with a brand image. Try to put yourself in each man's place as you read their stories, and consider the implications for your own branding decisions.

Q&A: PEREZ HILTON

Describe the origins of the Perez Hilton brand

After I created the character Perez Hilton, my alter ego or *nom de blog*, he over time started to take shape. I was aware of the power of appearance and appearances, so to this day, not always, but a lot of times what Perez wears on the red carpet is not what Mario, my real name, would wear in his every-day life. Appearance matters for everybody. When you go to a job interview, you want to look your best.

When I first started out, I wasn't thinking of myself as a brand, and I wasn't thinking of blogging (at perezhilton.com) as a profession. It really was just a hobby because professional blogging wasn't a thing when I started. Blogs back in 2004 and before were mainly just online journals. It was very first-person, a diary.

That seemed boring to me. I didn't want to do that. I wanted to talk about what I was naturally interested in, which was celebrities. It was such a different world back in 2004. Celebrity magazines weren't using their own websites to break news. *Us Weekly* and *People* and all of those publications were just using their websites in 2004 to get subscriptions. Since then it's changed drastically. It's also become a much more crowded field. And there's also been the prolif-eration of social media. In 2004, there was no Twitter, there was no YouTube, there was no Instagram, and Facebook was only for college students.

Could someone just starting out now achieve what you have been able to as a blogger?

I am a dinosaur of the Internet. Now if you want to enter the celebrity news world, unless you have corporate backing and tens of millions of dollars, it

FIGURE 6.3 Perez Hilton, a.k.a. Mario Lavandeira.

will be very difficult for you because everybody's doing it now. That's another big shift that's occurred over the last 11 years that I've been around. Celebrity news is now mainstream news, and nowhere is it more apparent than in 2016, a reality TV star being the Republican nominee for president.

Anything is possible on the Internet. It's still the great wild west. Plus, on the Internet, things happen so quickly. Everybody stands a chance. There are certain things you can do, though, to help your chances. One of those is: live in Los Angeles. Location is very important.

You can become successful wherever you are. But if you want to maintain success, I think location matters because ultimately, you need to reinvent yourself. You can't keep doing the same thing you've been doing. Like if you're a makeup blogger. That's what you're known for, and you live in Toledo, Ohio. Eventually that demographic of females of a certain age that loves to voraciously consume that media might start having children and become busier and grow out of that, and then all of a sudden your views are going to start dwindling. It definitely helps if you are in LA and able to do things outside of what you usually do.

What is the key to your success?

One of the reasons I was able to achieve success and maintain success is that I wasn't just working online. I was working all the angles concurrently. It was me being this new media phenomenon, plus also having the blessing of traditional media, and then also hustling and doing so many different things. I still consistently do radio. I've released books. I've done a lot of acting. Especially this year, I've done more acting than ever. It's about trying to be like Joan Rivers. That's my new model. The Joan Rivers model, which is just say "yes." The power of yes, people have written books on it. I like to call it "Yes, and." It's not only "I will do this, but I will do this, and. . ." Let me put some thought into how I can turn this one opportunity into something bigger. Or it's "Yes, I'll do that, then I want you to do this for me."

I feel like my success saved me. It gave me a purpose and a reason to work really hard and to care. If I had become successful in the corporate world somehow, I would've cared and I would've loved it to an extent, and I would've worked hard, but I wouldn't have cared as much or worked as hard as I do now because I'm working for myself.

Do you do anything to manage and protect your personal brand?

I don't really try to control my image. If anything, over the last few years I'm really just trying to be more authentic and hide less behind this character of Perez Hilton that I created, which is why I love Snapchat and Instagram stories because they're the most authentic glimpses into the everyday lives of people. Instagram proper is heavily curated and edited and filtered, but Stories and Snapchat feel more real, and people have really resonated with who I am through what they've seen through those platforms. After 12-plus years in the business, I'm at a point where I don't care, and I'm also a smart person. Today I read the headline "Amber Rose fans are upset at the host for this year's slut walk." I agreed to be a host for Amber Rose's SlutWalk [a protest against blaming the victims of sexual violence], and some of her fans are not happy that I am. You know what I did, I drew awareness to that article. I tweeted and Facebooked about it. Somebody else would've tried to ignore it or hope that it didn't pick up traction. I drew attention to it, and I hope it picks up traction. I love attention. I'd rather be talked about negatively than not at all.

How has your brand changed over the years?

Brands, like people, change and grow. If you don't, you're a 40-year-old who's still behaving like a 20-year-old, and people are going to think you're a d-bag. Brands die. They do. They go out of business. Evolution is necessary in life, both professionally and personally. For a while, in the trajectory of my 12-plus-year career, I found myself saying "no" to a lot of opportunities. My vision was almost myopic. I was so laser focused on just wanting a talk show. Joan Rivers' death affected me for many reasons. She died the same month I was celebrating my tenth anniversary of blogging, which was a real introspective moment for me.

Over weeks I internalized my whole life and career, and looked back at what I had accomplished, what I wanted still to accomplish, how I hoped to get there, what I hoped I had been doing right, what I had been doing wrong, and I realized that I had started turning down a lot of work for a variety of reasons, whether it be, "Oh, that's not a good fit for my brand, or oh, that's lame." I, as they say, started to drink the Kool-Aid. It happens. Sometimes you think you're too cool for school.

Joan Rivers' death resonated with me because I knew her and had the pleasure of working with her on multiple occasions. I did a guest appearance on her reality show on We with her daughter Melissa twice, plus she asked me to be a guest on her YouTube talk show. That's how much of a hustler she was. She had three shows on at the same time. She was doing *Fashion Police*, she had been doing a We reality show with her daughter Melissa, and she had a Web interview show called *In Bed With Joan*. Her philosophy was, as long as someone's going to pay me my quote, if the check is there, I'm there. And that really helped me change my thoughts on things because I want to be as blessed and lucky enough as Joan Rivers was to have a career for as long as I want to have it.

I started to re-approach things. I even went back and reached out to people who had offered me opportunities and I had said no to them in the past. For example, I had been asked to appear on this show *Celebrity Big Brother* in the UK, and I thought it was lame. I thought it was D-list. But I ended up doing it, and I got a big paycheck, so I was happy. I ended up being the most talked-about housemate in the history of *Celebrity Big Brother*, according to the social media statistics. I don't know if that's good or bad, but I'm happy with the paycheck.

Having children changed all of my motives for things. Now I'm all about, "How can I make more and spend less because I have two lives depending on me?" I also got asked to do this show a year and a half ago called *Celebrations*. It was a show on We hosted by David Tutera, a celebrity party planner. They wanted three and a half days of my time to film. The old me would've said, "Three and a half days of my time for We TV? Who watches We TV? Nobody. I'm not going to spend three and a half days of my life on this show." But the new me said, "Yes. If you want to do more television, you have to do more television. Say yes to this and also think of how to maximize the opportunity."

The show's concept is [Tutera] throws parties for celebrities. They asked, "Is your son having a birthday party soon, or do you want to have any kind of party?" I sat down to think about it, and I had the most brilliant idea: Let me throw a 10-year anniversary party for my blog. Then I'm drawing awareness to the mothership, and also, just as important, I used the party they paid for this really lavish event as an opportunity to invite my advertisers. So I made the people who were paying me feel special, I got to be on TV, and I used it as an opportunity to promote myself and my brand in every way possible. That's a great story to share when it comes to personal branding.

Back in 2010, I made a promise to be a more positive person and stop operating my website how I used to. I've continued to grow and evolve and make other changes on my website. Back in 2013, 2014, I instituted a "no kids" policy on my website. I won't post paparazzi photos of children on my site. I'll only post photos of celebrity kids if the parents post them on social media or if they take them to an event where they know there will be photographers.

When I first made the change, I tried too much to be like Oprah to the point of inauthenticity. I would constantly ask myself, "What would Oprah do?" But at a certain point I got lost. I'm not Oprah. I don't want to be Oprah. I'm not trying to be Oprah. I am just trying to be the best me possible. Now I don't mind having really strong opinions that would upset people.

Can you share any advice for those who would like to follow in your footsteps?

The best advice I could give is, "Ask yourself: Do you really want this? If so, are you really willing to do what it takes?" What it takes is devoting your entire life to it. This concept of balance that a lot of people in their twenties think they should have is not a real one. In your twenties, there should be no balance. It's all about work if you want to be very successful. That means everything has to come second. Personal relationships, friendships, your family, fun. All of that comes afterwards. Work must consume your life. Work must be your life. You must work harder than everybody else. If you are willing to dedicate your entire life to work for your entire twenties, you will be successful guaranteed. But it takes an insane amount of work. If you put in the hours, you will get the results.

Are there common misconceptions among those just starting out that you'd like to dash?

Ideas are not special. So many young people think ideas are special. They're not. Ideas are worthless. People are special. Two people can have the same exact brilliant idea. They can have the same exact revolutionary idea they think nobody else has ever thought of. The idea is not special. It's the person and how they implement that idea, what they bring to the idea, how they execute it—that's what is special. If an idea is so special, it should work on its own, right? No. But if two people have the same idea, but one person executes it one way and the other person executes it another way. One succeeds and the other doesn't. That shows you that the idea wasn't special. The person and what they brought to the table, how they executed the idea, that's what's special.

Do you plan to do this forever?

I love working. Granted, I don't love all aspects of my job. I hate that I spend so many hours a day on social media. That's something new that wasn't the case when I first started. There are so many platforms now, and I have convinced myself that I need to be on all of them because I *do* need to be on all of them. I still haven't gotten lazy 12 years later. I still really care about what I do, and I still want to excel, and I still want to grow and do better, and I'm still hungry.

I still love Perez. I'm still thankful because Perez Hilton made my life so much better. Perez Hilton allowed me the opportunity to financially support my family. My mom works for me. My sister works for me. My character definitely comes with baggage, and my baggage is more prominent than others', and maybe less desirable, but I embrace my baggage. Being Perez makes dating hard. It makes a lot of things hard. A lot of people still view me as the old Perez, the major d-bag, and a lot of people want to keep me trapped in the prison that is the past. But I don't live there anymore. I can't control other people's thoughts and feelings, and I don't really care.

What's next for Perez Hilton?

You'd think with success you'd be able to work less. That hasn't happened to me. But I don't have FU money in the bank yet. So I still have to hustle. I look forward to the day I have FU money in the bank when I can say I have enough money that I never have to work again. I may go a few days without posting on Instagram. A lot of what I do still is fear-based, and actually, that's something that a lot of successful people say. I remember watching an interview between J. K. Rowling and Oprah Winfrey, where they both had this fear of ending up poor again. I do too. I have that fear because I grew up poor. I am self-made. I don't want to mess things up. I don't want to go backwards. I want to keep moving forward in my life.

Q&A: THE SUCKLORD

Describe your brand

Suckadelic (suckadelic.com) is a bootleg toy company based in Chinatown, New York, owned and operated by a megalomaniacal supervillain called The Sucklord. He is the combination of an Intergalactic playboy and a street corner bootleg-bag-sold-in-basement proprietor type.

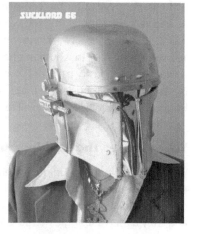

FIGURES 6.4 AND 6.5 The Sucklord, a.k.a. Morgan Phillips.

Describe your character

Sucklord is a title I created for myself to describe what I do, but it's not a character. This isn't some person I play on television or some sort of personality that I only turn on when I have to sell my products. Being The Sucklord gives me permission to be who I actually am, rather than having to be some normal person.

The whole thing I'm selling here is my unique personality and take on the world, and I just gave it a name, rather than use some pedestrian title like "Morgan Phillips." Thousands of people have that name, and it's not descriptive in any fashion. Throughout my process of self-actualization, I've come to be this particular person that has a disposition and a way of speaking and conducting himself and a way of editorializing and mythologizing himself, and I just gave it a name.

Where did the Sucklord name come from?

I started using "Suckadelic" first because years ago I made this *Star Wars* record. I made a little demo tape. I tried to get a record company and the *Star Wars* people to take an interest in it, and that was just not happening. I decided to put it out myself, but I recorded it myself, in my bedroom in my mom's house. It doesn't sound like a professional record.

I thought pretty much everything I do from now on, I'm just going to have to do myself because if I stand around waiting for a hand up, it's never going to come. So I'm going to produce everything myself, and it's going to suck a little bit because I have no resources. So I'm just going to call it Suckadelic so you have a heads-up before you even buy it and listen to it that it might suck a little bit.

I named myself after the company when I had to actually go out in public and represent this stuff. That worked out well for me because Suckadelic wasn't that much of a word in use, nor was Sucklord. That's part of branding. You want to make sure you don't have any conflict with another trademark.

If I'm at an industry party or I'm at an art opening, and someone introduces me to someone important, I make sure they introduce me as The Sucklord. Because that's a thing. People will remember that, and it also says something.

What makes the Sucklord unique?

What makes what I do unique is that I can go from one thing to another. I can make a piece of artwork. I can make a television show. I can do a podcast. I can make music. They all have a commonality because I created it, and they all serve a single narrative of expression. All these other people are wonderful, but they're not as complex and nuanced as The Sucklord. They have to stick to one thing, and I can do whatever I want.

In your Patreon campaign, you make a direct appeal for support from your fans. Is there any risk of the Sucklord selling out?

Part of the brand is doing things strictly for money. This is a grifting operation. If The Sucklord has to shill for Walmart to get a million bucks so he can throw that back into his Suckadelicking, I don't think there's any compromise there. If I only cared about money, I'd be working on Wall Street.

The Sucklord is intimidating. Brands need to be human and relatable. Are you concerned that showing too much humanity will undermine your brand?

If you watched [Bravo's] *Work of Art: The Next Great Artist*, Season 2, episode 4, you saw the humanizing effect children have on The Sucklord, and that didn't destroy my brand at all. In fact, it made me a more sympathetic character.

Do your fans understand the brand's function? Does the Sucklord persona ever keep them away?

I get people coming at me all the time. I have open hours at my facility here in New York, and people come from all over the world to see me. I get to meet tons of them, and every single one of them has been smart, interesting, creative, had something to say, had some aspect of themselves that made them interesting. I've never had a lame loser come over. People who seem to be attracted to what I am doing appreciate the faceted nature of it. There are certain people who do one thing, and do it well, and that appeals to some people.

Will you be the Sucklord forever?

I don't know if I'm going to keep using that title. I've created names for myself throughout my personal evolution. I've had other names before, but The Sucklord seems to be the most effective one. If there's any sort of continuity between the work I'm doing now and whatever it is I'm doing at 70, I don't see why that name wouldn't stay. It has served me well to this point, and if my brand is going to endure for the next 30 years, it would be stupid to change the name. Why change the name after you've made it into something? As long as I'm being true to myself, I don't think the brand is in trouble.

Do you have advice for young and new artists just starting out?

I tell them not to make any art at all, ever, and to do something else. This isn't any kind of life for anybody. I happen to be good at it because my combination of megalomania and masochism make it suitable to me.

I tell people, "Don't expect anything good to happen to you." You might have a great adventure and get a lot of creative satisfaction or have a lot of fun, but you may never get rich. A lot of people make the mistake that if they just grind, they'll get somewhere. I've done that, and it doesn't necessarily work. It's more about being consistent and smart.

You have to cut your own trail. That's what makes you an artist. That's what makes an artist unique and interesting and different and stand out. You need to do it in a way that nobody else did it before.

This is the only piece of advice I give any young artist: Come up with a name that is googleable. Whatever you want to call your art, whether you want to use your birth name or make up a jazzy logo or a snappy little saying or a graffiti name, google it, and if other stuff pops up, scrap it. That's almost the most essential thing. Why Suckadelic and Sucklord is so successful is because any instance in which you search for these things, you will find me and me alone.

Have others learned from your career success?

It has been applied by others to varying degrees of success, and others not so much. I leave it to others to figure out what to make of it. I'm a role model to a million people. I've got several dozen people who have completely copied my style and are trying to follow in my footsteps, and to them I say, good luck. I share whatever it is people want from me. If they want help or advice, I'm an open source kind of person. I put everything out there.

What does the future hold for the Sucklord?

Everything that I'm going to be, I've already created. Now it's just a matter of pushing it into other realms, getting out from under being this sort of underground lowbrow cult figure, and making more inroads into the established worlds of art and television and media, and to get out of the life of having to self-produce, self-finance, self-promote, and attach myself to some larger entities that can help me put what I do on a much larger footing. It does require a certain calibration. I've been trying to write a press kit and put together a deck, as they call it, and it's really, really hard to succinctly explain it to someone who doesn't understand.

What is Patreon?

Patreon (https://www.patreon.com/) is an online crowdfunding platform designed to help creatives raise continuous funding from fans and benefactors. Unlike the popular crowdfunding site Kickstarter (https://www.kickstarter.com/), Patreon is not about funding specific projects. Instead, it uses the old public television/radio model, prompting supporters to make recurring donations to support people who make all kinds of content, from written work to comic books to videos, podcasts, plays, art, photos, games, comics, or whatever. Supporters can pledge as little as $1 per project or per month. At the time of his interview, The Sucklord had 55 Patreon patrons who, together, pledged $568 a month to support his art. Many Patreon creators raise thousands of dollars per project or month.

Notes

1 Morgan Phillips interview.
2 "Trademark Process: USPTO." 2016. *Uspto.gov.* Accessed September 27, 2016. http://www.uspto.gov/trademarks-getting-started/trademark-process#step1.
3 "Top 10 Reasons to Register Your Trademark." 2016. *Findlaw.* Accessed September 15, 2016. http://smallbusiness.findlaw.com/intellectual-property/top-10-reasons-to-register-your-trademark.html.
4 "5 Reasons Not to File a Trademark Application." 2011. *OPEN Forum.* Accessed September 28, 2016. https://www.americanexpress.com/us/small-business/openforum/articles/5-reasons-not-to-file-a-trademark-application/.
5 "10 Popular Businesses Founded by Women" *Business News Daily.* Accessed September 27, 2016. http://www.businessnewsdaily.com/2156-women-owned-businesses.html.

7
CREATIVES NEED CONTENT

The creative field is broad, and there are countless ways to run a creative career these days. As the old barriers that once separated makers and creators from influencers and marketers erode, job descriptions merge and evolve. With this in mind, consider the creative careers detailed in Chapter 1 that rely heavily on social and new media skills. If you are old enough, you may recall a time when editorial and advertising functions in legacy media companies were once religiously maintained as separate.

As the Internet expanded, editorial offices slowly began to acknowledge the fact that maintaining a free and separate editorial product online was impossible. In much the same way, the once-separate worlds of physical and intellectual creation have merged. While once people had to choose whether they would work with their hands or their mind, now it is common for creative people to do both, and to even to support themselves through a combination of the two. In some ways this is the ultimate creative solution.

Now entrepreneurial professionals from Realtors, coaches, and consultants to artists and musicians find themselves in the position of either serving as their own promoters, social media managers, reputation managers, and content creators, or employing others to perform those roles. This has led to the creative development of many who previously could not easily express themselves in a way that aligned with their career choices. Consider the countless Realtors, mortgage brokers, and others in roles once segregated within office environments who now regularly blog or send out print or electronic newsletters through which they provide mostly content directly or indirectly related to their brand, along with content marketing pieces that make no clear connection to their brand but

FIGURE 7.1 Content isn't just for creatives.

Credit: Shutterstock ID#369324335

that help readers and viewers remember the source. This is the essence of content marketing.

We all look at media content enough these days to know that ever more voices are competing for a finite number of readers, viewers, and listeners. In fact, there are so many people around the world competing for the same online audiences that even those with the most to offer may struggle to even be noticed among the endless cacophony of voices clamoring for their attention.

The fact is that simply being a good brand, a competent communicator, or an entertaining social media presence is not enough these days. Nor is providing goods and services that people want. There is a simple reason for this: People do not consume media to be solicited and sold to. While they can be convinced to browse a website or even to buy something, there has to be more in it for them than a sales pitch. They don't consume media or act on an offer unless it has value to them. Creating value beyond a sales pitch is what content marketing is all about.

People will subscribe to your podcast or your e-newsletter, or will buy your goods or services, if they feel comfortable with you, engaged in a community you have created or curate, and most important, if they actually desire or need a product or service you offer. However, it is important to remember that these

FIGURE 7.2 Reach out to your community.

Credit: Shutterstock ID#379691755

days the relationship needs to be reciprocal and authentic if you expect to attract loyal and engaged followers.

This means your job just got bigger. Not only do you need to do excellent work bringing your expertise, products, and services to the people who want them (or who can be convinced to want them), but you also have to play multiple additional roles, possibly including community leader, manager, and cheerleader. In other words, unless you are a huge, faceless company like Target or Amazon (and you are not), you cannot simply be a salesperson and expect to succeed in the world of online marketing and promotion. You have to be a leader and a curator. Of the many things this means, one of the most important to keep in mind is that content is king. Content—which takes many forms—is what first attracts potential clients, and what keeps them loyal customers and clients.

If you are not already a content creator, communication professional or writer, you may find yourself in a tough position. What kinds of content should you generate beyond mere sales messages? The first thing to keep in mind is that content does not have be long and involved (in fact, it shouldn't), and it shouldn't take a significant amount of time to produce. To make the act of providing content sustainable—particularly if you are working alone or with a small number of people—you need to find some ways of automating the process. (Read more on automation in Chapter 8.) That means that instead of sitting down each morning at your desk, wondering what you are going to write, you make a plan that includes modifiable templates that will minimize the amount of new work you have to do by building on existing work.

Keep in mind that this is not just about social media. You should already have a social media marketing plan before you start thinking about content creation and curation. That means you should already be regularly posting to and interacting with other users on social media platforms such as Instagram, Facebook, Pinterest, and Twitter. You may already be using these platforms to post direct sales messages when, for example, new items become available in your online store or you start offering new services.

As you yourself know from your own reaction to receiving too many sales messages from even brands and people you respect or with whom you do business, hearing from someone only when they are trying to sell you something can get old pretty quickly. To leverage your brand's success online and via social media, you need to give as much as you get. In other words, you have to be a good citizen of both your existing community of followers and fans and of any new target markets you are trying to reach. Being a good citizen means contributing to the community without the expectation of a direct return. Consider it an investment in goodwill. And as most successful businesspeople know, a reputation for goodwill (essentially customer service) can work wonders for your brand.

There are two main kinds of content you can supply to your readers, viewers, followers, audience, or community. They are original content and curated content. Let's look at both types.

Original Content

Original content should be the easiest to come by (since you are the one supplying it) but the hardest to produce (because it takes time). Depending on your skills and comfort with writing, podcasting, video production, or other kinds of media creation, the most difficult thing about creating original content is determining what your audience would like to see and hear.

Selecting topics is often the hard part. Remember that content does not have to be (and should not be) all that long or extensive. People have limited time and short attention spans—particularly when they access your content on a mobile device. You will likely lose them if they have to scroll through dense text to grasp the point of your post, or if they have to watch more than three minutes of video.

Keep in mind that audiences respond well to messages containing information that is relevant to them. In general, content messages should be written in the second person point of view (i.e., "you"), as most of this book is (people like to be addressed directly), and deliver information you think your audience would like to know. Assuming your instincts about your audience are correct, this practice can win you much goodwill with your fans and followers.

Examples of this kind of content marketing include e-newsletters some local politicians send to their constituents, updating them on their work in the community, in the state capital or in Washington, or e-newsletters arts and crafts supply companies send out providing design ideas and tips to their customers. Marketing consultants, for obvious reasons, do a particularly great job in this

FIGURE 7.3 Share simple video messages with your followers.

Credit: Shutterstock ID#473101843

area, regularly sending helpful information of interest to those on their mailing lists, these days often by email.

In recent years, following the explosion of online entrepreneurship, an entire cottage industry has sprung up around helping struggling entrepreneurs market their businesses and increase their sales. One way they do this is by offering some aspect or part of their service for free as a preview to potential clients or customers. The hope is that if people like what they get free, they will be willing to pay for more. This strategy has an impressive track record for success. In fact, a variation on this strategy has long been used by salespeople in almost every industry to build a loyal customer base.

Whatever the form of your content, it should fit the forum and not waste words. Short, useful updates and news of likely interest to your audience are always acceptable. Keep in mind that increasingly users of social media want to see images and, particularly, video. While multimedia can be more time consuming to produce, those most successful at it have created their own systems to streamline the process.

Have a webcam setup at the ready so that all you need to do to create a quick morning message for your followers and fans is click "record," then "send." (Of course it may take a few attempts to master a performance that is free of awkward pauses, rambling language, and "um"s—but you'll get there eventually.) Make bulleted lists of your talking points, but don't memorize them or read from your notes. Keep them nearby for reference if you get stuck.

If you don't have much to say, try something fun that will get attention. Use a new filter or Instagram's Boomerang app to record a one-second video that loops continuously, often to hilarious effect. A one-second Boomerang video requires no editing. If a video falls short of your expectations, simply record a new one. Look for something that is moving, record it with your smartphone using the Boomerang app, then post it to Instagram. Yes, this counts as content. Just make sure it is consistent with your brand. It does not have to directly relate to your product or you, but it does need to reinforce your brand message, look, and feel.

Although you may be tempted to post a looping Boomerang video of your dog, unless your business is dog-related, that may dilute your brand—or worse. It could undermine your brand by confusing its message or making you look unprofessional. If you are a graphic designer, you could create and post a one-second looping video of you working at your desk or signing a sketch. If you create physical items, you could post a Boomerang video of a customer holding an item they just purchased from you. There are countless possibilities.

Keep in mind this is just one kind of original content you can create. It just so happens to be a particularly easy way to create content. Looping videos are fun and eye-catching, but they should not be the mainstay of your content creation. Your fans and followers may find this content engaging to a point. Overuse it, and it starts to seem gimmicky. People will tune out. When it comes to content creation, you need to keep things interesting by mixing it up. Look for opportunities in your daily life to capture an image or video that you can connect to your brand or that can connect your brand to something bigger in the news (i.e., an election, a snowstorm) to an anniversary (a milestone for your business) or a holiday (Halloween, New Years, etc.).

Like with almost everything else we discuss in this book, there is no set rule regarding what kind of content is appropriate for promoting your brand. Each enterprise, business, and individual is different, so the related content will necessarily be different as well. You may also want to augment your original content with other people's (credited) work. This can add variety and interest to your content, and promoting other people's (or other companies') content or products can help build your network.

Curated Content

Curated content is simply content you did not create. It is content someone else created and that you have featured or linked to, or highlighted in some way,

FIGURE 7.4 Curating content can be as challenging as creating it.

Credit: Shutterstock ID#303468863

always giving credit to the source. Curated content is useful in more than one way. On the most basic level, it is useful because it saves you from having to create so much original content.

As you may imagine or know from experience, creating appropriate original content to support your brand can be daunting. At the very least, it is time consuming. For that reason alone, curating content can help you maintain a regular posting or distribution schedule. Yet content curation can also play a more significant role in getting your name and brand out there. By referencing, reposting, or linking to someone else's content, you provide the content creator more exposure for their own brand. You drive more traffic to the sites and accounts of the content creator, which can then result in more traffic back to your sites and social media accounts.

As a general rule, the more connections you make to other sites, pages, and social media accounts, the better off you are. The online world is about connections. The more connected you are, the more likely people will be to find your sites and pages, along with those of others with whom you've connected. As long as you credit (and link to whenever possible) others' content, others will appreciate the attention. That's because the same rules about content marketing that apply to you also apply to everyone else you link to or connect with.

Curated content is also useful for bolstering or reinforcing your brand. By highlighting, redistributing, or linking to content created by others who share a similar branding message, you can leverage both brands. You help build a sense of community with those who share similar values, while allowing others to do the talking once in a while. This can be a refreshing break from a long string of content and social media messages in which you alone define your brand. Additionally, it can cast your brand in a more positive light in much the same way as reviews or testimonials from others can lend you or your brand more credibility than you'd gain from being the sole source of content and messages about your brand.

The process goes both ways. Your marketing goals should include creating content that others will want to curate, endorse, highlight, link to, or otherwise disseminate to their own communities and networks. Assuming your audiences do not overlap completely, this can bring both your content and the content of others to many more people, significantly expanding its reach and influence. This is a great way to leverage both your content and the content you curate. And of course it is a great way to build your brand.

Content Marketing Is Not New

For decades, savvy companies with a focus on quality published guides and manuals that specifically addressed the use or utility of their products. Then, toward the middle of the 20th century, custom publishing became common. Perhaps the most recognizable examples of custom publishing are inflight magazines, most of which are not created by the airlines they serve, but rather by subcontractors that create content assumed to be of interest to their clients' key audiences. More recently companies have found new ways to deliver content, in formats including blogs and podcasts, as means of extending their brands through content marketing. Now, of course, content marketing is also widespread across social media.

A particularly dramatic example of content marketing on a grand scale is afforded by the beverage company Red Bull, which has launched magazines, websites, YouTube channels, and feature films (through its Red Bull Media House) that go well beyond basic branding to create an entire lifestyle environment that seldom directly acknowledges the company that created it.

Content marketing has existed in one form or another for more than a century. Although it is somewhat more sophisticated today, companies have long produced content to support their brands. As early as the late 19th century, the tractor manufacturer John Deere is said to have been the first company to embrace content marketing by producing its own brand-building publication. According to brand marketing company Contently, John Deere's *The Furrow* magazine (http://johndeerefurrow.com/) is "the agrarian version of *Rolling Stone*."[1]

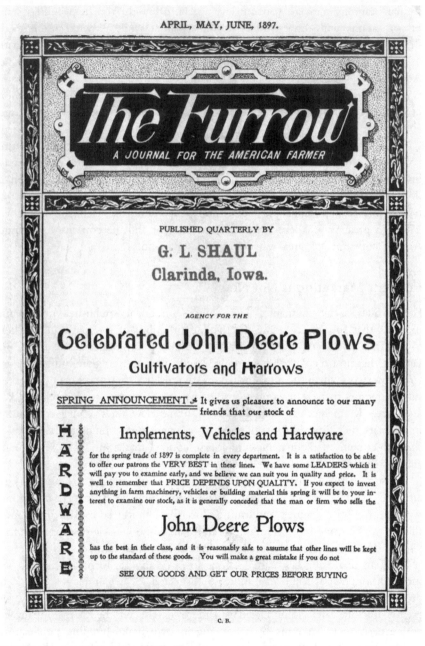

FIGURE 7.5 An 1897 issue of *The Furrow*.

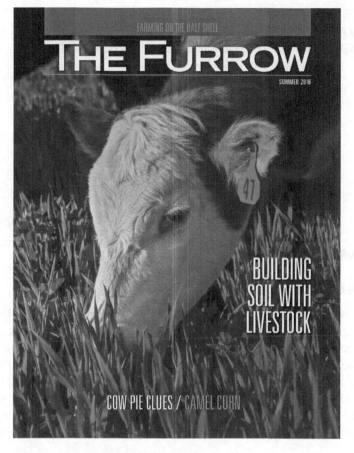

FARMING ON THE HALF SHELL

THE FURROW

SUMMER 2016

47

BUILDING
SOIL WITH
LIVESTOCK

COW PIE CLUES / CAMEL CORN

FIGURE 7.6 A more recent issue of *The Furrow.*

Instead of focusing on direct sales messages, *The Furrow,* a name that describes trenches plows dig for planting seeds, continues to represent a community and a lifestyle—which is exactly what branding professionals attempt to do today. *The Furrow* still helps extend John Deere's brand by bringing its core audience— mostly farmers in the United States and Canada—information that is useful and relevant to them. It also underscores the simple fact the company knows its customers, and understands their needs, desires, and interests. More than a century after its founding, *The Furrow* continues to publish stories that help build John Deere's brand reputation while bolstering its credibility and relevance among readers. Read on for *Furrow* editor David Jones' discussion of the magazine's significance.

Q&A: DAVID JONES, EDITOR, *THE FURROW* AND *HOMESTEAD*: JOHN DEERE PUBLICATIONS

FIGURE 7.7 David Jones.

Describe your career path

My first job as a communicator was in ag journalism. I fairly quickly discovered the bigger paycheck was in advertising and public relations. After maybe three years in ag journalism, I spent the next 15 to 18 years in advertising and PR, almost exclusively for agricultural clients. I came on the *Furrow* staff around four years ago. I've been with John Deere about 14 years. I'm a John Deere employee, and including myself, we have three full-time employees devoted to the magazine. The bulk of the content is created by—they are basically a full-time freelance staff. We have seven field editors on retainer.

Describe *The Furrow*'s history

The Furrow has always been created in-house or at least managed in-house. We first published in 1895. I believe we have been publishing continuously ever since. *The Furrow* is our flagship publication, but we also create *Homestead* magazine, which is more of a lifestyle magazine. When it was originally produced around 20 years ago, it was directed to rural property owners. We always referred to them as the doctors or the dentists who lived out of town on 10 or 15 acres. That publication has morphed slightly. It's a little more general now. We do some art stories. We do some travel stories. *The Homestead* audience is very difficult to describe. Basically, anyone who owns a piece of John Deere equipment could be a *Homestead* reader.

Homestead's circulation doesn't quite match up with the size of the potential audience, but one of the unique aspects of both magazines, *Furrow* and *Homestead*, is that they are partially subsidized by the network of John Deere dealers. John Deere pays to produce the magazine, and the dealers pay to mail it. So they pay a per-issue, per-recipient charge back to us to actually mail the magazines. It's not without a cost to the dealer, and times are tough in agriculture right now. Sometimes it's a tougher sell than others.

What is *The Furrow* about?

The Furrow is hardcore production agriculture subject matter for the most part. We also do some trend stories. There are usually one or two lifestyle-type stories in each issue of *The Furrow*. But by and large it is more technical—dealing with soil health or pest control or some other more technical aspect of production ag.

The Deere brand is about a connection to the land, a connection to place, and that's part of the mission statement of both magazines. We celebrate that connection to the land, and we tend to feature stories and sources that share that connection.

What is the secret to *The Furrow*'s success?

If there is a single key to the success and longevity of the *Furrow*, there is a very bright line between *The Furrow*'s editorial content and any John Deere corporate or product-related messaging. We do not talk about equipment in our editorial space at all. We don't talk about John Deere equipment. I have said before to groups that if you went back through at least the postwar history of *The Furrow*, I would be very surprised if you saw the words "John Deere" mentioned in the editorial space more than five or six times. We just don't do it. We take it even further than that. We don't depict John Deere equipment in the editorial space. We don't like for our sources to be wearing John Deere gear. If we have two photos to choose from—one with a farmer wearing a John Deere hat, and one without, we will always choose the one without. That has been the key to our success.

If John Deere owns *The Furrow*, why avoid mentioning the company?

We want the information we present to be seen as objective and unbiased. Since the magazine's beginnings, we felt like that was the key to acceptance among our readership. That kind of firewall between corporate and editorial has been in place since the magazine was first published 121 years ago. We carry advertising for John Deere products in the magazines, but as far as the editorial space goes, we want people to trust that what we tell them, we are telling them without an agenda.

Does John Deere have a presence anywhere in *The Furrow*?

We do have a couple of pages in the magazine that are typically devoted to more corporate messaging. On the inside of the front cover, that's typically where we may talk about philanthropy or volunteer events or that kind of thing.

We have maintained this tradition of editorial independence from John Deere corporate messaging for so long. We want to provide solutions, not just equipment. The magazine is a fixture, not just in John Deere, but in the global agriculture community. We are the highest circulation farm title in the world.

Who reads *The Furrow*?

The demographic for *The Furrow* would probably mirror the overall agricultural demographic—middle-aged and up, predominantly male, predominantly white. The average age of the U.S. farmer is between 56 and 58, primarily male, primarily white.

In our readership surveys, we always ask the question: "Knowing that John Deere publishes and pays for this magazine, and knowing that your dealership pays a part of it too, how does that affect your opinion of Deere and your dealership?" The answer is very consistently: "We have a higher opinion of Deere and the Deere dealer knowing this."

The vast majority of our readers know that it's a Deere publication, based on our longevity if nothing else. The ag audience is very astute. They're as quick as anybody else to recognize when they're being marketed to. By and large, they know it's a Deere publication. Based on our reputation of editorial independence, they are willing to overlook that.

What value does *The Furrow* bring John Deere?

The value is that it's getting read. If we were actively selling in our editorial space, I just don't think *The Furrow* would get read. My experience in ag journalism backs that up. Back when I started in the early 1990s, ag journalism had a really, really bad reputation. Back around that time magazines had discovered that they could really curry favor with their advertisers by running "sponsored editorial." A lot of the magazines were bad about it. Ag journalism in general got a pretty bad reputation back around that time. If some of my colleagues in ag journalism were being honest, they would say they are still working to overcome that reputation 15 or 20 years later.

The Furrow being above that fray ensures the magazine continues to be read, and our surveys back that up. We've got data that tells us that over half of our readers read every single word in every single issue, including the ads. It surprises even me. When I speak to groups about content marketing, that one always gets a gasp from the crowd, but it is the absolute truth. That's the value that our editorial philosophy contributes. That ensures that the magazine continues to be read rather than just tossed in the trash.

Authenticity Is Key

Although it should go without saying, authenticity is a prerequisite of successful content marketing. The reason is simple common sense: If people (your followers, fans, customers, or clients) believe what you say is true and real (instead of just a sales pitch), they will be more likely to value and buy into it. When your target audiences believe they are being marketed to—even if the message is not particularly aggressive—like you, they will probably turn away from it or ignore it. The bottom line is that people don't like sales pitches.

This is important to keep in mind when you are crafting your social media and content marketing messages. Although there is no hard and fast rule, when you communicate with your audiences, regardless of form or forum, make sure your sales messages are punctuated by at least as many non-sales messages—basically content that is relevant and of interest to your readers or viewers.

An oft-repeated "rule" of social media content marketing posits that the content you, the entrepreneur or creative, post or publish should be 30 percent original, 60 percent curated (i.e., retweeting, referencing, or otherwise highlighting words, ideas, or messages from another source), and just 10 percent calls to action (or sales messages).[2] The truth is that few but the biggest companies adhere to this informal rule. After all, creating and curating content takes a lot of time, and it can cost a fair amount of money, depending on whether you hire a content marketing specialist to do this work for you (which you shouldn't need to at first—although you may eventually consider assigning some part of the job to a subcontractor or automation company; more on that in Chapter 8).

It doesn't take much social media research to determine that the vast majority of those promoting themselves or their businesses online don't follow the 30–60–10-percent rule. This shouldn't come as a major surprise. Few independent businesspeople and creative professionals were trained in marketing, and directives to publicize their products and services using social media do not suggest doing much more than direct promotion. Only someone with some training in marketing or entrepreneurship would imagine that promoting or disseminating other people's content, or creating content not directly related to their sales message would make a bit of sense. In fact, from a strict business perspective, content marketing doesn't make much sense. But it also doesn't take much more than a basic understanding of human psychology to understand why providing useful or entertaining content that doesn't directly promote or sell is an excellent investment in your target audience's future loyalty and trust.

Like all people, your audiences seek out and value real relationships and communications that are not contingent on an expectation of sales. How many people do you know who invite conversations with random telemarketers? None, of course. They're probably not interested in what the telemarketers are selling, and the telemarketers are only interested in selling. That's why the arrangement doesn't work. But the dynamic shifts completely if the content creator shows she has something more to offer, building trust by demonstrating that she understands and values the people in her target audience, considering them members of a loyalty community rather than customers waiting to be exploited.

For the most part, people want authentic content. There is no strict definition of authentic content. All it means is that the content is real, useful, entertaining, and not explicitly about making sales. Realtors tend to be particularly good about anticipating people's wants and needs. Some of the most successful Realtors make it their business to engage communities of current, past, and potential clients through content marketing.

Steve Matsumoto, a Realtor based in Carlsbad, California, has taken the "content is king" message to heart by actively maintaining a contact list, and communicating with those on the list through regular newsletters, postcards, and email contests. Matsumoto's newsletters, on folded slick paper that arrives in the mail, are not all sales messages. In fact, almost none of the content Matsumoto sends to his community is directly sales-oriented. While the newsletters often include the listing and sales prices of local homes, most of the content has nothing to do with real estate.

Matsumoto updates readers on his young family (trips to Disneyland, adopting a new dog). He also shares parables, jokes, and entertaining stories—none of which have much or anything to do with real estate. At a glance, some of the content may seem strange. (In the interview that follows, Matsumoto reveals that some of the stranger content is actually produced by a marketing company.) Why, his readers may wonder, is Matsumoto recounting a story about X? The answer is simple: Because readers remember him—long after they've forgotten his stories. What may at a glance seem off-point is actually brilliant content marketing.

Q&A: STEVE MATSUMOTO, REALTOR AND CONTENT MARKETER EXTRAORDINAIRE

FIGURE 7.8 Steve Matsumoto.

How does content marketing apply to real estate sales?

Journalism has changed, and real estate has changed too. Real estate has become much more relationship-driven, and therefore much more agent-centric. Agents have had to go out and create more individual brands to attract and retain customers. If agents want to work through referral, they might do marketing that's more content based. That's what differentiates them. If you work for a brokerage, you need to put the brokerage information on your card somewhere, but it's like, "How small can I shrink it?" If you're a new agent out of the gate, you leverage the brokerage's brand. But the more you go on, the less you need that brand, and the more you want to develop your own brand.

How has the internet changed real estate sales?

The Internet has done real estate a favor. There was a point where 10, 12 years ago, all this real estate data was suddenly available on the Internet: Realtor.com, Zillow. Houses were even being sold on eBay. There was this scenario where people thought real estate agents would be put out of business because all the information was out there. We had been brokers of the information. Now we're interpreters of the information. I really think the Internet did real estate a favor in that regard. Now there's too much data out there. I want to help people get through all that and help them interpret it so they can make better decisions.

What is your brand?

I went through a couple of exercises a few years ago to really center in on what it was. Crafted loosely. I didn't pay any outside consultants.

I would say my brand is "real estate broker and math dad" because I used to be a math teacher, or "former teacher and real estate broker." I didn't formally set out to have a family-oriented, dad brand, but that's who I am. It would be hard for me to be anyone else. That's probably the key thing about branding. You can't stray too far from who you are.

For most people, their house is their largest asset. You can't just be, "Hey, I'm mister slick salesman. I'm going to sell your house as quickly as possible," There's a need to tell your story. There are a lot of real estate agents out there. You're creating a tribe, you're creating fans.

A couple years ago I made the decision to start sending mailings to my neighborhood, which isn't a logical place to "farm" for prospects simply for the fact that the neighborhood doesn't turn over all that much. For me, the distinguishing factor was that I live there. That holds a lot of value to people.

The Lake and Cannon newsletter is a logical fit for my brand. There's a school at Lake and Cannon, my kids are in the school, and we're very active in the community. My kids are 9 and 7, so they're still in that prime parenting wheelhouse. Because home and family are front and center for me, they're very logical to talk to people about.

The newsletter has the real estate meat and potatoes, the data, but it also has some personal stuff in it too. One part of the newsletter is a tale of what's going in my house. I put out 200, 300 words every month or two, and that's just an interest of mine. Readers feel like they know me. There's a family aspect, and local credibility.

Every year in December, I do a major Christmas party. It's a breakfast with Santa. A lot of marketing budget has to go toward this. If I look at return investment from it, it's absolutely worth every penny. It's a pancake breakfast, and at one point Santa shows up, and there are pictures with Santa. The inspiration for this was I was with my kids. They were little. We were waiting in a long line at the mall for Santa. I was like, ugh—there's got to be a way to elevate this experience.

Describe your content marketing

I mail the newsletter, which is 11 x 17 inches. It comes in the mail folded in fourths. It's a little more substantial than the postcards that go out. I think that shows a sort of permanence. I'm committed. It comes out every other month, so you know that you can count on that. I'm more cognizant of Realtors who mail a postcard once a year or twice a year because I'm paying attention.

I am by no means a graphic designer. I've had some help from professionals in our company. We have some marketing people who have put together pieces of it. I've had a photographer take some of the pictures. Others are just stock photos that I have or my professional headshot. I plug in the content every other month, and away it goes. A printing house in Orange County mails out 450 copies.

The postcards come from a company called By Referral Only. That's from a real estate coaching and marketing outfit. That's their content. By Referral Only works with Realtors around the country to do those sort of marketing machines. They do the monthly "Fun Day Monday" emails. It's a monthly drawing for contacts and past clients, and my boys and I shoot a short video of the drawing. We pick a name out of a hat, and the winner gets a $25 Amazon.com gift card. I've gotten such incredible feedback on those videos. Every month I could probably find a more interesting and better contest question, but I'm not going to spend the time doing that. People don't even enter the contest, but they always comment on the videos. That has been worth its weight in gold in terms of the goodwill and the branding that's come through the videos. It's very soft marketing.

Why do you do content marketing?

I'm trying to build my base of raving fans—people who have done a deal with me—and build that following. If someone's going to trust you with their most valuable asset, they have to know, like, and trust you.

I'm more inclined to do business with people with whom I've already had that relationship, or if it's an introduction from someone who already does know, like, and trust me. So I'm partway down that path anyway, as opposed to meeting someone outside a house and starting from complete scratch.

Do you ever turn down work to protect your brand?

Everybody would love to be at a point where they can pick and choose who they're working with, and I can't tell you that I'm there right now. But to some degree I think there are some things that are a more logical fit with my brand, and I focus on those.

Have you made any mistakes along the way?

My first year in the business, I spent $3,000 on a website, and it was the biggest waste of money. It was essentially a business card out in the black hole of the Internet.

Can you share content marketing tips for others?

I teach new agents, and one of the things they have to do for their brand is write a biography. They have a really hard time doing it because, they're like: "I don't have any clients."

But you start off with some reflective questions to match up people's image of you and your self-image. You could call up 10 clients and ask them: What's the first word that comes to mind when you think of me?

A branding question in real estate would be something to the effect of, "How do I want my clients to feel when they work with me?" I ask, "Did you ever buy or sell a house before? What did you like? What didn't you like? Think about that question." One of the best phrases I remember from a marketing book is: Who are your customers and what are their problems?

You also want to come up with a plan. If you have to reinvent yourself every month, you're going to exhaust yourself. If you have a map, even if you deviate, at least you have a plan in place.

Use what you have. I've decided that I like to write, and I think that I can write competently. So that's something I've decided to use. I wouldn't recommend starting a blog if you don't like to write or can't write. If you don't like yourself on screen, find a way to use video where you minimize your presence in it. Use whiteboard animations or shots of a neighborhood.

Go out there and become the expert in something so people subscribe to your blog or watch your videos. For example, are you familiar with what a natural hazard report is? It's a report on the geography of your house. Someone could write 100 words on that, then if someone ever googles "What is a natural hazard report?" they could find you. And maybe they'll go to your website.

If you are the one purveying the content, people will find you on the Internet eventually. People will find you if they have the need. Right now I need my house painted, so if you knocked on my door and wanted to talk to me about house painting, I'd probably listen. But if someone were to knock on my door to sell me a security system, I'm not interested.

What's next for your content marketing?

Right now video is the frontier where the cutting-edge people are. What I believe about video is, going back to that authenticity, I think the real estate community wants to see the goofy handheld videos rather than the slick production stuff. So, for example, the "Fun Day Monday" results show is just my iPhone, and my wife videos it.

Some people are doing Facebook Live in front of their open houses, and using video to promote themselves or houses in a clever way. Most people have a hurdle over video, over their physical image. It stops a lot of people from doing that. We've got a ways to go from the Realtor who has their 20-year-old picture on their card. But video is where the most interesting personal branding and content stuff is going on now.

We have an agent here who used to be a cameraman for local news. Not surprisingly, he uses video quite a bit to market his properties. You've got to use what you have, and you have to do some reflection on what your brand is.

Notes

1 "The Story Behind 'The Furrow'." 2013. *The Content Strategist*. Accessed July 24, 2016. https://contently.com/strategist/2013/10/03/the-story-behind-the-furrow-2/.

2 "Rallyverse." 2016. *Slideshare.net*. Accessed July 27, 2016. http://www.slideshare.net/ Rallyverse?utm_campaign=profiletracking&utm_medium=sssite&utm_source=ssslideview.

8

YOU ARE AN INFLUENCER

If you have followers on social media, you are an influencer. The influencer role has value for a number of reasons. Since the dawn of advertising—and more today than ever before—exposure, access, and influence are the key currency of business. The value of access and exposure to select audiences of particular sizes is what determines the cost of advertising. This is not a new concept, but it is important to keep in mind as you launch or maintain branding campaigns on social media. Although advertising venues and practice have changed dramatically over the last several decades—just as journalism and media have been transformed by advancing technology—the underlying principles remain the same.

Let's briefly consider the era of mass media advertising, romanticized mostly for those not old enough to have lived through it by the popular TV show *Mad Men*. The mass media advertising business model, while not as influential as it once was, still exists in broadcast television (mostly network stations) and terrestrial radio (a frequency picked up by a radio). This traditional model entails offering content for free, then selling advertising time that is worth more as the number of viewers or listeners exposed to it increases, and that fluctuates based on the relative desirability of the demographic exposed.

The value of a demographic has traditionally been determined by the likeliness of the group of people the demographic represents to buy a product or service. In the mass media days, the most appealing demographic to advertisers was 18-to-34-year-olds. Depending on the product type (i.e., technology, movies, household goods, etc.), the young people targeted in that ideal demographic were either male or female. These consumers, went the thinking, were early in their consuming lives. Winning them over early could mean decades of loyal consumption.

FIGURE 8.1 Viewer demographics are more difficult to track in the on-demand era.

Credit: Shutterstock ID#409650142

In the days of the broadcast media's domination, demographic consumer groups were broadly segmented, in basic terms, because media choices were limited. As the Internet has matured and our technology choices expand, entertainment is increasingly moving toward an on-demand model. Further, as both creating and consuming media have become easier and less expensive, the sheer amount of content available and ways to consume it has resulted in a deeply fragmented media marketplace that is much more difficult to measure.

In years past, media research companies such as Nielsen sent paper logs to randomly chosen American television viewers to record what TV programs they watched and when they watched them. Measuring media consumption habits has become much more challenging in recent years, and will no doubt become even more so as people watch less broadcast TV and scheduled programming, instead turning to on-demand streaming services like Netflix and Hulu, or watching and sharing videos through YouTube and mobile apps.

The value of your social media influence is determined by both your number of followers on various platforms and networks, and the engagement of your followers, which is then determined by the degree of interaction and exchange as compared to the overall following. This is less complicated than it sounds.

Because engagement looks different on every social network, there's no one measure that applies to every scenario. That fact established, one could, for instance, compare an individual's total number of Instagram followers to the average number of likes she gets on the photos she posts to the social network. Those kinds of data may be revealing for Instagram specifically, but not all social networks work the same way, and not all are equally valuable for all audiences, brands, and messages.

For instance, likes on one platform cannot be compared to follows on another. Likewise, popularity on one platform may not be equal to popularity on another. What matters most is popularity and engagement on platforms favored by your key audiences. If you have a robust following on Twitter but your key audiences are not big Twitter users, your popularity on this platform is not so meaningful. While popularity on channels largely ignored by your key clients and customers probably couldn't hurt, your time and energy is much better spent focusing on channels your audiences use heavily.

Measure Your Influence

As of this writing, the nearly century-old media measurement company Nielsen is preparing to take a new tool to market that will attempt to provide accurate information about media consumption across screens and platforms. Nielsen claims its Total Audience Measurement Tool will be able to track media consumption on mobile devices as well as on television sets. The company has even partnered with Facebook to glean more demographic information from people who consume content on their mobile devices, matching viewers' self-reported demographic information (i.e., age, sex, geography, and other characteristics) with their viewing habits.[1]

Why should you care about measuring media consumption habits? Simple: Because it is now up to you to do just that for your audiences. What Nielson is only now preparing to do, you should already be doing for your brand's engagement channels. Otherwise, there's no way to know if what you're doing works, if your messages are reaching their intended targets, or if you need to change your strategy.

Remember that just like mass media outlets, you have the power to affect and influence those who consume your content. That makes you an influencer. And that has value.

Although you may not yourself enlist Nielsen to research your audiences and influence, there are now many tools available that you can employ to learn more about the desires, interests, and characteristics of your audiences, people who are either current or potential clients, as well as customers or employers. The most common and reliable tool used to measure reach and engagement online is analytics data. Happily for entrepreneurial journalists and other creative professionals, there are numerous sources of analytics data available to those who use social media and have an online presence.

We discuss search engine optimization and Google Analytics in detail in Chapter 10. For now, simply consider the value of your influence online in terms of what you may want to do with it. While you start at zero on every social network and in every community, over time, especially if you become and remain an active participant on these platforms, you will build your community of followers.

FIGURE 8.2 Influence is about more than just numbers.

Credit: Shutterstock ID#217152226

While increasing followers is key to spreading your influence, and with it, awareness of your brand, keep in mind that numbers alone don't tell the whole story. Increasingly, as more individuals and institutions around the world sign onto social media to compete for attention and media consumers' limited time, engagement becomes a more important measure of success than mere numbers.

For the most part, social media engagement is great for brands. However, not all social media platforms are equally valuable to all brands. And success means different things on different platforms. Even within a particular social media platform, success may be difficult to measure.

One can have thousands of followers on Instagram while receiving only a small number of likes on the typical image she posts. That might show that while the community is large, engagement is low. This is important to understand if you hope to increase the impact of your messages. Simply reaching people without engaging them points to wasted time and resources. Why spend both attracting followers who will never show the slightest interest in your brand? It just doesn't make sense.

In recent years, social media platforms including Instagram, Facebook, and Twitter changed their algorithms to promote engagement while attempting to marginalize spammers by reducing the visibility and reach of their messages. This is part of a larger movement across social media to emulate and increase human interaction to support a more authentic experience for legitimate users. The reason for this is simple: Since the earliest days of social media, individuals and organizations have found new ways to exploit the medium for profit, frustrating legitimate users and degrading everyone's online experience.

In June 2016, Instagram reorganized the way posts appear in users' feeds to favor engagement and, the app's developers argued, to increase the likelihood that users would see posts that were more relevant to them. Among Instagram's explanations for changing its algorithm was its argument that users missed a large number of posts they would find relevant when they appeared chronologically. By favoring posts with more likes and comments, Instagram pushed users to post higher quality content that would receive more likes and comments. For users to find audiences, simply posting content was no guarantee they'd be noticed, or their posts viewed, liked, and shared.

Although there was much concern and consternation about the algorithm changes when they first went into effect, they did not ultimately prove as damaging as many had initially feared. Like with most technology changes, people were slow to accept, and the issue soon disappeared from tech blog headlines. The bottom line is that engagement is the new measure of social media success. Presenting a brand in any way that could be perceived as spammy could prove fatal.

Leverage Your Influence Through Partnerships

You already know that if you have followers on social media, you are an influencer. That's great news. However, you may actually need to reach more people in order to achieve your branding objectives. While it's essential to continue to expand and cultivate your social media identity, you may eventually need to leverage your current reach by partnering with another influencer.

FIGURE 8.3 Leverage your own brand by partnering with others.

Credit: Shutterstock ID#316493429

While partnering with social media influencers isn't difficult, it *can* be difficult to determine the right partners. Although it's not an exact science, choosing social media partners is a delicate process. Selecting an online or social media partner is about more than just the number of each party's followers, and whether a particular brand has an acceptable reputation. It's mostly about determining how each brand can help the other. This is a nuanced idea. It requires an in-depth knowledge of your brand and audience, as well as those of potential partners.

First, let's consider the matter of complementary focus. How do you determine what kind of social media accounts would align well with your brand? There are at least a couple ways to approach this. The obvious strategy would be to approach accounts that are similar to yours. If you are an advertising copywriter, reach out to other advertising copywriters. If you are a social media manager, reach out to other social media managers. This approach makes a certain amount of sense. If you are involved in the same business type, the fit may seem natural. In fact, there's likely some overlap between your followers and audiences. But this isn't wholly advantageous. In fact, if the overlap in audiences is significant, there may not be much for either party to gain.

You want to choose a partner whose brand resonates with a similar audience, but that does not compete directly with your brand. For instance, it may not make much sense for two brands that sell content marketing solutions to forge a partnership. Because the services they offer are the same, instead of potentially increasing the profile and sales potential of each, the brands may cannibalize each other.

Let's assume, for instance, that you're a freelance social media manager, offering potential clients content creation and management services. Instead of partnering with someone in the same line of work, you may want to partner with a designer who specializes in creating logos for online entrepreneurs or building websites—or with people who do both. Partnering with other creatives who offer services to similar audiences might allow you to offer special deals to customers who could be convinced to bundle services (i.e., logo and Web design, content creation, social media management) to save money and increase efficiency. It can also mean increased sales or growing client lists for both parties.

Now let's consider the degree of influence or number of followers. An ideal social media partner has slightly more influence than you do. This means they may have a few hundred more followers than you do, but not a few thousand more. If a potential partner has too few followers, their value to you is limited. Always look ahead to those who are more influential or more successful at getting the word out about their business. As a general rule in business, keep your focus forward, concerned with those you admire or would like to learn from instead of on competitors coming up from behind.

Don't forget that leveraging social media influence is a two-way street. While others' social media profiles can bolster your own, it's important to keep in mind that you also must also have something to offer. This means you should expect to grow a solid social media following before approaching others for partnership. How big a following is needed is up to you, although 1,000 is a good minimum for most platforms.

Let's take the example of an Instagram partnership. Perhaps you have 1,000 followers. You're not likely to get the attention of someone with 30,000 followers. With 30 times as many followers, they don't stand to gain much from partnering with you. Instead, look for people with 1,500 or 2,000 followers. The relationship is more equal and there's much more upside potential for both of you if your number of followers is similar.

An additional challenge is the fact each social network operates differently, which means that partnerships on one platform may not logically extend to partnerships in another. Each social network and the devices people use (i.e., desktop or laptop computers, tablet computers, mobile phones) claim different shares of various user demographics. For instance, core Facebook and Twitter users skew older, while millennials gravitate toward mobile apps such as Snapchat, and social media users around the world favor apps that may not be as well known in the West.

Unless you've identified potential partners independent of the platforms on which they reside, it may make more sense to start with the platform, then research potential partners for each. Don't forget that partnership is about mutual benefit. While you hope a social media partnership will bring more reach and exposure for your brand, you want the other party to get something out of it as well.

While it's impossible to completely control the way your brand is received online (such things as who follows your brand, or who likes your posts or official Facebook page), you can control the associations you make on behalf of your brand. Consider the following example of how this might work.

A graphic designer who creates logos and a Web designer may wish to partner on a more professional platform such as Facebook or LinkedIn pages, where they can cross-promote each other's services through links, testimonials, and discounts or package deals for potential customers of each or both creatives.

That same graphic designer may also wish to target a younger demographic by cross-promoting on Instagram. Let's imagine a partnership between the graphic designer and an indie rock band. Both have Instagram accounts, and each can promote the other simultaneously, reaching both their own followers and each other's. The graphic designer posts on Instagram a photo or video of herself holding up a poster for the band that promotes an upcoming show, and provides a link to the band's Instagram account. The band can then post a photo or video of the poster, crediting its designer and providing a link to her Instagram account.

This kind of cross-promotion not only leverages the reach of both accounts, but it also creates a sense of goodwill and strong positive associations for both the designer and the band, who appear to have promoted *other people* instead of themselves. The social media community rewards users who seem selfless or who promote others before themselves. Ironically, this kind of "selfless" promotion actually winds up doing more to promote the self than more direct attempts. This is why forging social media and online partnerships is such a valuable strategy for entrepreneurial creatives.

What follows are some other examples of types of creatives who could find synergy on social networks.

- Entrepreneurial journalists, content creators, text and video editors, Web developers, live streamers, social media managers, graphic designers
- Invitation designers, wedding photographers, videographers, clothing designers, florists, event planners
- Graphic designers, bands, event planners, custom printers
- Content creators, social media managers, Web developers

From these examples, it should be easy to see how synergies among creatives can help with cross-promotion by leveraging the audiences of each. This is the beauty of thoughtful partnerships.

Despite the obvious upsides, you'll want to explore all the implications of a particular partnership before entering into it. This isn't just about avoiding associations with disreputable brands and online identities. It's also about maintaining a clear branding message. It's difficult enough to quickly convey ideas clearly online and through social media, where attention spans are notoriously short. Muddying your brand message by partnering with an individual or company that has no logical connection to your brand could mean the difference between recognition and confusion, between a possible new lead and a quick dismissal by someone who sees a lack of coherence or professionalism.

Protect Your Influence

Although it is often among the milder concerns of individuals and companies on social media, associating your brand with other brands or individuals that are highly politicized or connected with controversial ideas or concepts could potentially undermine your brand. For the same reason a brick-and-mortar business would be wise to avoid planting campaign signs in its front lawn, it is wise to avoid possibly turning off customers or clients by taking a political stance, even in a passive way.

Of course in the highly connected and ever changing world of the Internet and social media, it's impossible to prevent all possible negative associations. Further, problems may appear long after you have connected your brand to a social media account or identity. You can't control everything—particularly others' behavior.

For example, you accepted another Pinterest user's invitation to post content on their popular board, "Places to Visit Things to Buy." At some point after you started posting content on the board (and months before a presidential election in the United States), someone changed the board's cover image to a picture of two prominent American Democrats surrounding the text "STOP ELECTING IDIOTS." This created an association between the political ideas expressed through the board and your brand, which you have probably worked hard to keep apolitical.

While leveraging your reach by partnering with other people (often strangers) is a key social media strategy, it does come with some risk. That said, there is some risk involved in every public interaction you have online. Companies that are too risk averse to fully engage in the online world or that try too hard to control their online presence miss out on some of the Internet's best features, including global interactivity and engagement.

Further, if a company is too controlled in its social media management, presenting only a corporate face and refusing to fully engage, potential clients, customers, and followers will be turned off and may disengage as a result. Smart organizations and individuals understand that the beauty and strength of social media and online interactivity is the fact that users, customers, and fans can engage with and develop connections to individuals and brands in ways they were not able to in the days before social media. In other words, you can't win if you don't play.

Make the Connections

Just because you build a professional blog, maintain active social media accounts or consistently distribute targeted content doesn't mean your audiences will be able to find any of it. Even if it is readily available, your content needs to be both compelling *and* easy to access. That's what marketing is all about. Keep in mind that while you are probably active on several social media platforms, the norms, limitations, and expectations of each is different, as are their respective

FIGURE 8.4 You may not understand Snapchat, but you can't afford to ignore it.

Credit: Shutterstock ID#427370260

audiences. Because some social media platforms, like Facebook and Twitter, are losing market share as younger uses gravitate to more real-time apps like Snapchat, simply targeting one or two platforms with which you are comfortable will likely prevent you from reaching large swaths of potential followers (and ultimately clients and customers).

Keep in mind that you may not be the target demographic for your own brand. Just because Snapchat may frustrate or annoy you does not mean you can ignore the platform completely. In a 2015 Slate article, "Is Snapchat Really Confusing, or Am I Just Old?: A 32-year-old's Hopeless Quest to Understand America's Fastest-growing Social App," technology writer Will Oremus observed that Snapchat's user interface can be tolerated only by those 25 or younger.[2] But that doesn't mean he, at 32, could ignore it.

Essentially a photo messaging app for your smartphone, Snapchat's defining characteristic is that its messages disappear after a few seconds. The app is famously popular with millennials, who remain its majority users. There are now more than 60 million daily Snapchat users in the United States and Canada.[3] If North American millennials are any part of your marketing strategy, you can't afford to ignore Snapchat. If you can't find a way to incorporate it into your social media marketing strategy, hire a millennial employee or intern you trust to take care of it for you. While this may sound like the bad advice CEOs received years ago, instructing them to hand the social media reins over to the interns since no one was paying attention anyway, at least with Snapchat, messages that don't quite align with your brand quickly disappear.

It now almost goes without saying that each time you post a new blog entry, video, photo, podcast, or anything at all, you should be using sharing tools to maximize your content's reach. The more you can cross-market and cross-post your content, the more exposure you will generate for your brand. Most hosting platforms now offer built-in solutions for publishing posted content on other platforms, and countless plugins (add-ons to your basic site software) will do everything from sharing content on a schedule to prompting visitors to sign up for e-newsletters or create loyalty accounts for special perks. WordPress.com offers its own built-in plugins, which provide simple stats (a stripped-down version of Google Analytics) and search engine optimization among other basic tools. If you use WordPress.com, enable the Publicize tool to share the content you post to your Facebook, Twitter, Google+, LinkedIn, Tumblr, Path, or Eventbrite accounts. Set up Publicize by going to your WordPress dashboard, clicking on "My Site," then "Sharing." There you will be prompted to connect your social media accounts.

If you host your own site (instead of using a free WordPress.com site), you can choose from more sophisticated plugins, including options for more comprehensive search engine optimization and analytics, ecommerce, and other resources for increasing the effectiveness of your communications, improving your reach, and growing your community of followers. To find the plugins that are available for your blog or site, simply google "WordPress.com plugins," "Shopify plugins," or "plugins" + "your software (replace this with the name of your site software or host)."

Make a Plan

Even if you don't use Hootsuite to manage your social media content distribution, you can refer to the Hootsuite blog for helpful resources. Hootsuite does exactly what it tells its users to do: Create useful content and make it available for free for those who may find it valuable. Although there's no expectation that you will become a paying Hootsuite customer if you find the company's content useful, you will likely develop positive feelings about the company for the free value it provides. Then later, if you find yourself looking for a company to assist with your social media campaigns, Hootsuite will probably come to mind.

The 2016 Hootsuite blog post "Six Social Media Templates to Save You Hours of Work"[4] provides an excellent example of useful free content. This post, by Evan LePage, offers downloadable PowerPoints and templates to help you track and manage your social media posts and campaigns. You may find No. 4, Hootsuite's Social Media Planner, particularly useful. For each day, this customizable spreadsheet lists times and social media platforms on the Y axis, and on the X axis, it provides space to add each post title, its contents, the link, and (to complete later) the number of clicks it receives. Download the Social Media Planner here:

https://blog.hootsuite.com/wp-content/uploads/2014/12/Social-Media-Content-Calendar-Template-January-2015.pdf

Automate Incoming Content

Now that you've established that you are, in fact, an influencer, and that your time has value, your next task should be determining how to make the best use of your power of influence given your finite resources. One of the best things about being an influencer on social media and online is that, assuming you have a smartphone and a fast, reliable Internet connection, achieving online influence is free. The greatest cost to you is time. (It may, though, cost you a little money to save time by using tools like the content automators over the next few pages.)

For most people, the idea of distributing content is every bit as daunting as creating or curating it. For those who also work other jobs, this can be a particular challenge, rising to the level of a job in itself. Even those for whom running and marketing their own business *is* their day job may struggle to get it all done. To keep the task from eating up all their time, they maintain a content marketing schedule, and automate at least part of the distribution process to get the job done. You, like them, need a plan.

FIGURE 8.5 Don't waste hours every day looking for content. Automate the process. *Credit*: Shutterstock ID#164143403

We established the utility and importance of curating content in the last chapter. The question we consider here is where to find content to curate, and how to build the curation process into your daily routines so that finding and disseminating it is less time-consuming than creating content from scratch, and distributing each post, podcast, photo, pin, or video individually. Without a streamlined process and go-to sources of reliable content, curation could start to interfere with the business or brand it is intended to support. Keep in mind that your time is likely your most valuable resource as an entrepreneur. Despite the common expression, you can't simply make more time.

A good content marketing plan will keep you from wasting time casting about for content every morning or even every day. Although your content marketing plan can take any form, at the very least it should outline steps you plan to take at designated times each day (and probably each week and month) to find, gather, curate, and distribute content. You probably already have a few go-to sites, apps, podcasts, or even newspapers or radio stations you rely on for daily news. Keep checking these and other news feeds covering topics that align with your brand. What follows are some resources that can help.

BuzzSumo (http://buzzsumo.com/) is an online research tool that allows for sophisticated searching. Type in keywords and timeframes to find content aligned with your brand and relevant to your audience and community. You can filter them by type, separating written content from images, videos, and infographics. Content is shown in ranked order based on how extensively it was shared on social networks. You can then select stories or items to share based on their popularity across social networks.

Reddit (https://www.reddit.com/) has been around for a long time (more than a decade, which is an eternity in the Internet era). Although the interface is clunky and old, Reddit, which resembles an online bulletin board from the 1990s, remains a useful tool for finding trending topics online. Popularity of Reddit posts increase or decrease based on upvotes and downvotes from the community. Like BuzzSumo, Reddit is a search engine for online content. But it's more than that. Both highly personal and democratic, Reddit is a passionate community of committed users. That means news can be skewed when the community takes ownership of a particular issue. Keep this in mind when you're searching for stories.

Feedly (https://feedly.com/i/welcome) is a good resource for collecting and reviewing fresh content from around the Web. You can create a free account and set up alerts for topics related to your brand. Each topic includes information on specific content sources, including the number of readers, how many articles the source produces each week, and whether the content is delivered in abstract form or at full length. Simply choose a topic (i.e., news, food, tech, design, startups), and select among several feeds for each. Select which sources you would like to follow, and as new content becomes available from each source, it will appear in your Feedly feed. This way you can simply select all the sources that may provide useable content, and scan them in one place. The process is simpler and less-time consuming than randomly searching the Web for potentially relevant or useable content.

Pocket (https://getpocket.com/), a Chrome browser extension, is also a great way to collect content online, and access it from various devices. Pages and posts saved to your Pocket get synced across your devices running Chrome. When you find relevant content online, you can save it to your Pocket, then return to it later, when you're ready to curate it for your own audiences.

Scoop.it (http://www.scoop.it/) functions similarly, as does **Curata** (http://www.curata.com/). Compared to its competitors, Curata has less of an indie feel. Its website conveys a notably corporate interface, focused on marketing and sales. As of this writing, the Curata home page emphasizes sales, specifically mentioning "supply chain."[5]

Google Alerts (https://www.google.com/alerts) is another way to bring potentially relevant content to you instead of having to spend time searching for it. Google Alerts allows you to choose keywords and create an RSS feed that will deliver items containing your keywords to your email address.

Sites that highlight original content may provide more consistently high-quality content. For example, **Medium** (https://medium.com/) is an attractive repository of mostly thoughtful blog entries. Medium is searchable, and includes collections of related content that you may return to regularly for content relevant to your brand.

Instead of actively searching for content that may be relevant to your audience, you can automate the search process using a tools such as **Content Gems** (https://contentgems.com/), which filters content on the Internet and social media for the search terms you select, then emails it to you in a digest. You can then pick and choose which items you would like to bring to your own audience.

Automate Outgoing Content

Now that you know where to find online content, you may want to consider how to disseminate it without letting it take over your life. With all the social media platforms and options now available, strategic distribution of content is not only important but also necessary given the increasing time commitment. Without efficiency, one can easily find themselves lost in an ongoing quest to continuously post the right images, videos, text, and other information to the appropriate networks. It can consume entire days.

There are now a large number of apps available for those who would like to automate content across social media platforms and the Web. **Hootsuite** (https://hootsuite.com/) may be the most famous and the most established. (It was founded all the way back in 2008, the dark ages of social networking!) Hootsuite allows you to schedule and automate posts to Facebook, Twitter, Instagram, YouTube, LinkedIn, and Google+. Hootsuite offers a free plan and four paid plans, each allowing progressively more uses, shares, posts, analytics, and other functions.

Others content automators include:

- **Buffer** (https://buffer.com/)
  - Integrations: Facebook, Twitter, Instagram, LinkedIn, Google+, Pinterest
  - Membership levels: 5, including a free option
- **SocialOomph** (https://www.socialoomph.com/)
  - Integrations: Facebook, Twitter, LinkedIn, Tumblr, Pinterest, RSS feeds, blogs, and Taiwan's Plurk
  - Membership levels: 2, free and professional
- **SproutSocial** (http://sproutsocial.com/)
  - Integrations: Facebook, Twitter, Instagram, LinkedIn, Google+
  - Membership levels: 3, none free (although they do offer a free 30-day trial)

Influence the Influencers

Influencers are (at least on social media) bold and confident. They aren't pushy or demanding, but they stand by their online content, and they're not shy about promoting it. After all, they need to assume they have something important to share with their audiences—and they do. There's no reason to be shy about that. The only catch is that they must be mindful of what they do share, carefully balancing promotional content with a much larger proportion of useful or interesting non-promotional content.

While social media influencers must promote their brand without reservation or hesitation, they must be careful to not be perceived as self-promoters. Instead, they should be seen as purveyors of relevant, high-quality content. By providing useful content to their audiences and followers, their brand will quickly become indispensable. People will seek out the brand based on useful content the brand has delivered in the past. (Consider the Hootsuite example in the previous pages.)

In recent years, an entire cottage industry has grown up online to serve the needs of individuals and small companies looking to promote their homegrown brands. The smart people who have created sideline consulting and branding businesses to augment their own e-commerce businesses may understand the rule of relevant content better than anyone else. Although the technique is hardly new to sales, these online consulting firms are huge proponents of the strategy that encourages potential new clients to sample a certain amount of relevant content for free in the hope that clients and customers will then eagerly pay for more.

These new professional online influencers are some of the best creators and distributors of relevant social media content anywhere. They understand online branding better than almost anyone because they've worked hard from the early days of social media to promote their own brands. They were early adopters,

FIGURE 8.6 Influence the influencers by teaching what you've learned.

Credit: Shutterstock ID#352387571

and they learned the lessons of those on the vanguard of emerging technology. In most cases, they found partners and professional groups early on that helped them leverage their own influence by combining it with others'.

Because the online marketplace is now so crowded, these Internet influencers understand that the lessons they learned promoting their brands are highly in demand among others now hoping to achieve similar success. They are, in other words, some of the Internet's most successful influencers. But they won't be the last. Although you may be far from being able to promote yourself as an online branding coach, you can still apply the lessons of these online influencers to promote your own brand and perhaps someday become a powerful influencer of other influencers.

Notes

1 "7 Things You Need to Know about Nielsen's New Tool." 2015. *Broadcastingcable.com*. Accessed August 15. 2016. http://www.broadcastingcable.com/news/currency/7-things-you-need-know-about-nielsen-s-new-tool/146053.
2 Oremus, Will. 2016. "Is Snapchat Really Confusing, Or Am I Just Old?" *Slate Magazine*. Accessed October 1, 2016. http://www.slate.com/articles/technology/technology/2015/01/snapchat_why_teens_favorite_app_makes_the_facebook_generation_feel_old.html.
3 "Forbes Welcome." 2016. *Forbes.com*. Accessed October 1, 2016. http://www.forbes.com/sites/kathleenchaykowski/2016/09/26/snapchat-passes-60-million-daily-users-in-the-u-s-and-canada/#4c98befa34dc.
4 "6 Social Media Templates to Save You Hours of Work." 2016. *Hootsuite Social Media Management*. Accessed October 2, 2016. https://blog.hootsuite.com/social-media-templates/.
5 "Content Curation & Content Marketing Platform." 2016. *Curata.com*. Accessed August 7, 2016. http://www.curata.com/.

9

CHECK YOUR SKILL SETS

It seems a new media platform appears every day, and for independent content creators, that means another new addition to an already bulging portfolio of social media, blogging, curation, and sharing sites that must be regularly fed and maintained. In Chapter 7 we discussed the content side or branding in detail. This chapter goes into a bit more depth, addressing some of the technical considerations behind creating and distributing the content you create.

Written Communication

Although its importance is often downplayed in a world rich with multimedia, we cannot afford to forget that solid writing skills are at the heart of any communication. If you cannot express yourself clearly in writing, you will not likely succeed as a content creator. Every day we are surrounded by all kinds of content. We consume content deliberately and on-demand, but also absorb it accidentally, through our mobile devices and other ubiquitous media. Most people now receive news updates and messages throughout the day, in a number of forms across a variety of platforms. We know this because we live in the same media environment as those with whom we hope to connect. We understand how many people and messages compete for our limited attention throughout each day. We know first-hand what it takes to break through the constant media barrage and get our attention with a message with personal relevance.

Like others, we complain that we are overwhelmed by the amount of media we receive and must sift through—or simply ignore. For this reason, it is easy to see why media coverage has become shorter and more digestible. When was the last time you sat down to read a long news story? (Maybe you never have.) While traditional media such as newspapers may have once favored long articles, media consumers today prefer short items that can be quickly read on smart-phones or mobile devices. You know this because you are one of these consumers. Your time is as limited as anyone else's, and you are just as likely to be reading and consuming on the small screen of a smartphone or tablet computer. You routinely make split-second decisions about what to read or watch. You know exactly why news and media consumers may spend time reading a one-line Instagram post or watching a minute-long video, while longer posts or three-minute videos will likely be ignored—or marked for later, then lost to the sands of time.

This move toward short-form content across all media does not, however, mean that standards have slipped. In fact, as content becomes shorter and more compressed, the demand becomes even greater for writers and producers to make more impact in less time. Consumers want their news and information as quickly as possible, using the smallest number of words. Creators of video content also need to practice compression to attract and keep viewers' attention despite increasing competition from other content creators clamoring for their share of local or global viewership. In today's crowded and competitive marketplace, shorter is almost always better. Shorter content allows people to consume more information and entertainment in less time. As time becomes the global economy's most precious commodity, efficient use of time remains a primary goal.

As Twitter has shown us for many years, writing a clear, concise, accurate story with a limited word count is much more challenging than covering all

FIGURE 9.1 Writing skills are still essential for content creators.

Credit: Shutterstock ID#367928828

the relevant facts in a long article or feature. Impeccable written and oral communication skills have always been necessary for journalists, but now these skills are even more important to entrepreneurs and creatives who, in increasing numbers, must represent themselves to potential clients, customers, and audiences. Even more important than being able to write and talk well is the ability to change communication styles for different situations and platforms.

Across much of social media, character counts or attention spans—or both—are limited. Yet that doesn't mean the same clipped language that may be acceptable for Twitter will also work on Instagram, Facebook, or another platform with fewer space restrictions. Keep in mind that even if a platform (Instagram, for instance) allows you to make a lengthy post, that does not necessarily mean you should or that anyone will read it. Key is to study and internalize the conventions of the stars of each platform. Even though communication style is not often articulated by the platform, it is not difficult to learn the norms and standards by paying close attention to what successful members of the community are doing. Like with all things, it's usually a good idea to embrace the conventions of any field's most successful practitioners.

Oral Communication

Oral communication skills remain essential for any professional, regardless of field or specialization. As we just discussed, our potential audiences have limited time, and every day it seems there are more other people and entities competing to access a bit of whatever time is left after all the daily requirements of life are met. Now, just as clear, concise writing skills are required of anyone competing for people's already limited time and attention, so is clear, concise oral communication.

FIGURE 9.2 Creatives and entrepreneurs of all kinds need excellent speaking skills.

Credit: Shutterstock ID#193643762

Are you a good writer? Are you a good speaker? If you aren't a professional communicator, the answers to these questions may not be immediately apparent. The bottom line is that everyone, regardless of their current skills, can improve through practice. Even if you are already a good writer and oral communicator, your existing skills may only get you so far. In a world of almost countless media outlets, it is unlikely your natural writing or communication style will be a good fit for all. In fact, you could be an excellent long-form writer and struggle to write well in a more succinct or shorter format. You may be a fine creative writer and struggle with academic style. Your style or tone will likely need some tweaking for each venue. This is normal.

Variations in Style and Tone

If you are accustomed to writing or speaking to a particular audience, what you may need most is to try your hand at communicating in different contexts. Focus on one platform at a time. Read as much content as you can, then translate some of your existing writing into the platform's style. Keep in mind that not every example on social media or online is worth emulating. Find the most popular and successful accounts (by checking the number or followers or the amount of inter- action generated by posts), and pay close attention to their communication style.

Here are a few questions to consider when evaluating communication style:

- How much text is there?
  - Is it brief or long?
  - Does it tell a story?
  - Is there other multimedia content? If so, how is it handled?
- What is the content's tone?
  - Is it serious or silly?
  - Is it complete, or is it intended to pique interest?
  - Does it address the reader as if he or she are insiders or part of a special community?
- What is the writing style?
  - Do writers rely heavily on slang or insider language that is exclusive (or near-exclusive) to particular groups?
  - Do the writers use emoticons? If so, how?
- What is the content itself?
  - What is the purpose of the message? To entertain? To sell?
- Are there direct sales messages?
  - Does the content creator offer coupon codes or other enticements to buy or to sign up for additional content or an e-newsletter?
- What are the norms and interaction protocols?
  - How do people respond to posts and content?
  - How do content creators respond to comments on their posts?

Improve Your Writing

If you are not already routinely communicating with particular audiences, you may need to simply build your writing and speaking skills. This may be particularly challenging if you need to communicate in a non-native language. Unfortunately, there is no easy or quick way to build your writing skills. The best—and only—way to build your skills is to read everything you can get your hands on, and write every day. Editing other people's writing can also be a great skill-builder.

Here are a few suggestions for building writing skills:

1. Read a newspaper or news site every day. Choose a longer story, and summarize it in a single paragraph. Write a version for at least three different platforms (i.e., Twitter, Facebook, Instagram, Pinterest, etc.)
2. Create a personal blog about a topic of interest. Make at least one new blog post of approximately 250 words every day.
3. Exchange writing with someone else. Critique each other's work and offer suggestions for improvement.

Remember the key to improving your writing, like building any other skill, is consistency. Work on your writing every day, and it will improve.

Improve Your Speech

Being a clear, compelling speaker, as you surely know, is more than a matter of writing well. Speaking clearly and, for most people, addressing live audiences, can evoke stress and even fear. In office jobs, most workers get few opportunities to speak publicly. Most would consider that a good thing. Yet if you are the face of your company and are working to establish its brand, you can expect to have to talk to potential clients and customers. You will also likely have to address large groups from time to time. The sooner you start to prepare for that eventuality, the better off you will be. Even the most experienced public speakers can fall out of practice if they haven't addressed a crowd for some time. Regardless of your experience level, it is essential to practice your skills in a no- or low-stakes environment.

Here are a few suggestions for building oral communication skills:

1. Volunteer for leadership opportunities at work or in your community that will require you to address groups.
2. Join your local Toastmasters International chapter (www.toastmasters.org). Toastmaster members from all professions and regions improve their public speaking skills by presenting to each other on a regular basis, and both receiving and providing feedback on presentations. Like with writing, oral

communication skills take time to develop. There are no shortcuts. The only way to significantly improve your skills is through practice.

3. Create an introductory video for your website. You should do this anyway. Forcing yourself to write and present a script or outline introducing yourself and your brand is one of the best ways to improve your oral communication skills. Editing your presentation to fit a one-minute introduction will require you to critically examine your speaking style, and determine how it may be improved. Before you finalize or post your video, make sure to have a friend or trusted colleague watch your video and provide honest critique. It is likely you will want to record your video one, two or more times to address the weaknesses you or your critics reported.

Your Brand Online

As you have read countless times in this book so far, consistency is essential for creating a professional look and feel for your brand. Even though business is increasingly conducted through mobile devices and via social media, the overall presentation of your website still determines to a significant degree whether people will trust you and want to do business with you. Remember that visitors to your website and social media landing pages usually make decisions about the quality and trustworthiness of your site within just a few seconds. Success requires you to make an almost instantaneous positive impression. As the saying goes, there's no second chance to make a first impression. If a visitor to your site determines it is unprofessional, it is unlikely that visitor will ever return.

When much or all of your business is conducted online, the impression your website makes in the first 30 seconds often determines whether you will gain a follower, client, or customer, or you will be dismissed as an amateur—or worse, a crook. Lacking the opportunity to make a human connection, your online presence says it all. It is your job to ensure it has only positive things to say.

Without face-to-face interaction with those with whom you do business or plan to do business, people have less to go on when making decisions about whether to trust a person or a company, and consequently, whether to trust them with their personal and financial information. Often, as both a consumer and provider of goods and services online, you are limited to only images, text, and in some cases, video. While all of these media can make powerful impressions, they will never surpass the power of in-person engagement.

Given this fact, it is incumbent upon those of us who represent ourselves online to maximize the impact and impression power of the images we present to the world. Let us consider some of the ways we do that, and why.

For many online entrepreneurs, the venues for making impressions are limited to the Web and mobile media. In both of these venues, images are the primary means of making impressions. These images may include photographs and graphic design elements, type treatments (i.e., fonts and type size), and layout, among other subtler factors. All of these items are vitally important in forming impressions of you or your company because in the absence of other factors traditionally used to make judgments about individuals or companies, they may mean the difference between attracting a client or an audience and turning away or tuning off potential clients. Online, people decide whether to stay on a site in mere seconds.

Design, images, content, and functionality must not only be top-notch, but they must be thoughtfully considered in order to reinforce, not undermine, the brand. Logos, photos, type treatments, and other design elements that represent your brand online and on marketing collateral such as business cards, invitations, posters, T-shirts, or other printed material should be simple, clear, compelling, and consistent. Consistency, as we discuss in other chapters, is key to building and maintaining powerful brand identities. Without the recognition that comes from consistency, a brand may fail to make an impression, and can easily fall from audiences' consciousness. A consistent, visually strong brand is the best advertising your brand can get.

Although each brand is different, and there are no universal rules governing the way photos and other branding images should appear online and in print, there are several guidelines anyone interested in building or maintaining a brand should carefully consider. Creating a professional presence for your brand, and building trust among current and prospective customers, clients, and employers is no simple process. It can be done, but it is never finished.

The trust factor is central to building a successful brand online. Unlike selling, promoting, or representing in person, when your primary venue for representing yourself is the Web and the tiny screens of mobile media, the anonymity of the platform remains a significant and constant challenge. Unlike those who see clients in offices or customers in stores, you have to build trust through indirect measures.

Consider what you look for when determining whether you can trust a website with which you are unfamiliar. What kinds of things do you consider? Perhaps you check to see whether the URL is secure or you scroll to the bottom of the home page to find any clues identifying the site's ownership. Maybe you click on a "contact" button to see if getting in touch with the company is difficult—or even possible.

While it may take a few minutes to determine whether a site is legitimate, there are several highly important factors that can nearly always ensure that visitors will quickly dismiss your site as either amateurish or untrustworthy. What follows are a few of the most important things to get right when presenting your services, your products, or yourself online.

Develop a Website

Although many brands now become ubiquitous through social media, your brand still should have a website to serve as its online headquarters and the landing page for social media accounts. Anyone who does business online should have a professional website. Fortunately, a professional-looking website is now so easy to produce, you should not need to hire a professional to do it.

Journalists and creatives need fewer Web skills than they used to. Because the available free tools are so much simpler these days than in years past, less training and fewer specialized skills are needed to create basic websites. Unless you plan to be a coder, don't bother learning how to code. The visual (not html) editors that are built into software like WordPress, Wix, Squarespace, Tumblr, or Blogger have made creating Web pages and posts almost as easy as creating a Word document. Despite this, knowing a little html may be a good idea for occasional troubleshooting. It is, after all, helpful to be able to take a quick peek at the underlying code when text or images behave unexpectedly in a post. Thanks to the Internet, it is easy to make small tweaks to code without knowing any html at all. Want to make the email address on your contact page a link? Just Google it.

Here it is, thanks to W3schools.com:[1]

<a href="mailto:webmaster@example.com">Jon Doe</a>

There are now several robust software options for building an attractive and functional website without knowing code. Some people like Wix or Squarespace. Shopify is a favorite for e-commerce. But the stalwart of website creation remains WordPress, the world's most popular platform for blogging and creating websites. Once the only option for regular people (not trained Web designers or coders) to build and host a basic website using an attractive template, WordPress is no longer alone in its ease and functionality. That said, it has been around for so long, and has such a large and loyal user base, WordPress.com is still a great option for most.

With the abundance of options now available to everyone with Internet access, there is no longer any excuse to have a website that looks unprofessional. The tools are just too abundant, inexpensive (often free), and easy to use. With no shortage of website themes or templates available for use on a variety of hosting platforms, there are likely to be several that will serve you well. Website themes are basically design templates for showcasing content online. They render unnecessary much of the work once associated with creating websites. Simply choose a host and select a theme that will work on that host. Website themes work so seamlessly today it is easy to forget that you are even using one.

Let's assume you are using WordPress to host your website. You are a photographer, and you would like to showcase a portfolio of your recent works to share with current and potential clients. Selecting an appropriate theme is as simple as Googling "wordpress portfolio themes." Your search will pull up dozens of potential themes you may want to try on.

If you use or plan to use a free, WordPress-hosted WordPress.com site, simply navigate to wordpress.com/themes. There are thousands of WordPress themes

FIGURE 9.3 Don't design your own website. Buy an attractive theme.

Credit: Shutterstock ID#113161615

available. Your biggest challenge may be browsing hundreds and selecting only one. The good news is that if you eventually find that your theme no longer works for you, it is likely you'll find one that will better present your content.

Because the search for the perfect theme can be overwhelming, it's important to have some search guidelines in mind to streamline the process somewhat. For instance, if you're a photographer, artist, or graphic designer, you may want to limit your search to portfolio themes. Navigate to the search window on Word-Press' themes page, and you will find a few categories that may help focus your search. You can choose among sites for different kinds of content (i.e., travel, business, wedding, food, music), different features (featured images, custom header, infinite scroll), the number of columns you want in your layout (one, two, many), color schemes, and free or premium.

You should know that WordPress.com sites (they call them "blogs") are hosted on a WordPress server and you, unless you pay a modest yearly fee that will allow you to customize your site, will not have access to the stylesheet that determines how the site looks and functions. In recent years, WordPress.com has introduced a number of paid upgrades that allow users of the company's hosted blogs options once limited to WordPress.org users who used the company's free software on a non-WordPress hosting platform. Domain mapping was among the first paid upgrades WordPress offered. It is inexpensive, and well worth the cost.

Domain mapping allows you to customize the URL of your WordPress.com site. When you register for a free WordPress.com account and create your first blog, the URL will look like this: yourname.wordpress.com. Because that URL is long and does not look professional, you should pay to customize your WordPress.com blog with your own URL. You can buy your domain directly from WordPress.com, or from a domain (URL) registration and hosting company such as GoDaddy (godaddy.com), Register (register.com), Network Solutions (networksolutions.com), or a number of other competitors. On any of these sites, you can search for the domain you want until you find an acceptable domain that is available.

If you see that a domain that you are interested in is available, purchase it quickly because domains have a way of becoming unavailable soon after they are searched for. In 2008, Network Solutions was sued for "domain name front running," or reserving domain names that people searched for, in what the company denied was an effort to force customers to later buy those domains from them.[2] The practice was in a legal gray area at the time, and domain registrar Go Daddy was accused of the same practice in 2012. Although public criticism seems to have brought an end to front running allegations, it is still a good idea to buy a domain you like as soon as you find it is available.

If you purchase your domain from WordPress.com, it will replace the default WordPress domain. If you purchase your domain from another company, you merely need to direct visitors to your blog to WordPress servers. This is called updating your name servers, and you can do by logging into your account with your domain registrar, and typing in WordPress' server names (currently NS1. WORDPRESS.COM, NS2.WORDPRESS.COM, and NS3.WORDPRESS.COM). WordPress.com support (en.support.wordpress.com) provides step-by-step directions for domain mapping and pretty much anything else you may want to do with a blog.

On the WordPress dashboard (which you can get to by typing in your domain name followed by "/admin."), you will want to set your site (or blog) to "private" in the Settings > Reading menu until you are finished building it out. WordPress.com has an excellent community-based support site and easily searchable information on building websites and blogs. New users can start at the support home page (en.support.wordpress.com), where online tutorials and videos provide step-by-step guidance on creating and updating sites.

Website Functionality

There may be no worse advertisement for yourself or your services online than having a dysfunctional, slow, or difficult-to-navigate website. A poorly functioning website may not be immediately apparent to yourself because the version

You have reached the
borders of the Universe

404 Error Page

Please, keep calm
and return to the previous page

FIGURE 9.4 Don't let a poorly functioning website turn off potential clients and customers.

Credit: Shutterstock ID#334772408

of the site you see and interact with may be different from that seen by others. When checking the functionality of your site, make sure to view it on a different browser, or at least log out of your administrator account to view the version seen by the general public. In some cases, these two versions can be wildly different.

When you check your site as an outside visitor, make sure to click on several pages to determine whether links are working properly, and to determine whether anything (like a large image file) is significantly slowing the page's load. Also check any links to external pages or multimedia (such as video) hosted on different sites or servers. You will want to perform this kind of check at least monthly, and more often if you make significant changes to your site.

There are also services you can employ and apps you can install to check the functionality and speed of your website. Nibbler (nibbler.silktide.com) is an excellent free tool (with an advanced paid version) for checking your website's viability and effectiveness in maximizing its potential as measured by accessibility, experience, marketing, technology, popularity, and other characteristics. Check your website with Nibbler or another service to find recommendations for improving your site's visibility and reach. Some of the possible recommendations are of a simple nature (i.e., include more text on your pages, increase the number of links to the site, include meta descriptions for each page and each image to help Web browsers find them and provide them in search queries), use consistent image sizes, link to social media accounts (Facebook, Twitter), and maximize engagement with people who may find your site through these accounts.

Meta Tags

Meta tags are informational snippets of code that describe something (like an image or a page), making whatever they describe discoverable by search engines. They play an important role in search engine optimization (SEO). Most website developers and themes make it easy to add meta tags, and it is important that you do if you want people to find your site. Tags in general are among the main ways people find your online content. Although they function somewhat differently on different platforms, social media tools such as Twitter and Instagram also rely heavily on tags to make content searchable and discoverable.

It should be obvious why relevant, direct text is essential for engagement online and on social media. In addition to tags and meta tags, text is also searchable. While the actual words and phrases used in search is of key importance, keep in mind that the more words there are on a Web page, the more likely the page will appear in searches. This is a simple matter of having more searchable content.

The rule of more is simple enough. In basic terms, the more content—including words, images, and multimedia of all kinds—that exists on a site, the more there is for search engines to find. This does not mean that you should overload your site with wordy content, but that you should maximize the amount of relevant content you include.

FIGURE 9.5 Keep working on your keywords.

Credit: Shutterstock ID#230066236

Your Brand's Look and Feel

It almost goes without saying that online images should be appealing. Yet this fact cannot be stressed enough. Attractive photos are among the most significant factors in increasing engagement in a website or social media account. It is easy to understand why.

Of course the quality of your photography and other images will not matter if your website template is unattractive, poorly organized, or difficult to navigate. Assuming you have fixed any problems in these areas, you will want to focus on maximizing the quality and effectiveness of your photos and other images. While there are no set rules governing aesthetics for all websites, there are several basic rules that should apply to all.

Photos and Design

When Instagram filters first allowed even amateurs to share attractive photos that were optimized for social media back in 2010, suddenly everyone with a smartphone had the ability to create professional-looking photos. Professionals now face a unique challenge in trying to distinguish themselves from the pack. How can entrepreneurial journalists and branded creatives produce higher quality images than the amateurs?

Here are a few tips:

Frame thoughtfully. Take your time to ensure that everything you want in the frame is there, that heads aren't cut off, that trees and lamps aren't growing out of people's heads. Consider the foreground and the background. Remember that viewers with fresh eyes will see everything in the frame—even the background.

Consider the rule of thirds. This guideline for framing photos attempts to avoid the boredom of centered images by dividing the frame into a nine-square tic-tac-toe board. To create more drama, energy, and elegance, the photographer or photo editor should ensure that the main image is roughly aligned along one of these lines, with about one-third of the frame occupying the space between the image and the closest edge, and (particularly if the subject is a human or animal) facing toward the negative space that occupies roughly two-thirds of the frame between the main image and the farthest edge.

Light adequately. You can't lighten a photo or video that was shot with inadequate light without introducing grain and "noise." Grainy photos look bad. While a photo's background can be shaded, it is essential that the main image in the frame is well lit and visible. You don't need a professional lighting kit to adequately light an image, but depending on how regularly you plan to shoot photos for your website or social media, it may be a good idea to invest in two or three inexpensive portable shop lights on stands from your local hardware store. If you don't want to invest in additional lighting, you can also use available light. Indoors, bright lamps without their shades may be sufficient.

Many photographers and documentary filmmakers use only natural light. Natural light is a good alternative to studio light if you don't mind restricting your shooting to times when available light is good. Of course, "good" is a relative term, and it depends on the look and feel you want to create for your photos and your brand. For outdoor shoots, natural light is almost always preferable to studio lighting. Daytime shots outdoors are usually bright enough (often they are too bright and require subjects to move to shadier areas or away from direct sunlight), and most contemporary digital cameras will automatically adjust brightness levels.

Professionals often use three-point lighting to ensure that the subject of a photo is well lit from all angles with no harsh shadows on the face. In three-point lighting, one main light called the key light because it is the brightest light, points toward the subject at an angle from one side. Another light, the fill light, illuminates the side of the face that the key light left in shadows. It is usually less bright and positioned slightly lower than the key light. A third light, sometimes called a hair light or a back light, illuminates the subject from the back, sometimes creating a halo effect.

FIGURE 9.6 Lots of light helps make your photos look great.

Credit: Shutterstock ID#294852302

Under most conditions, cameras on smartphones and other mobile devices will produce images adequate quality for the Web. However, if lighting, colors or contrast are extreme, a DSLR camera may be necessary to produce high-quality images. Keep in mind that when the sun is bright, the more interesting shot may result from shooting into the sun. In the days before digital photography, photographers were often cautioned against shooting into the sun to avoid shooting an image in which the subject would appear as a darkened silhouette. But digital photography is more forgiving, and often with careful positioning, the sun or other light source can create a halo or a dramatic sunburst around the subject.

You may have heard of "the golden hour," which is the hour or so just after sunrise and before sunset when outside light is particularly warm (with a yellow or orange tint) and shadows are extreme. Shooting at the golden hour can create drama and heighten artistic effects, though it is not good for representational photography in that it tends to distort the subject.

Clarity and Purpose

Photos—especially those that are intended to represent products—should be clear and accurate. While you can (and in most cases should) use photo editing software to improve your photos, you also want to make sure that you do not modify the photos to the point that they misrepresent reality. Depending on the purpose of the photo (to represent an item or to create a mood), you should opt for either simple clarity or dramatic distortion, and use these techniques consistently. Featuring both abstract and representational images on your website or social media accounts can muddy or confuse your brand.

If you produce physical products, photographs of portfolio items or items for sale should be well-lit, in focus, and complete. Place the objects on a neutral background (white is usually recommended, except for white or extremely light items), and photograph it from all important angles (i.e., front, back, sides, top). Of course if you are simply trying to create a mood or a tone, representational images may not be important.

If you are using a camera with manual settings, adjust for depth of field and exposure. If you aim to show an accurate depiction of an item, with less loss of focus for items behind the main point of focus, you will want to adjust the f-stop to the highest number, which results in less light hitting the camera shutter. Lenses differ, but selecting an f-stop of f/8 or higher (ideally f/16 or f/22) will result in a greater depth of field and a flatter, less dimensional image. It will also allow less light into the lens, in turn requiring more exposure time. This means you will want to put your camera on a tripod to avoid camera shake and blurry images.

However, if you would like to emphasize detail on an item or person, you will want a shallower depth of field and a lower f/stop. This will result in a more dimensional image, bringing the focal point into sharp focus while blurring out the background, foreground or both. This will let more light through the shutter, allowing you to use a faster shutter speed. Before you adjust f/stops and shutter speed, you will want to set the ISO on your manual camera.

ISO should always be the first and last adjustment on your manual camera, and it should reflect overall conditions in the room or environment. The brighter the environment, the lower the ISO. If you are shooting in bright sun, for instance, you may want to start with ISO 100, which tempers some of the sunlight in the image, reducing the likelihood of overexposure. Conversely, if you are shooting indoors, you will likely want to start with an ISO of 800, take a few test shots, and make the necessary adjustments before starting the shoot. Change the ISO when the shooting environment changes, but if the shooting conditions do not change, you should adjust the f/stops and shutter speed before touching ISO.

Consistency

As we mentioned earlier, photos on your website or social media accounts should have a consistent look. If you apply filters or other treatments in editing, make sure to apply the same filters or treatments to all your images. Also make sure that images that appear in the same space on a website (like a gallery, carousel or showcase) have the same aspect ratio, or ratio of an image's width to its height. This means that images are proportionally the same. They may be square or rectangular with a vertical or horizontal orientation. It is important that images that occupy the same space have the same aspect ratio so that they look consistent when users browse through images. For instance, if one image is smaller than the previous image, it may appear with unattractive vertical or horizontal bars on each side.

Size

Most website themes have recommended image sizes. It is generally a good idea to follow these recommendations to ensure the highest quality images with the fastest load time. Images that are too large or that your site has to scale down will slow a site's loading. The longer it takes for a website to load, the more likely visitors will be to leave before engaging with content or making a purchase.

Logos

You may not need a logo for your entrepreneurial pursuit. However, depending on what kind of business you have, a logo can be a critical part of your branding campaign. For most companies and organizations, logos are among the most important ways of establishing and reinforcing brands.

The first question you may have is: If you had a logo, where would you use it? Here are a few possibilities:

- On your website
- On your business cards
- On your stationery
- On your email signature

Even if you do not sell products and have not established a legal company, a logo can be one quick way to reinforce your branding, increase recognition of your brand, and convey professionalism. However, you do want to keep things in perspective and avoid the temptation to overpromise or mislead with a logo design that could suggest slick commercialism or might look junky.

Most likely, if you are an independent contractor running your own social media, editing, art, or consulting business (to consider a few examples), you want a simple but memorable image. The same rule is generally true for larger companies too, although they do enjoy a bit more leeway in their designs. After all, consumers do not have the same expectations of larger companies that they do of individuals. They do not expect to enjoy a degree of intimacy with a large company the way they may with an individual.

As an individual providing goods or services directly to the public, who you are is extremely important to your current and potential audiences. Any miscalculation or incorrect assumption (such as failing to realize certain words or images may be offensive to some people or have another meaning in a different language or culture) in the creation or maintenance of your brand image or message could be damaging.

Regardless of the size of your enterprise and whether you need a logo right now, anyone engaged in professional communication needs to understand the power and potential of logos and other brand images. The good news is that logos are easier and less expensive to make now than ever before. For most people's purposes, a basic brand image can be easily made without hiring a graphic designer. When it comes to designing a successful logo, there are no hard and fast rules. However, there are dozens of guidelines and tips—most of them available through reputable marketing sites online.

According to Creative Bloq, a blog run by London-based online publishers Future, there are some fairly specific rules to live by.[3] These include the following.

Simplicity

Above all, a successful logo is simple. It is streamlined, stylized, and easy to recognize at some distance. Simplicity is essential for a few reasons. Not only does it keep the image recognizable, but it makes the logo easy to reproduce on advertising and promotional materials that may require simple designs for reproduction.

A complex logo may not even be reproducible in some media. If your logo design does not translate well to other media, it may be time to simplify.

Endurance

You don't want to create a logo with elements that are so closely associated with the time that they will look dated and need redesign in a few years. You have probably noticed that logo designs, just like fashion, may become trendy. This may amount to an unfortunate success for the designer who was so successful, others later copied or incorporated elements of his design.

A good example of an iconic image that was a victim of its own success when it debuted in the late 1980s is AT&T's blue-and-white-striped sphere. It has been updated and modernized in the decades since its debut, acquiring a three-dimensional look, but to anyone who was aware of such things in the late 1980s, the original two-dimensional logo seems hopelessly dated—mostly because it was so widely copied at the time.

AT&T was not the first company to use a circle in its logo, but it was among the first to give a circle a three-dimensional effect by changing the thickness of lines within the circle. Another company to do this was Continental Airlines, which debuted a spherical white-on-blue logo in 1991. According to Wikia, the new logo took more than a year for the brand strategy and design company Lippincott and Marguiles (now Lippincott) to research and develop, in addition to a smaller, less detailed logo that would read better online and in small print.[4]

FIGURE 9.7 An updated version of AT&T's iconic logo.

Credit: Shutterstock ID#190380671

FIGURE 9.8 United Airlines incorporated some of Continental's logo design after the companies merged.

Credit: Shutterstock ID#87128146

So successful was the then-decade-old logo that when Continental merged with its rival United Airlines in 2011, the new company kept the United name and Continental's brand image.

In 2010, when the airlines' merger was announced, *Fast Company* writer Alissa Walker argued that the use of Continental's simple white-on-blue globe image squandered United Airlines' rich brand image. Interestingly, celebrated graphic designer Saul Bass designed United's colorful "U" logo as well as the iconic red circle logo that Continental's white globe replaced in 1991.[5] Bass also introduced the Bell System's simple and elegant bell logo (a progenitor of the current AT&T logo) from the 1970s. Bass' designs were so powerful that they remain widely recognized to this day, more than a decade after his death.

Originality

Among the challenges of great logo design is the competing demands of simplicity and originality. As one would imagine, it is more difficult to be original with fewer lines. In designing a logo, as with any other creative task, seeking inspiration from existing designs is essential. Yet it is just as important to take care that that inspiration does not, even inadvertently, end up as part of your "original" design.

If you are designing your own logo, make sure you invite at least a few other people who are at least somewhat familiar with brand images and logo design to review your sketches or prototypes. Ask them to honestly assess whether your creation reminds them of an existing logo or design. If it does, compare the two images side-by-side to determine the extent of the similarity. If it is more than a passing similarity, you need to go back to the drawing board. Keep in mind that it is never okay to start from an existing logo or image, and modify it. Simply adjusting someone else's image is unethical and illegal. You could be sued for copyright violation. Bottom line, if you have any doubts about how similar your design is to someone else's, retire your design and start again.

Ease of Recognition

To increase brand recognition, restrict your logo to limited colors, and make sure it works well in black-and-white. Even now, as you have seen in this book, images still sometimes appear in black and white.

Easy Online Logo Creators

There is no shortage of basic, easy-to-use, and often free Web-based logo creators today. They include the following, all of which offer a similar product. Simply type your text, choose a type style, add a basic graphic element (a flower, crossed

FIGURE 9.9 Online logo creators can help you create simple branding images.

Credit: Shutterstock ID#217636597

arrows, a big "X," etc.), then download your image. Check out the half-dozen listed below. There is some, albeit limited, variation among them.

- Online Logo Maker (www.onlinelogomaker.com)
- Logo Generator by Spaces (gospaces.com)
- Hipster Logo Generator (www.hipsterlogogenerator.com)
- GraphicSprings Logo Creator (www.graphicsprings.com/start-your-logo)
- Logoshi (www.logoshi.com)
- Logaster (www.logaster.com)

Graphic Design Basics

You don't need to be a graphic designer to create an attractive or compelling website, social media profile, or collateral materials (business cards, brochures, stickers, etc.). But it helps to know the basics when you set up your site or send out postcards for an upcoming show or event. The following are from Robin Landa's Graphic Design Solutions.[6]

Format

Basically, what is the medium for your design? A webpage, a postcard, a billboard, and an Instagram post, by their very scale and size, have different requirements. Proportion and aspect ratio are particularly important here because vertical orientation and horizontal orientation have much different requirements, as do the square formats favored by social media. Consider the size and shape of the final image.

Balance

Visual balance may be intuitive. In short, it is about ensuring that what appears on one side of an image is balanced by a similar number and size of images on the other side. An observant person will notice—and probably be bothered by the off-kilter appearance of—images that appear mostly on one side or in one section of an image.

Visual Hierarchy

This is exactly what it sounds like: arranging images in a way to show importance. Particularly useful with text, visual hierarchy draws the viewer's eye from one point to the next.

Emphasis

Emphasize, or draw attention to, a section or part of an image by isolating it, placing it in a conspicuous spot, changing its scale or contrasting it with other design elements.

FIGURE 9.10 The best design incorporates visual balance.

Credit: Shutterstock ID#234442405

Rhythm

In design, rhythm is about creating patterns. A consistent or coherent sequence of images, colors, or design elements can create a sense of continuity. Similarly, breaking the established rhythm can signal a change or departure from established patterns.

Unity

In graphic design, unity is about ensuring all the elements of a design work well together as a whole. A unified image may include photos, illustrations, text, and other elements.

Shoot Video

When it comes to engendering user trust and engagement, there is simply no better tool than video. For obvious reasons, video is the closest proxy to face-to-face communication that you can get in the online world. Video is powerful because it allows the creator to reveal herself, her expertise, and her products in more dimensions over some span of time.

While online videos should be short (ideally three minutes or less, and closer to one minute when possible), even brief videos provide much more than the highest quality photos. If you are selling yourself, your expertise, or your products, presenting yourself on video quickly provides your viewers, visitors, and whatever communities you are part of a much more complete version of who you are and what you are about. You can establish or reinforce trust through video by telling your story and expressing passion about what you do. Paired with an authentic, well-written "about" page, it can go a very long way toward reassuring visitors that you are a human being, and that you will deliver what you promise to on your site.

Your brand and the kinds of goods or services you provide will largely determine the kind of video—or videos—you want to feature on your site or on social media. Fortunately, you probably already own the basic tools necessary to capture useable Web video. Most people now have a choice of personal mobile devices that record video, including smartphones, tablets, computers, DSLR cameras, and video cameras, and the quality of their video recordings is remarkably high—particularly for the Web, where you should sacrifice some quality in favor of load time.

The average price points on this equipment have decreased dramatically in recent years, and it is now possible to get high quality for little money. A good rule of thumb is to buy the best camera you can given your budget, although if you are new to video, you may want to start with a simpler, lower-end camera (or even an iPhone) before upgrading to a professional or "prosumer" camera. Depending on your plans for video, you may not even need to upgrade to a dedicated video camera. With proper lighting, the iPhone can produce surprisingly attractive video, and there are many attachments, including lenses and microphones, that can help improve the captured image. If you decide to upgrade to a professional-quality video camera and budget is an issue, buy used from a reputable company such as B&H Photo in New York. They rank their

FIGURE 9.11 Use your smartphone to shoot video.

Credit: Shutterstock ID#103532255

equipment according to condition (much of it is almost undistinguishable from new), and even allow returns.

Thanks to current and constantly improving smartphone technology, most people in the developed world own the minimum necessary technology to produce a decent video or podcast. At a 2016 "Tech Day" event at the International Documentary Association (IDA) in Los Angeles, veteran cinematographer Kirsten Johnson told the crowd of mostly new and early-career filmmakers that for most of her career she shot with expensive, state-of-the-art equipment that could not produce images as high quality as those produced by today's smartphones.

If you have a smartphone, you can create acceptable video. The 2015 film *Tangerine*, an official selection at the Sundance film festival, was shot entirely on the iPhone 5s (albeit with the help of a few special lenses, apps, and stabilizers). You can even do some editing within social media platforms, or simply post raw video. Although your raw video may not look as polished as video that has been professionally edited, the proliferation of media across the Internet and social media has lowered our expectations, allowing us to enjoy raw or sloppily produced video for the authenticity it may represent.

Edit Video

Editing tools are no longer as daunting as they once were. You do not need to be a professional film editor to produce slick, professional-looking video. The questions you may want to ask yourself about producing professional-quality video include when it might be worth it, and whether you have the time, skills, and resources needed to do it well when it is.

While shooting video may be necessary, editing video may not. Increasingly, we are able to perform simple edits right in our devices or social media accounts. But for those who want a more polished presentation, a professional editing program may be necessary. There is no shortage of powerful tools now available for editing video, from high-end programs such as Adobe's Premiere Pro to Apple's somewhat less expensive (but just as good) Final Cut Pro, to dozens of free or nearly free options such as Apple's iMovie or Windows' Movie Maker. Some companies, like the cinema-grade video camera company Blackmagic Design, now offer their hardware with software (in this case DaVinci Resolve) built in. Regardless of the tool you choose, most video editing tools these days utilize the same basic functions, varying mostly in terms of how many additional features each offers.

Depending on the work you produce, its length and purpose, you may not need highly developed video editing skills, though it is a good idea to have a basic familiarity with how these tools work just in case. At the very least, you should know how to cut video into clips of a few seconds each, create effective transitions between clips that, taken together, create a logical narrative, and add music or voiceover. You should also know how to publish, post, or share your videos when they are finished.

Like with Web hosting options, you now have a number of choices for hosting your videos. YouTube is still the most popular, and includes some limited options for on-the-fly editing. Vimeo is preferred by professionals who want to share their videos in a space less cluttered and junky than YouTube. Choose either service. If it doesn't work for you or your audiences, try another.

For those who avoid extremes, there is a growing middle ground between raw, unedited video and slick, highly polished video. Aside from social media, where quick, less polished work is the norm, many now produce video that is a step above raw, with some editing to suggest professionalism or to keep audiences from growing bored with overly long videos, without veering into the realm of a corporate ad campaign. This middle ground between the two extremes of video production is actually also where most corporate video is heading these days as well. Audiences tend to be suspicious of overly produced content on the Web or on social media. In response, companies are adopting some techniques best known for independent work to lend their brands authenticity. Millennials and young people in general tend toward suspicion of big companies and brand names. The good news is that you do not have to worry about competing with million-dollar ad campaigns on Instagram. The bad news is the indie look some companies are bringing to their social media marketing can create some brand confusion and make it even more difficult for independent content creators to stand out.

Authenticity is a term that appears throughout this volume. Although the desire for authenticity may wane in coming years, it is at a high point at the time of this writing, perhaps in response to trends toward depersonalization in the early years of the ubiquitous Internet. Beyond being simpler, faster, and less expensive to produce, raw video is often coveted for its authenticity and ability to build trust by forging a human connection. In a media environment in which access to publishing tools is nearly ubiquitous and the old gatekeepers are gone, entrepreneurial journalists and creatives must find ways to not only build their brand identities in a crowded marketplace that is quickly expanding, but to show followers, and potential clients and customers that they are legitimate, real, and trustworthy.

Although its growth was not as deliberate, the use of raw video to establish legitimacy and authenticity is not a new thing. You may recall the explosion of television dramas, films, and even commercials shakily shot with hand-held cameras in the 1980s. This documentary style of shooting—a clear departure from the smooth Steadicam studio shots of old situation comedies and classic television commercials—shocked and thrilled audiences who were not accustomed to watching professional media that, aside from the higher picture resolution, resembled home movies. Shaky hand-held shots conveyed a degree of realism audiences had never before seen on mass media. So successful was the technique that few viewers would even recognize it as a technique today. Shaky video is so commonplace these days that several plug-ins for video editing software such as Final Cut Pro include a wide assortment of camera shake effects.

Way back in 2012, Huffington Post blogger Graham Milne complained that shaky camera effects in *The Hunger Games* made him literally queasy. Explaining the effect's emergence on the mainstream, Milne wrote, "From a critical standpoint, letting the camera bounce around invokes the realism of documentaries, placing the audience member in the middle of gritty, cheap life and death, not in the safe, million dollar air-conditioned artifice of a soundstage. 'Shakycam' in *Saving Private* Ryan helped to convey the rawness and bloodiness of the D-Day invasion the way the bolted-to-the-floor approach of the '60s John Wayne war epics didn't."[7] He also noted how the technique helped build suspense in the faux-reality horror film *Blair Witch Project*.

You may not be shooting a big-budget Hollywood film, but you may be using some of Hollywood's techniques to connect with and build trust among your audience. Realtor Steve Matsumoto, whose interview excerpt appears in Chapter 7, uses raw, unedited smartphone video to connect with his community of online followers. Matsumoto, whose brand focuses on family and home, said his viewers and followers "want to see the goofy handheld videos rather than the slick production stuff."[8] This is because the goofy handheld style aligns well with his personal brand. If he wanted to establish himself as a fast-talking urban Realtor serving the needs of single young professionals, he may have opted for a more polished look, which can be achieved only through editing.

Clearly, there is no one right way to create and use video to establish, maintain, and build your brand. How you use it should reinforce your brand's tone. Most important to remember is the fact that whatever choices you make in representing your brand (and there are countless choices to make), you must make those choices consistently. If your brand image or tone is inconsistent, the brand itself will broaden to the point of unrecognizability. The brand will essentially disappear.

Audio Basics

Although you will likely record audio along with your video, there may come a time when you need to capture audio independently. Unlike video, which should be no longer than a few minutes (and ideally less than two), stand-alone audio can run longer since listeners can be mobile. Just like traditional broadcast radio, recorded podcasts and streaming audio content can be played while driving, running, exercising, or working. Like with every other technology skill set discussed so far, there are countless tools now available for recording high-quality audio. Even so, it is essential to keep in mind that audiences will tolerate low-quality video more easily than they will tolerate low-quality, scratchy, or staticky audio.

FIGURE 9.12 Lots of apps now allow you to record quality audio and even calls on your smartphone.

Credit: Shutterstock ID#344550671

In general, you don't want to use video equipment to record audio. The built-in microphones on even pro-grade video cameras are improving but still should not be used to record primary audio. If you are recording in the field, a cinema-quality portable digital audio recorder can be purchased for less than $100. (Search for "Zoom digital recorder.") If you are recording at length—a podcast, for example—you may want to set up a professional-grade recording studio complete with fixed microphones in a small space lined with plenty of acoustic foam to absorb echo and improve the sound quality. (Read more about equipment in the "Podcast" section, which follows this one.) But a professional-quality setup is not necessary, as podcasts are now sometimes recorded from a Skype session or other voice over Internet (VoIP) service and edited using a simple program such as Apple's Garage Band or the free, open-source Audacity.

Even if you aren't able to invest in expensive microphones for your podcast, at the very least you want to record using USB headsets, which should produce acceptable sound. Always avoid using the built-in microphone and speakers on your computer because their quality is comparatively low, and recording without a headset can create echoes and feedback that may be impossible to fix in the edit. As with any time you record audio or video, make sure to find a quiet place without audible interruptions. And don't forget to silence your phone.

Podcast

Podcasting became popular in the first years of the new millennium, shortly after the iPod was first developed, popularizing portable media. At that time many declared podcasts a fad, and predicted the medium's ultimate decline into obsolescence. In those early days, before cars were routinely built to accommodate iPods and smartphones, podcasts were mostly informational and blog-like. They were conceived as audio blogs. As text-based blogs (originally conceived as "Web logs") began losing ground to microblogs (on Twitter, for example) and other shorter forms, attention spans also shrunk for audio content. At around the same time, as media prognosticators began to ring the death knell for podcasting, noting that no one was interested in hearing someone else talk for an extended period of time, the media transformed itself again.

In keeping with the convergence of all other media, podcasting, in its maturity, morphed into more of an alternative to broadcast radio. By the middle of the first decade of the new millennium, people were already familiar with satellite radio and other ways of receiving radio-like content. Once Apple made it easier to subscribe to podcasts, and automobile manufacturers began equipping vehicles with ports and outlets for iPods and other mobile devices, interest in a more broadcast-oriented kind of podcast grew. Podcasters began directing their recordings as if they were radio shows. Many shows began to feature more than

FIGURE 9.13 You don't need much equipment to record a podcast these days.

Credit: Shutterstock ID#102463826

one personality, and the medium became more conversational and engaging than the one-way content of the old days.

Entrepreneurial journalists and other professionals took advantage of the portability of the format—the ability to download recorded podcasts and listen to them on their own schedule—to create entertainment and educational programming as well as talk shows that resembled those on broadcast radio, except available on demand and without so many advertisements. And the overhead costs were minimal.

There are now many highly professional podcasts that are recorded in dedicated studios (or in people's garages) that utilize high-end production equipment, including studio microphones. But many podcasts are now recorded using available equipment, then edited with Audacity or Apple's Garage Band. The entry barriers to podcasting are now quite low.

Q&A: GERALD GLASSFORD, PODCASTER

FIGURE 9.14 Gerald Glassford.

Why podcast?

The first thing when it comes to podcasting is it shouldn't be intimidating. It is very easy to acclimate oneself to the podcasting world. Very easy and inexpensive. For virtually nothing, with the right clicks and the right downloads, you can make a show that's worth listening to, that's appealing to a large audience and that's also marketable, not only in the podcasting realm but from a broadcasting, video, and audio experience as well.

What kind of equipment do you need?

It depends on whether you want to make an audio or audio-visual experience. Connection to the Internet is key, and then the recording equipment that you need. A p.c. cam of some type, and also a microphone that is going to produce a quality stereo feed, that has low distortion, and that's something that when you play it back, it's easy to listen to. If you host your own show and your audio is not good, how do you expect to build an audience?

Audacity is a great place to start as far as basic editing. That is an absolutely free program that you can get online. I cannot compliment that program enough for what it's done for my podcasting career.

How did you start podcasting?

It started out with a friend of mine. We had an idea of starting up a video game news and information website called Game Source back in 2009. For a while we were writing articles on the video game information scene, and working through our social media accounts, but we felt like we wanted to do something more to ingratiate a larger audience and inform them of all the great things we had to offer. I like to listen to myself talk sometimes.

In 2010, we started our first Game Source podcast, and 149 podcasts later, we have arrived at what I can say is possibly a good 45 to 90 minutes of very good conversation about the video game world. In 2015, we decided that we would add content or things that people wanted to talk about such as movies, television, comic books.

I was speaking with a friend one time about starting a radio network locally in town. I wanted to include an entire world of pop culture. Rob McCallum, who's the director of Nintendo Quest and Missing Mom, which is his latest documentary, suggested Pop Culture Cosmos. From there we were shopping around to radio networks all over, high and low, here in Las Vegas. We could never come to an agreement on where we wanted to market the show. Whether it was due to us being charged too high a price or at a time when we didn't think we would get an audience. We decided to make Pop Culture Cosmos a podcast. I was able to, after many weeks of persistence, get a spot on the schedule for the Podcast Radio Network. It is the number one podcast station currently across the Internet. I'm very happy to be part of that schedule. As of right now, it's on Monday nights.

For three years we also did podcasting shorts where it was just one person. They were almost like an opinion page. We would shout out an opinion on the video game scene that would last anywhere from 5 to 15 minutes, and we produced about 100 of those. We broadcast the Game Source podcast on a biweekly basis, but one of our sponsors here, a local video game store, Retro City Games, has asked us to record Pop Culture Cosmos every Wednesday. It gets edited down to a one-hour format for the Monday airing. I add into the hour some pre-recorded material. I recently did an interview with the author of the official book regarding the history of the Coleco company. It was a very stimulating conversation on ColecoVision and the Cabbage Patch Kids.

I have an excerpt of that interview on the podcast and other interviews I tape across the week at other people's convenience. I throw that in there along with the footage that I get from Retro City Games. The added bonus is I do a visual stream of the initial feed off of social media. In this case, Facebook Live. I did it previously on YouTube. It gets sent to people's Facebook channel and to various social media before it even becomes an audio podcast.

I try to mix it up instead of just keeping it a studio format. I love doing shows from a live location. It seems like it's more interesting to consumers when I do. I do a weekly show from a gaming store, and we have other things planned. We are going to be trying to do it from movie theaters when *Dr. Strange* and *Rogue One* come out. We'll try to do a live podcast from there. At CES [the Consumer Electronics Show], I've done dozens of recordings and interviews over the years. Those are always added bonuses. People seem to like it when you're down in the trenches and not just from a generic studio location.

It's also the most rewarding when you can talk to someone at length in an environment that they're most comfortable in, because you don't always get the answers you're looking for when you're hooked up on a Google hangout or you're hooked up on a Skype conversation.

Has your podcasting been profitable?

In the past, Game Source used to get hundreds of downloads for a single airing. It was not heavily marketed—only through our social media. We had no paid advertising for it. So the potential is there if someone wanted to buy into their program and believe in their program, they can get a large marketplace if they want to. When I was making money podcasting, and I hope to do that again, I was selling advertising. If you hear the Pop Culture Cosmos show now, you will hear that we are running advertising on it.

I've made deals in the past with entities we do reviews on if they want to sponsor. That's basically how most people in streaming these days get their funds—either visually through Twitch views or YouTube through clicks and views, and then watching the advertising on that. Or if you're able to make arrangements with companies to run their commercials, that's a heavy source of advertising, especially on the larger entities such as PodcastOne. CBS has its own network as well.

There's a reason why so many famous individuals are now doing their own podcasts. That's because of the revenue they get from the parent company that is making deals with the advertisers on their podcasts.

If I can make near what I made in the retail and car rental industries, I will be a happy man.

Can you share any tips for potential podcasters?

I highly recommend to anyone who wants to do podcasting, if you're going to do it, you need to do it on a consistent basis so you have an audience that will follow. If you have iTunes, when that show hits, it will hit on a regular basis. The podcast networks that make a substantial amount of money, they all drop on a schedule and they always drop on that schedule, whether you're going to listen to it live or download it, or if it comes up on your iTunes automatically. Once your podcast is not on a regular basis, you're going to lose a lot of consumers.

It is also essential to find quality, reliable people to do this with. Do not go at it alone. If you have a collective that shares the same vision, it is so much more to your advantage. At Game Source, when I was getting in daily content and I was seeing thousands of Web hits, and I thought it was going to be something substantial, that was because I had a consistent 7 to 10 people who were sending me content on a regular or semi-regular basis who were committed and saw the future in the long run, but for the most part since you're dealing with a volunteer staff and you're dealing with something that is not going to make you money right off the bat, you have to have a passion for it that's not going to run out anytime soon.

It's mostly about getting it out there. Getting people interested. Constantly pushing. Constantly getting people's attention. iTunes is now just a sea teaming with podcasts of various interests. You're going to have to sit down and decide, How are you going to stand out?

What's next for you as a podcaster?

We're still in the process of trying to sell the show to other avenues. Once we get to a level where we feel comfortable, I'm going to go back on the road and pitch small stations around the country. If we are able to do that and get any kind of success with that, even though it's going in an old-school direction, going back to traditional radio, it's an avenue that may ultimately prove to be successful long term because it's not what everybody is doing.

Notes

1 "HTML Address Tag." 2016. *W3schools.com*. Accessed September 30, 2016. http://www. w3schools.com/tags/tag_address.asp.
2 "Network Solutions, ICANN Sued over Domain Front Running." 2011. *Techcrunch*. Accessed September 30, 2016. https://techcrunch.com/2008/02/25/network-solutions-icann-sued-over-domain-front-running/.
3 "65 Expert Logo Design Tips." *Creative Bloq*. Accessed July 5, 2016. http://www. creativebloq.com/graphic-design/pro-guide-logo-design-21221.
4 "Continental Airlines." 2016. *Logopedia*. Accessed July 5, 2016. http://logos.wikia.com/ wiki/Continental_Airlines.
5 "The New United-Continental Logo: Flying a Little Too Close Together." 2010. *Fast Company*. Accessed July 5, 2016. http://www.fastcompany.com/1638794/new-united-continental-logo-flying-little-too-close-together.
6 Landa, Robin. *Graphic Design Solutions* (Boston: Wadsworth, 2011).
7 Milne, Graham. "Why I'm Sick—Literally—of Shaky Cameras." 2012. *The Huffington Post*. Accessed September 27, 2016. http://www.huffingtonpost.com/graham-milne/ shaky-cameras_b_1380069.html.
8 Steve Matsumoto interview.

10

TIME FOR A TUNE-UP

In the previous chapters, you learned the basics of personal branding for entrepreneurial journalists and creative professionals. You considered your brand's unique positioning. You worked on defining your niche and audience.

After you had the basics down and created a framework for planning your brand, you learned how to build your brand and differentiate it from the millions of other brands out there, likely thousands of them similar to yours in some respect—or perhaps in many respects.

You then worked on describing and defining your brand through story and images. You considered brand platforms and messages. You learned options for creating, managing, and assessing communication campaigns to support your brand. You even explored using partnerships to leverage your brand potential while helping others leverage theirs.

Your brand is starting to come together. You've begun your business plan, and worked on strategy. You have a better idea of your personal and professional goals.

In an increasingly crowded online creative marketplace, you know it takes more than talent and hard work to get ahead. If you're reading this book, talent and hard work aren't among your problems. If you do have a problem, it's most likely that not enough people are seeing your work.

It's an unfortunate but unavoidable reality that you can be doing really great work and still escape wide notice. And if no one is noticing, it doesn't matter how creative, intelligent, or even unusual you or your product are. That is why branding is not just a nice-to-have but is now a need-to-have for anyone attempting to build a creative business online or onsite.

Happily, you now have the tools to create a brand that is sure to get attention from readers, listeners or viewers. Although you may have not yet had the

FIGURE 10.1 Doing great work isn't everything. You also need to let people know it exists.

Credit: Shutterstock ID#457160080

opportunity to create your brand—or to improve your existing brand—eventually you will have to concern yourself with managing the brand, which is the focus of this chapter.

If you don't yet have a well-developed brand, consider a hypothetical brand or an existing brand with which you're quite familiar. You may want to explore the topics and lessons of this chapter through the lens of one of the brands we considered as a mini case study in Chapter 3. Ultimately, once your own brand is established, you'll want to return to this chapter to review and develop strategies for assessing the success of your brand based on progress toward the goals you defined when you created your strategic plan.

Depending on how much time has passed since you wrote your strategic plan (or if you've even written your strategic plan), it's possible that your goals have changed. Before you even begin to assess your progress toward the goals you established, you'll want to review the goals themselves to determine whether they're still relevant and appropriate to your brand. It makes no sense to hold onto—much less evaluate the success of—obsolete goals. So throw them out. Replace them with new goals, if appropriate, but only if the new goals make sense. Avoid the temptation to keep the same number of goals you started out with. Holding onto irrelevant goals is a waste of time at best, and can damage your brand at worst.

Measuring your progress toward your goals is an extremely helpful exercise for any brand. At its highest level, it should help you determine which of your activities, habits, or practices are supporting the brand, as well as which may be damaging the brand. Use this invaluable information to determine which activities and practices you should continue, and which you should cease. The general principle here is simple: Build your brand by continuing to do what brings positive results while learning from what brings negative results.

Check Your Measures

Is your brand successful? Sure, you might have a general idea of its success, based on anything from sales and revenue to clicks on your website to the number of followers you've gathered through your various social media accounts. But this information is purely anecdotal if it's not tied to specific measures. No matter how much information you gather or how reliable the information may seem to be, one unassailable fact remains: It means nothing if it's not measureable. In other words, if you can't compare your progress toward a specific goal to a specific reference point, you're not doing assessment at all.

There's no special science to assessing brand success. Rather, assessment is a commonsense process that works precisely because it's so simple and straightforward. Once you have the roadmap to success and have established the milestones along the way, you're more than halfway there.

Measuring brand success is a simple matter of following the rules you established for yourself when you created the assessment plan as part of your strategic

FIGURE 10.2 There is no one way to measure your performance.

Credit: Shutterstock ID#227362342

plan. If you were specific and detailed in the creation of your outcomes, the truly hard work is over. Now all you have to do is gather evidence and compare it to your projected outcomes. If you were thoughtful and thorough in the development of your measures, your analysis should be simple and yield clear results.

There is no one set format for or way of designing measurement tools. You can build yours as a spreadsheet that directly and succinctly presents the basic information. Or you can build yours into an elaborate PowerPoint presentation. Any number of businesses will design them differently to suit their particular needs. No need to get fancy if the plan is just for yourself. Unless you have shareholders or potential investors to report to, it doesn't matter how your plan looks or is formatted. All that matters is that it asks the right questions and that it yields relevant information that informs the strategic plan. Below are the basic requirements of an assessment plan. You may be surprised by how simple they are.

Assessment Plan Components

- Timeline
- Goals
- Short term
- Long term
- Degrees of achievement (i.e., meets, exceeds, does not meet)
- Measurable outcomes

Before we apply these terms to a hypothetical scenario, we should define a couple terms. Although "outcome" and "goal" are often used interchangeably, their meanings are different. A **goal** describes an ideal future state. For example, your goal may be to achieve personal financial freedom. This is a broad concept or idea, and it is not directly measureable. An **outcome**, on the other hand, is a specifically measureable achievement that directly illustrates the degree of progress toward a goal. On the way toward achieving the above goal of financial freedom, you might, for example, determine this outcome: To have maintained $25,000 in a savings account for at least one year.

Let's consider a hypothetical measure developed as part of the strategic plan. This measure is for an entrepreneurial journalist who is developing her brand as an investigative reporter covering the growth of B corporations, or benefit corporations, in the United States. Unlike standard corporations that exist to serve shareholder interests, B corporations are for-profit businesses certified to benefit not just shareholders, but also society at large by embracing principles of social and environmental responsibility.

SAMPLE ASSESSMENT MEASURE FOR A HYPOTHETI-
CAL BUSINESS BLOG

Goal 1: To become the go-to site globally for news and information about B corporations.

Objective 1: Grow electronic newsletter subscription list to 100,000 within three years of launch.

TIMELINE/ OUTCOME	Does Not Meet Expectations	Meets Expectations	Exceeds Expectations	Actual
YEAR 1	Fewer than 25,000 newsletter subscriptions	25,000 newsletter subscriptions	More than 25,000 newsletter subscriptions	
YEAR 2	Fewer than 50,000 newsletter subscriptions	50,000 newsletter subscriptions	More than 50,000 newsletter subscriptions	
YEAR 3	Fewer than 100,000 newsletter subscriptions	100,000 newsletter subscriptions	More than 100,000 newsletter subscriptions	

Formative Assessment

One of the great things about working (with audiences, clients, or customers) online is that there is so much data available every step of the way. You don't need to—nor should you—wait three years to assess how you did in year one, or at any other stage of the process. As soon as you have enough data to analyze, you should at least start looking for trends. They can identify current problems that you'll want to fix now.

Pretend you're the business blogger who created the sample goal and outcome table above. You're most likely tracking subscriptions to your newsletter more frequently than once a year. You may even be checking the signup list in your online campaign manager account daily. Although you can't draw any reasonable or helpful conclusions from a snapshot of a single day, checking in every few weeks or once a month to see if you are on track to reach the objective isn't a bad idea.

Halfway through year one, at the six-month mark, you notice your subscription list is at only 5,000. It's not exactly a disaster, but if your year-end goal is 25,000, you are significantly behind.

Can you make up the remaining 20,000 new subscribers in the next six months? That depends on a number of things.

Keep in mind that you set your own goals, and if you're working alone, only you know how hard you're working to achieve them. This is why it's important to keep track of your time and how you use it. If you're already spending several hours a day developing your newsletter subscriber list, you may determine, for example, that you simply have no more hours each day to dedicate to the task. That means it may be time to reassess one or more of your outcomes or goals.

Reassess Brand Goals

Especially when you are just starting out, you may often find yourself guessing at your goals and outcomes. Lacking the data needed to develop realistic and relevant goals, you are forced to make a number of assumptions about what success may look like for you. Often, when we look back at our expectations at the beginning of an undertaking (a career, a job, a marriage, school), they scarcely resemble what actually happened. For this reason, especially in the early years of building your brand, you should seek out any available opportunity to collect data or feedback, and, if necessary, adjust your goals based on new insights and information.

At what point should you reconsider a goal? There is no strict science about this, but there are a few signs you can look out for. They include:

- You have a gut feeling. This is simply a growing sense that the initial goal you set for yourself may not be appropriate, or that you're working too hard to achieve it.
- You are not on track to achieve an outcome. Continuing the example above, you have grown the newsletter subscription list for your blog to 5,000 in six months. At this pace, you will fall far short of your objective (25,000 subscriptions) for year one.

FIGURE 10.3 Don't wait until you're in trouble to revisit your goals.

Credit: Shutterstock ID#279604145

- You have become less interested in the goal. This is not uncommon in the early stages of an enterprise. In the first weeks and months after launching a brand, you learn more about branding your business and yourself than you will learn about these processes once your brand is established. This is when you're most likely to learn that your initial goals may not have been as relevant or appropriate as you had once thought.

Regardless of why you may think a particular goal no longer works for you, there's no harm in reassessing or changing it to better fit your improved knowledge and understanding of the enterprise, its ability to connect with potential audiences, and how challenging it will be to convert online visitors into readers, subscribers, or clients. It may, for instance, take several months of tracking your website's statistics to develop a good sense of how many people are regularly visiting your site, where on your site they're landing, where they click once they are on your site, how long they stay on your site, and whether you have managed to convert them by, for example, convincing them to buy something or to subscribe to your newsletter. As with all statistical analysis, it becomes more meaningful as more data are gathered.

As you reassess your goals in the first weeks and months of launching your brand, you will likely find that your initial projections were off. You may find that they were too ambitious, or maybe that they were too conservative. The latter is always a pleasant surprise. Naturally, it is satisfying to exceed your goals. However, exceeding a goal in this initial stage of goal-setting often points to a need to revise expectations. After all, it's easy to exceed a goal that was set too low. Because your goals at this point are for your own use, to guide the growth of your brand, the more realistic they are, the more useful they will be. So while it may be tempting to set overly conservative goals for yourself, only to easily exceed them, this will not help you achieve meaningful goals.

Of course, it is also possible to legitimately exceed your goals—not by aiming too low with your initial goals, but by performing better than you had expected to. You will know if this has happened after you've hit one or two assessment milestones. Assuming you developed the sample worksheet in the previous pages to measure the growth of your brand as a business blogger, by the time you reach your first milestone (the one-year mark), you should have a pretty good idea about how realistic your initial objectives are. If, at the end of year one, you have grown a subscriber list of 23,000 or 27,000 people, you can safely conclude your goals are realistic. If, however, your subscription list failed to top 5,000, or skyrocketed to 50,000 in a single year, you should reconsider your goals.

Build on Success

Let's assume that you were able to attract 30,000 subscribers to your newsletter by the end of year one. Clearly, you are doing something right. In fact, you are probably doing a number of things right. If you plan to grow your brand by capitalizing on its current strengths, it's important to determine what you are already doing right.

So you have attracted 30,000 newsletter subscribers. How did you do that? The answer to that question is likely complex. Key is keeping good records of efforts to promote the newsletter, including when and how often you promoted it, through what channels you promoted it, and how. The relative success of each method, channel, and technique may not be clear without some additional data. Any time you sign up subscribers or collect data from those who visit your site, you have a new opportunity to conduct research on your audience. This requires a delicate balance.

Every time you initiate an interaction with a visitor to your site, you must consider the visitor's (the potential subscriber's) cost-benefit analysis. For example, the more onerous, time-consuming, or complicated you make the process of subscribing to your newsletter or blog, the greater the visitor must perceive his or her benefit in order to make the transaction worthwhile. If the visitor expects great potential benefit from signing up on your site, he or she will be willing to tolerate a few questions (such as, "How did you find out about the newsletter?"). Conversely, the less benefit the visitor expects to receive for signing up, the less tolerant he or she will be of additional questions or the additional time required to answer them.

We discuss attracting brand supporters and strategic partners throughout this book. Our exploration has included finding, attracting, and incentivizing potential visitors, customers, and clients.

Continuing with the example at hand, let's say you included in your newsletter subscription pop-up not just the subscriber's name and email address, but also an additional question: "Where did you learn about the newsletter?": (a) Facebook, (b) Twitter, (c) Instagram, (d) the blog, (e) other. Although this is just one quick additional question amounting to some 15 seconds of the subscriber's time, the information it can yield is priceless. If you see that a majority of your subscribers learned about the newsletter from Facebook, for instance, you would be wise to focus on Facebook messages as an ongoing vehicle of growth for your brand—with one fairly substantial caveat: Social media and their usage trends change almost daily.

This means that just because Facebook may be generating the greatest percentage of referrals to your site, this may not be the case for long, as social media platforms and usage trends are in a perpetual state of evolution—particularly among younger demographics. While older people may have embraced Facebook as a simple way to share information and images with family and friends, younger people's use for and demands of social media are in flux. As this group is particularly conscious of trends and eager to try new things, they are less likely to be loyal to a particular online platform or site. This goes for not just Facebook and Twitter, but also for your blog or site.

But if online trends can change by the day, how can you plan a successful online strategy? This is a legitimate question, and a common one among those just beginning to navigate the challenges of developing a successful online brand in a very crowded marketplace.

It's worth noting at this point that none of this is an exact science. Data are helpful guides, but they aren't a panacea. Much of the work of developing and building an online brand is as simple as keeping your eyes and ears open all the time. In other words, there are no unassailable truths about the online world because the online world is perpetually in flux. Using it to its greatest potential means never making assumptions, but simply paying close attention to what works and repeating those successful tactics until they no longer work so well. On the flip side, equally important in the online world is paying close attention to practices that may not be working well, and either transforming them or discontinuing them as soon as possible.

Learn From Mistakes

Many marketing and branding professionals are fond of saying that mistakes are more valuable than victories, assuming you can learn from them. Indeed, often the only lesson we take away from success is that we need to keep doing what we are doing. That is neither very deep nor very helpful. Odd as it may seem, failure presents a much greater opportunity for growth than success. So cherish your failures—but make sure to learn from them.

FIGURE 10.4 You'll make mistakes. Learn from them.

Credit: Shutterstock ID#357339065

Returning to the scenario above, let's say you have fallen far short of your expected outcome for year two. You came close to achieving your expected outcome of attracting 25,000 subscribers by the end of year one. You can rule out the possibility that the outcome you established was unrealistic. But by the end of year two, when your expected outcome was 50,000 subscribers, you managed to attract only an additional 10,000, leaving you with around 35,000 subscribers—far short of your initial objective.

How could you have fallen so short this year? The potential reasons are many. The first thing to consider is comparison to year one, which was much more successful than year two. What changed between year one and year two? What are you doing differently now?

Consider your successes during that same time. Maybe paid Facebook ads had the most impact on growing your subscriber list, based on what subscribers reported during the signup process in response to the question: "Where did you learn about the newsletter?"

Did fewer subscribers in year two report being directed from Facebook? If so, why? Did your paid Facebook promotions lapse? Did Facebook change its policies in a way that reduced the number of people it directed to your site? Or is Facebook use declining among your target demographic?

Build in Ongoing Assessment

Developing a brand is a complex process covered in previous chapters. Now comes the hard part: managing your brand. It is much easier to create a brand than to keep it going and growing over time. Sustainability is impossible to determine without assessment.

Assessment is key to any enterprise's long-term survival. In order to achieve all you set out to when you first developed a brand, you must set goals for the enterprise, and measure your progress toward those goals by defining clear, measurable objectives. You must compare your actual performance with the performance you anticipated when you defined your objectives. If your performance varies wildly from your expectations, you should consider whether your objectives and goals were realistic. It may take some time—and data—to determine this. It will be easier to determine how realistic your objectives and goals are once you are able to compare your performance during two or more time periods.

Once you determine that your initial objectives and goals were realistic, you have a baseline against which to measure your actual achievement. The point of this exercise is to capitalize on your successes so you can increase their impact and grow your brand, and to stop doing things that either do not help or that may actually damage the brand.

It is important to keep in mind that once a brand achieves success, the story isn't over. Brands that remain successful over time are not just maintained, but evolve over time to meet the needs of those they serve. A successful brand manager has a keen understanding of the marketplace and, most important, the particular segment of that marketplace it serves. As the world changes—and it does, particularly online—so must a brand. A brand cannot afford to stand still for a minute.

Measuring the impact and reach of your campaigns is central to evaluating your success and planning to achieve future goals. After all, how could you begin to understand where to steer your business initiatives if you do not know what aspects of your campaigns are working, which are not, and what kinds of adjustments may be needed to help you achieve your goals.

Measurement is a term you need to be intimately familiar with if you are not already. You set goals for your enterprise as part of your business plan. To determine the degree of your progress toward those goals, you need some kind of measure. This can be much simpler than it sounds. In fact, it is as simple as the fact you cannot know exactly how far you have traveled, how much carpet you need to install or how much oil you need to add to your engine without some kind of measure. The same rules apply to achieving your determined outcomes.

It's seldom easy to determine your outcomes, much less how to measure your progress toward achieving them. You will have laid the groundwork for measurement when you created the business plan for your enterprise. This challenge was difficult enough. Now you want to closely examine your goals and outcomes, identifying logical milestones on the way to achieving them.

Most of the measures we use these days are related to activity online, particularly on social media. There are at least a couple reasons for this. For starters, since they involve computers, they leave an electronic trail that is easy to measure. More important, though, most people in the key demographics you would like to reach are heavy Internet users. They spend countless hours online, many of those hours on mobile devices. A third possible reason why online measures are probably appropriate for determining the relative success of your venture is because it's likely that most of your business—particularly its promotion—now takes place online.

As you may already know, the gold standard for measuring all kinds of online activity and engagement is Google Analytics. This free service from Google provides a wealth of information on the performance of your websites.

Google Analytics is free to all users. However, unless you host your own website or have access to your site's back end controls, you won't be able to use it. This means that if you have a free WordPress-hosted account (from WordPress. com, not WordPress.org), or if you use another free hosted blogging platform, you don't have access to the technical information Google needs to provide you with specific analytic data. That doesn't mean there is no analytics data available to those with free, hosted accounts.

For instance, WordPress.com provides users with some rudimentary analytics information relevant to visits to your site, including clicks, search engine terms visitors used to reach your site, referring sites, and the posts and pages on your site that have received the most visits. WordPress.com also provides information on the most popular day of the week and time of day for visits to your site.

The following pages explore the basic information Google Analytics tracks for users.

Learn From Google Analytics

If you have administrative access to a website to which you would like to drive traffic, you would be wise to open a Google Analytics account. Google Analytics, which measures website traffic, clicks, and the behavior of those who land on websites, is free. While it is true that Google is in the information business, primarily Google is in the advertising business. Providing access to and analysis of the behavior of visitors who land on your sites is unquestionably a helpful free service. Google figures correctly that those who are interested in knowing more about how people interact with the websites they run or manage will likely also be interested in driving more traffic to those sites. These people may not need much encouragement to also invest in a Google AdWords account.

Google AdWords is an online and mobile advertising platform intended to increase traffic to websites based on keyword search ads and display ads that appear on websites and mobile devices. Although the business model and

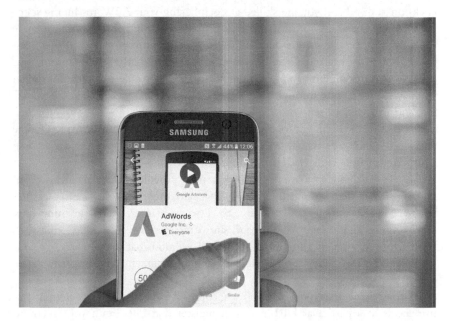

FIGURE 10.5 Google AdWords can help improve online performance through pay-per-click ads.

Credit: Shutterstock ID#426446308

management of keyword- and phrase-based advertising is more complex than most advertisers care to know, in general terms, advertisers (people like you who are trying to drive traffic to your sites) select groups of keywords or specific phrases likely to be relevant to potential clients or customers. Assume, for example, that you are the advertiser, and you want to build awareness of your brand online, and increase the number of people who visit your website. You choose a few words and phrases that your potential customers may use when searching online or on their mobile devices for the kind of goods and services you supply.

We discuss the strategic selection of keywords throughout this book, but for the sake of this example, we'll assume that you've selected a few great keywords and phrases. This means that every time someone types one or more of them into a search engine (like Google's own), you bid against others who have also selected those words and phrases for the privilege of Google showing the searching person your ad. Because Google is not able to show on each search the ads of every person who placed a bid on the search terms, the ad of the person with the highest bid (more on that later) shows up.

The advertiser (you) pays the bid price only when the person shown your ad clicks on it. Because the bidding process takes place in a fraction of a second throughout the day, unless you opt for manual bidding (which is almost impossible given the timing), there is no way to know exactly how much you bid each time your keywords or phrases appear. You will know afterwards, if someone clicks on your ad and you are skilled at deciphering your AdWords billing statement. There are strategies for making your bids more competitive, but ultimately the only way you can ensure that you do not spend more money than you want to is to set your maximum daily budget. This ensures that you stay within your daily, weekly, or monthly budget, even if you are not able to determine what you pay for each click through to your site. This is called pay-per-click advertising, and it is easy to see why.

We discuss the bidding process in more detail later. Let's now return to Google Analytics, which, as you will recall, is the research tool you may use on its own or in conjunction with Google AdWords.

Google Analytics is a robust tool that may provide more data or ways of looking at data than you need or want. That said, there are a few basic measures you will likely want to pay attention to if you are interested in learning how users engage and interact with your site, strategies for increasing your site's popularity, and strategies for increasing the likelihood that those who visit your site will take a particular action, such as signing up for an email list or e-newsletter, or making a purchase.

It's free to create a Google Analytics account. As long as you have administrative access to a particular URL, you can register that URL with your account. You can register any number of sites you own or manage with Google. After you register your site, it will appear on your Google Analytics home page. Here you will see a few basic measures, including sessions, average session duration,

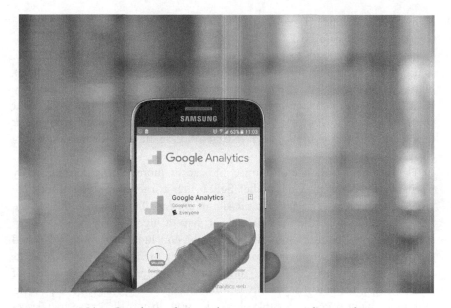

FIGURE 10.6 Using Google Analytics is key to assessing online performance.

Credit: Shutterstock ID#445690864

bounce rate, and goal conversion rate for a particular date range. A popup menu in the upper right will allow you to adjust the range.

Let's look at three key terms.

Sessions: How many times someone clicked anywhere on your site or on its related pages.

Avg. Session Duration: The average length of time one who clicks on any page on the site remains somewhere on the site before clicking out.

Bounce rate: The percentage of times anyone who visits your website clicks off without visiting any page beyond the page they landed on (a single page visit). Bounce rate is a measure of user engagement with or interest in your site's content. The higher the bounce rate, the less engaging your content and the more you may want to consider adjusting it to increase engagement or, as an ultimate goal, conversion. Average bounce rates differ according to site type, construction, and goals.

Generally speaking, an ideal bounce rate is between 26 percent and 40 percent. The average is closer to 55 percent. However, bounce rate may not mean much in certain situations. Specifically, if conversion—whatever the conversion goal is—does not require visitors to click through multiple pages, bounce rate is irrelevant. For instance, on one-page sites, blogs, or news sites where visitors may only need to visit one page to achieve engagement goals, it may not matter if visitors click beyond the landing page. However, in most cases high online engagement is a main goal.

If you have a website to promote your brand and encourage visitors to take some action (signing up for an e-newsletter or making a purchase, for example), high engagement is best. The question you may want to ask yourself is exactly what high engagement means to you. One question you may ask is whether you want visitors to your site to click through many pages, or would you prefer they spend more time on the landing page (placing an order or making a purchase, for example).

The relative importance of bounce rate can be more reliably determined by pairing this percentage with another figure such as the average length of time visitors spend on each page or on the site in general. This is where the average session duration could be revealing. If you have a high bounce rate and short average session duration, you can reasonably conclude that those who find themselves on your site either do so by accident or do not find its contents particularly compelling. Keep in mind that the assumption in measures of website engagement is that visitors will remain on sites for as long as possible, visiting as many pages as possible along the way. Eventually, every user leaves a site, so negative-sounding terms like "bounce" or "drop-offs" can be misleading.

Despite this, the behavior of your site visitors is potentially useful information that can lead to important conclusions. If, for instance, you are able to direct a large amount of traffic to your site, but this traffic leads to few conversions, you can conclude that your search engine optimization is good, but your content is somehow lacking. This may be due to a number of factors, although common reasons for poor user retention include low-quality images and photography, clunky site navigation, and poorly written or wordy content.

More common, particularly for newer sites, is the dual problem of few visitors and low retention. Lacking visitors to your site is mostly a matter of search engine optimization. This scenario provides no insights into the quality of site content because there is no way to determine how engaging users find content if the users are not making it to the site in the first place.

Click beyond the Google Analytics home page, and you will find more detailed information about your audience, those who visit your website. The "Audience" section provides information about people who visit your website, such as age and gender. Other categories of audience characteristics include language and geography. Additionally, Google Analytics will provide you with information about the kind of technology people use to access your site, down to the smartphone or tablet model, or desktop computer browser and operating system, and even the Internet service provider (ISP). Knowing the kind of technology people use to reach your site can help you make decisions about site design and layout, assuming you want to maximize the ease and utility of site navigation for the largest share of your audience.

This information may be more technical than what you need to run a basic website, but it is worth exploring, even if you do not at first know exactly what to do with it. Generally speaking, the more you learn about your audience and the visitors to your sites and social media accounts, the higher the quality and outcomes of your decisions will be going forward. The lesson is simple: Learn all you can when you can. Information that does not seem to have immediate utility may come in handy later. So review it and keep it in mind for possible future use. It may take a few weeks of examining your Google Analytics data for any useful trends to emerge. Remember that although the statistical information Google Analytics provides is neutral, objective, and reliable, it is hardly the last word in your audience research. In fact, it may be more useful as a starting point.

A Deeper Dive

One of the nicer aspects of Google Analytics is that you do not have to be a pro use it. You can use it for basic information or can dig in to locate ever deeper degrees of detail. Clicking beyond the "HOME" tab to the "REPORTING" tab in the top navigation, you will find a somewhat more detailed list of information, including, for your selected time span, not only the number of sessions, but also the number of users, the average number of page views per session, and average session duration.

You can also see the percentage of visitors to your site that are new or returning, the language they used in their search, and the country, state, or city from which they originated their search. You can even see the resolution of visitors' screens, which can help in determining how to size your images in a way to maximize visual quality while minimizing load time.

In the "Behavior" section (on the left-hand navigation), you can make comparisons that may help you make adjustments in how your site is designed or how one navigates within it. The information presented here includes comparisons between visitors' session duration and page views. The "Users Flow" section in the left-hand navigation allows you to track visitors' progress through the pages on your site, specifying users' flow from page to page, and at what page the visitor left the site.

It is important to remember that Google Analytics, like all analytics data and statistics, is not an exact science. While it is possible to draw fairly reliable conclusions based on some of the data Google Analytics provides, using this tool to drive traffic to your website and improve the user experience for those who land on it, many of the adjustments you make based on your data will and should be considered trial and error. This means you make a few adjustments based on your findings (for instance, what pages visitors land on most frequently, what—if any—other pages they click through to, how long they stay on each page, and whether their visit results in a "conversion," which is whatever your

FIGURE 10.7 Keep tweaking your SEO for better online performance.

Credit: Shutterstock ID#379383847

end goal is for visitors to your site, such as signing up for an e-newsletter or making a purchase). Make a few adjustments, then wait a couple weeks or a month to compare your findings before the change to current numbers.

One of the most common and easiest changes to make is to tags. Tags are the words and phrases attached to elements of your website, from posts, images, and videos, to the pages themselves. Adjusting tags or keywords, which are the terms people type into search engines that bring them to your site, is an ongoing process. Because keywords are easy to change and they are central to getting noticed online, these will probably be the most frequently tweaked elements of your site. Google Analytics will provide you with a detailed analysis of how your keywords and phrases perform (how frequently they bring people to your site or content). It is an excellent tool for learning search engine optimization (SEO) as it applies to your brand.

Considering all you may learn about keywords that perform well or perform poorly when it comes to bringing readers and viewers to your content, it can be tempting to make sweeping changes to everything all at once. This is never a good idea. As the Google reps themselves warn, if you make too many changes at the same time, it is difficult to determine exactly which change is responsible for which effect. If, for instance, you stumble upon a few great new keywords, resist the temptation to include these keywords in every place you can. Instead, apply these keywords thoughtfully in a few well-targeted places, and wait to see if they make a difference. If you later find that they made a positive difference (and only then), you may want to make the same adjustments elsewhere.

Search Engine Optimization and Choosing Keywords

Selecting keywords to draw people to your content is somewhat more nuanced than simply choosing the most popular search terms. A simple rule to keep in mind is that the more popular the keyword, the greater the competition for it. In other words, if you select a keyword employed by thousands of other people to bring traffic to their content, it will be more difficult for your brand to stand out from the crowd. The reasons are simple. First, if the keyword is popular, it is likely also quite broad. If you are trying to establish and differentiate your brand, employing broad keywords is not a good idea. Remember, you want to attract visitors to your site or your posts who are actually interested in your content.

When it comes to online search, it is better to have fewer well-targeted visitors to your site than large numbers of visitors who either are not that interested in your content or are unlikely to become your brand's customers or clients. This is particularly important if you use paid search such as Google's AdWords, and Google charges you every time someone clicks through to your site based on a keyword that may be overly broad. Assume that you are a freelance copy-editor. Among the keywords you selected to bring traffic to your site is "writing." When someone who used the keywords "best American writing" clicks through to your site, is not only a missed opportunity to reach someone who needs an editor, but it is not fun to know that Google charged you for that mistaken click. This is why it is important to choose highly specific keywords that describe your brand's niche, and why simply selecting popular search terms may actually waste time and money. Linking your Google AdWords account with your Google Analytics account will allow you to more easily understand trends and behaviors of those who visit your site.

Google AdWords

If your Google Analytics account is linked to your Google AdWords account, you can access AdWords in the left-hand navigation of your Analytics "Reporting" tab. Under the "Acquisition" heading, you will see the "AdWords" link. The first item in this section is "Campaigns." This is where you can learn more about the performance of any AdWords campaigns you have created. If you have one website or landing page to which you hope to drive visitors, it is likely that you have just one campaign. By default, it will appear as "Campaign #1." In this row, you will find the number of clicks your campaign produced, how much you have been billed for those clicks, your average cost per click, the number of sessions (visits to your site), the bounce rate (discussed earlier), the average number of pages visited per session, the goal conversion rate (the percentage of visitors who completed an action such as signing up for an e-newsletter or making a purchase), the actual number of conversions, and the goal value (the value you assigned to each conversion, multiplied by the number of conversions).

Click on the campaign (Campaign #1 by default), and you will find, again by default, "Ad Group #1." Assuming you have just one campaign to increase traffic to your website, this will be your only ad group. Each ad group you create associates a specific set of keywords with a specific set of ads. You may have as many or as few of each as you wish. It is easy to get lost in terminology at this point, but the concept is actually quite simple.

Remember, keywords are the terms people use when conducting an online search. You select terms to bid on based on which you think people who are interested in your content will be most likely to type into a search engine. When someone actually types that term into a search engine, you and everyone else who has placed a bid on that term compete for the opportunity to show a clickable ad (which looks just like a regular search result, except it is preceded by a box with the word "Ad" in it). When you set up your campaign, you also set maximum bids for selected search terms or keywords. In a fraction of a second after someone types that term into a search engine, Google compares the maximum bids of everyone who has selected that term, and shows the highest bidder's ad.

When you first establish your AdWords account, your keyword selection will be experimental. Regardless of the keywords you choose, check in a couple weeks after selecting them to see how they performed. This is among the most important learning experiences afforded by Google Analytics and AdWords.

Although you should have connected your Google Analytics and AdWords accounts, if you are looking for AdWords data, it will be easier to click out of the Analytics window and into AdWords. This will bring you directly to your pay-per-click or paid search data. Here, you will see the same "Campaign" window you saw in your Analytics account, and you will be able to make changes and adjustments to your campaigns. In the main AdWords window, the first choice you have to make is determining your daily budget. How much are you willing to pay each day for clicks through to your site from your Google ads? Although your daily budget can be $1, keep in mind that a competitive bid for your keyword is likely to be close to $1. Setting your daily budget this low means that you may get zero to one click per day, which may not be particularly helpful in driving traffic to your site.

After choosing your AdWords budget, you need to make a few more choices. If your budget is small or you are just starting out, you will probably want to select "Search Network only." This means your ads, when they appear, will show up as text listings like any other search results, but with the "Ad" box icon to the left. Other options include "Display Network" ads and video campaigns that run on Google's YouTube site. While keyword searches trigger search network ads, display network ads can appear on any of Google's ad platforms, including mobile networks and Google's YouTube site. If your product is video-oriented, you may want to create a video campaign that runs across Google's display networks and on YouTube.

Although there are a number of options you can choose among for your campaign, the most important is selecting keywords. In AdWords, you will find a "Keywords" tab in the top navigation. Click here to choose your keywords. There are five options for selecting keywords. They are: broad match, broad match modifier, phrase match, exact match, and negative match.

Broad match is exactly what it sounds like. Selecting this option will trigger your bid for not just your selected keywords but those that Google determines are similar. Google's example shows that with broad search, a term like "women's hats" may also trigger searches for "ladies' hats."

Broad match modifier includes variations of your keywords and changes in the order they appear. Synonyms do not appear. Like with Boolean searching, with broad match modifier, you include a plus sign in front of each term you want to include.

Phrase match will trigger your ads based on your selected phrase and similar phrases.

Exact match is also exactly what it sounds like. Your ads can appear if someone searches for the exact phrase you selected.

Negative keywords allow you to choose keywords while ensuring your ads are not triggered when certain terms are present. Simply type your keyword, followed by the negative keyword with a minus sign in front of it. For example: "clothing-children's."

Google defines "close variations" as "misspellings, singular forms, plural forms, acronyms, stemmings (such as floor or flooring), abbreviations, and accents."[1]

Google keeps the keyword selection process simple by allowing users to simply type the terms they would like to include in their keyword lists. Yet understanding basic Boolean search strategy can help ensure you get the results you are looking for when selecting keywords and phrases. Boolean searches include phrases inside quotes (to denote exact matches, preserving everything that appears inside the quotes as a single, fixed phrase). They also allow the use of plus and minus signs immediately in front of words to be, respectively, included or removed from the search.

For each keyword you choose, you can automate the bid process, allowing Google's processors to determine the best strategy for you, or you can change your bid strategy manually, possibly increasing your bid for the keyword to increase its likelihood of appearing on the first page of a relevant search. If your daily budget is low ($5 or less, or even $10), keep in mind that increasing the percentage you are willing to bid on a particular keyword may limit the number of clicks you receive overall. For instance, if your daily budget is $3, and you raise your bid for a particular keyword, bringing it closer to $2 for a single click, that day's budget may be exhausted as soon as someone clicks on that keyword.

On the plus side, your ad will appear in a more prominent place, and the person who clicked on it may be a particularly good match for your customer profile, which could increase the likelihood of conversion. However, it is also possible that the person who clicks on your high-profile ad either does so by mistake or soon realizes that they are not interested in your content after all. This can be an expensive mistake, not only for the money you have spent attracting the wrong person to your content, but also for the opportunity cost you pay in exhausting most or all of your daily budget and limiting your opportunity to reach people who may actually be interested in your content.

Bid strategy is one of several options you may want to leave in its default position at first, until you enter your keywords and collect at least a couple weeks of data to determine whether or to what degree they accomplished your goals for them, and what adjustments you may need to make to your campaign.

Mid-Campaign Corrections

Let's assume that your AdWords campaign has been active for a couple weeks. Now is a good time to see how your search terms performed, and to determine what kinds of changes you may want to make to your campaign to increase its likelihood to attract well-targeted potential clients and customers to your content while minimizing the number of bad leads and mistakes that end up costing you money and opportunities.

FIGURE 10.8 If your current path isn't getting you anywhere, try another one.

Credit: Shutterstock ID#192230474

In your Google AdWords account, the keywords and phrases you selected should be prominent. On your home page, you will see a summary of your keywords' performance. For the selected time period (which you can select from a scrolling menu in the top right corner of the home page), you will see the number of clicks for each keyword; how much each keyword cost you based on the number of clicks it received; "CTR," or the click-through rate, which is the ratio of users who clicked on your ad to the number of people who saw it; the number of impressions, or the number of people who saw your ad; the "Avg. CPC" or average cost per click; "Avg. CPM" or cost per thousand impressions; and "Avg. Pos Status," or in what position (first, second, third, etc.) your ad appeared.

Generally speaking, the closer an ad is to the top of the first page, the greater the likelihood that someone will click on it. If the position is eight or less, your ad probably showed up on the first page. This is where you want your ad to appear. There is a dramatic decline in views of search results that appear on or after page two. Although the specific numbers vary by study and report, by one account, only 10 percent of searchers make it past the first page of search results.[2] In addition to page position, you also want to pay attention to the CTR, or click-through rate. If a keyword is under 1 percent, it is not performing well.

Another highly important area for scrutiny appears as a subtab under the "Keywords" tab toward the top of your AdWords campaign home page. Look for the "Search terms" label. Clicking here will reveal the actual search terms that triggered your ad. Some of these terms may surprise or annoy you— particularly if they describe something that is quite different from what you had in mind when you carefully selected your AdWords search terms. In some cases, it may be difficult to determine both how the actual search term used became associated with your keywords, and then why the person who ultimately clicked on your ad did so considering they would not likely find what they were look- ing for on your site.

Although there is no exact science to explain why they appear, search term errors are often an additive problem. This means that terms or phrases have been added to your chosen keywords, sometimes making them absurdly specific. For example, your chosen keyword was "social media management," and an actual search term that brought someone to your site was "plus size model manage- ment." Although one or two words may match, the person who clicked on your content was clearly looking for something much different than what you provide. Although this mistake may cost you only $1 or so, those dollars can add up and eat up your daily AdWords budget.

For this reason, it is important to check your search terms on a regular basis. When you pull up the list, simply click on the empty box to the left of each invalid or misleading term, then click on the box at the top of the list labeled "Add as negative keyword." This will ensure that no one using this keyword in the future will be shown your ad. It will also help focus your campaign and make your AdWords budget go further. Remember it is an ongoing process, and despite the detailed data involved, it is far from an exact science.

One of the nicer aspects of being a Google AdWords customer is that you can call the company periodically for free education and advice. Soon after you join as a new member, you will receive emails suggesting you call for free analysis of your campaign strategy. Take advantage of this free service. Just as you want your clients and customers to be satisfied with the service you provide, Google wants you to find their services valuable. That means their goals align with yours. If they see that your campaign is wasting money by targeting the wrong people, they will tell you so.

On the phone, an AdWords rep will walk you through options and choices you may not have even realized existed. For example, on one call to Google a couple weeks into a new campaign, an AdWords rep suggested a customer capitalize the first letter of each word in her campaign to increase the ad's visibility and likelihood to be clicked. While there was no scientific reason explaining why people are more likely to click on ads with capitalized words, the research had proved it. It is unlikely the advertiser would have realized this on her own.

This brings us to the one aspect of your AdWords campaign that is at least as important as your keywords, if not more so: your ads themselves. Too often, in our quest for the perfect keywords, the ads that appear when people use them are an afterthought. In each campaign, you will find the "Ads" tab on the top navigation, to the left of the "Keywords" tab at the time of this writing. (User interfaces change quickly. If important tabs and links move, they usually do not go far. Finding relocated Web features is often a matter of considering its most logical location. This kind of thinking is what drives those who specialize in improving the user experience.)

Under this tab, you will find a prominent button with the word "AD" in all caps next to a plus sign. Click this button to start building your ad. Write as many ads as you like, but two to five is a good number. Click on the "text ad" option, and an ad template will appear, guiding you through the process of writing your ad with the help of previews and sample ads. With limited character counts in each of three lines, your creative process will be reduced to an exercise in compression. Your competing challenges will be to use popular keywords in a focused way to ensure only likely clients and customers see your ad, while staying within restrictive character limits.

Under these circumstances, writing a nuanced ad is almost impossible. The best you can do is to focus on including your most important keywords, and build short lines of text around them. Again, like with selecting keywords and tweaking SEO, this is not an exact science. When you return to your AdWords dashboard in a couple weeks, take another look at your ads with your highest-performing keywords in mind. If your ads do not match your keywords, it may be time to revise your ads.

IMPRESSIONS VS. CONVERSIONS

Two of the key terms used to describe activity on a website are **impressions** and **conversions**. At its most basic, an impression is a single exposure of the brand message (or ad) to a target viewer.

For example, you have a Google AdWords account for which you have agreed to pay a certain amount of money (usually a few cents, with actual rates varying as part of an instantaneous bidding process in which you compete against others hoping to make an impression on someone who has entered a particular keyword—it is best to let Google's computers manage the bidding process).

The analytics reports you get from Google show the number of impressions, or the number of times your ad was displayed (or the number of people who were exposed to your ad). "Conversions" is a general term, and can be described differently on various analytics reports depending on the conversion goal. A conversion is some kind of action on the part of the visitor, user, or customer. That action may be clicking on an ad, clicking to a page, making a purchase, or subscribing to a newsletter.

The number of conversions, regardless of the action described (clicks, sales, signups, etc.), is naturally smaller than the number of impressions. In fact, it is usually much smaller. Consider the fact that an average conversion rate is 1 percent, and that 5 percent is a strong conversion rate. This means that for every 100 impressions you make, you can expect around one person to act. And that does not necessarily mean they will become a reader, subscriber, or customer. Let's say your keywords-based Google ad makes 1,000 impressions in one day. Maybe 10 people will actually click on that ad. (Remember, these are clicks you pay for.) And maybe one of those people will actually subscribe to your newsletter or buy your product. Those are pretty long odds.

Unless your product (your brand) is well defined and narrowly targeted, you could wind up paying a lot of money for pay-per-click ads and getting little or nothing in return. Yet even if your pay-per-click ads generate little or no revenue, what you learn from Google's AdWords analytics reports is invaluable for anyone launching or managing a brand. Combined with Google Analytics, which is a free service to anyone who hosts their own website, the data you can collect on your brand performance and the needs and habits of your audience can offer among the most useful information available for assessing brand success.

We discussed search engine optimization (SEO) in more detail elsewhere in this chapter. While improving your SEO skills can help bring more people to your website or blog, analyzing impressions and conversions can help determine what you may be doing wrong (or right) to attract, maintain, and grow a loyal audience or client pool.

Analyzing impressions vs. conversions will help you understand whether any difficulty you may be having in growing your brand is due to a failure to attract the attention of potential viewers, or your failure to maintain their attention after they land on your site. While the former may prompt you to reconsider the way you get the word out about your brand, the latter points to a much larger problem: The content on your website or blog is not engaging. Both are extremely valuable wake-up calls for a struggling brand.

ANALYTICS AND ADWORDS GLOSSARY

Bid Usually automated by Google AdWords, your bid is the amount of money you offer to pay when competing against other bidders to have your ad appear for those who have typed one of your keywords into a Google search.

Bounce rate is the percentage of visits to your site, page, or other content that do not continue past the landing page. Bounce rates should be low, unless there is no expectation that visitors will click past the first page they land on.

Budget Usually expressed as a daily limit, your budget is the maximum amount you are willing to pay for clicks on your keyword-generated ads.

Campaign is a group of advertisements for the same thing. You may have only one campaign to drive traffic to your website or build your contact list.

CTR, or click-through rate, is the percentage of those exposed to your ad who click on it.

CPC, or cost per click, is what you end up paying when someone who sees your ad clicks on it.

CPM, or cost per impression, is the price you pay for 1,000 impressions. This number depends on how many people who see your ad click on it, and how much you end up paying for each click.

Conversions are the ultimate goal of your campaign, or what you are driving a visitor to your website to do. If you sell goods, a sale is a conversion. If you are building a client list, each new person or e-mail you add to your list is a conversion.

Engagement is a less precise term that refers to the relative amount of interaction one has with a website or with other online content.

Google Analytics is Google's free research tool, allowing those who manage websites to learn about who visits their site, from where, and at what time, as well as the pages they visit and how much time they spend on them.

Google AdWords is Google's online advertising platform. Advertisers bid on online ad placements to drive traffic to their content. Link it to Google Analytics to learn more about how your ads perform and what changes you may need to make to them.

Impressions is the number of times people are exposed to your ad based on their relevant Web searches.

Keywords are the words or phrases you select to trigger your ads. There is more competition for popular keywords. The higher the demand of the keywords you choose, the higher the minimum bid may need to be to be competitive against other bidders for the same term.

Organic search refers to unpaid search results, or the results of a search that excludes paid advertisements.

Paid search refers to search results that are advertisements.

Position refers to the placement of an ad triggered by an online search. The first ad on the first page of search results occupies position 1. The second ad occupies position 2. In general, you want your ad position to be 8 or less to appear on the first page of search results. The percentage of those who click past the first page of search results is quite small.

SEO, or search engine optimization, is the process of selecting keywords to maximize their likelihood to attract users to your site or content. SEO uses many of the measures listed above to determine the quality of keywords and phrases in online search campaigns.

Build Your Own Assessment Measure

Consider your personal brand or a brand identity you would like to create. Establish one primary goal for your brand and one objective to measure your progress toward achieving that goal. Your answers to the following questions could serve as one part of a complete assessment plan for your brand. Feel free to replace the timelines (i.e., "Year 1," "Year 2," "Year 3") or outcome designations (i.e., "Does not meet expectations," "meets expectations," "exceeds expectations") with your own. (For a completed example of this form, see p. 178.)

Name and describe the brand in 150 words or fewer:
Goal 1:
Objective 1:

TIMELINE/ OUTCOME	Does Not Meet Expectations	Meets Expectations	Exceeds Expectations	Actual
Year 1				
Year 2				
Year 3				

Target Your Tags and Keywords

Regardless of whether you subscribe to Google AdWords, you should periodically assess the tags and keywords you use to attract people to your website or blog. If you are paying per click on these search terms, you could be wasting your money. At the very least, choosing more targeted terms should improve your search results and increase the likelihood that those who land on your site actually want to be there.

For this exercise, you will compile the 10 most frequently used tags or keywords on your website or blog. The objective is to assess the strength and relevance of your keywords, and to identify similar keywords that may better target your audience and turn more impressions into conversions.

Enter each term individually into Google Trends (www.google.com/trends), a site that provides analysis of Google searches. Complete the following table. You may want to add additional terms to analyze over time.

KEYWORD/TAG	Interest over time (upward or downward trend)	Regional interest (top three countries)	Alternative terms (top or rising terms)
1.			
2.			
3.			
4.			
5.			
6.			
7.			
8.			
9.			
10.			

1. What can you conclude from this analysis?
2. How might you improve your keywords and tags for search engine optimization (SEO)?

Notes

1 "About Keyword Matching Options: Adwords Help." 2016. *Support.Google.com.* Accessed September 19, 2016. https://support.google.com/adwords/answer/2497836?hl=en&authuser=0.
2 "The First Page of Google, by the Numbers." 2016. *Protofuse.com.* Accessed September 19, 2016. http://www.protofuse.com/blog/first-page-of-google-by-the-numbers/.

11

MANAGE YOUR TIME

Among the biggest challenges of entrepreneurship and working for yourself is time management. When your days aren't rigidly defined by the hours you are required to be at your desk, it's up to you and you alone to manage your work hours. For most motivated entrepreneurs, the risk is not working too few hours, but rather, allowing the creative work you love take over your life to an unhealthy degree. The very fact that you love your work makes you susceptible to the kind of schedule that can lead to burnout.

You know you can't make time. But you can manage it. Even though you may not go into an office every day and your days aren't measured by lunch hours and rush-hour commutes, you should still keep a schedule or calendar. There are countless productivity apps now available to help you manage your time and schedule. Just search for "productivity" in the app store.

That said, while a fun calendar app may tempt you to overschedule yourself or account for every minute, try to be realistic. Understand the usual flow of your day, including the activities that consume most of your time, and how your time may be better spent on a typical day.

For the entire week before you plan your basic schedule, track your daily activities in a log, online or on paper, and leave time to review it at the end of the week. The way you actually spend your time may differ significantly from how you think you spend your time, and knowing this will help you limit the time you feel you waste, while helping you create a realistic schedule.

Just as it is for most people who work in offices, those working alone or independently routinely find themselves engaged in tasks or conversations they had not planned for when they considered that day's to-do list. Working at home or in your private studio doesn't prevent interruptions from phone calls, e-mails, or even in-person visits. Working at home may also make you more

FIGURE 11.1 Despite what some people say, you can only manage time—not make it.
Credit: Shutterstock ID#296562803

available to handle family emergencies or other family-related concerns than you would be working in a remote office.

It's worth mentioning that time management for entrepreneurs isn't just a matter of planning and keeping track of your own time. It's also about educating those around you about how, even though you may be at home, you're still at work. You may need quiet, and you may need to work without interruption for hours at a time. For some family members—particularly children—this can be a tough rule to enforce. "I could be in an underground cave," said Realtor Steve Matsumoto in an interview excerpted elsewhere in this volume, "and my kids would find me."

Accept the fact that despite your best intentions to carve out uninterrupted blocks of time dedicated exclusively to work, you will be interrupted. The phone will ring. You will get an e-mail that requires immediate attention. There will be a knock on the door. Interruptions are inevitable, and you should plan for them by building time for them in your schedule.

If you anticipate a particular project will require an hour of your time, schedule yourself for 90 minutes. That will allow you to take a needed break (taking a short break after every hour of work, even if that simply means standing up and stretching, will boost your energy levels and increase your effectiveness afterwards), and it will keep you from getting behind if you're interrupted.

When you sit down to create your plan for the week or the day, avoid the temptation to overschedule. If you schedule your workday too tightly, you're

FIGURE 11.2 It may be hard to hide in a home office.

Credit: Shutterstock ID#73796224

likely to start running behind fairly early in the day, leaving you way behind by the end of the day. This can be discouraging, and it can make it more difficult to stick to a schedule in the future. Set reasonable goals for yourself, and you're likely to achieve them. Achieving your goals will motivate you to shoot even higher in the future.

Entrepreneur magazine has reported extensively on time management through the years. There's good reason for this. Time management remains one of the greatest challenges to independent workers, and it becomes ever more challenging as new media and technology compete for our already limited time.

Among *Entrepreneur's* time management tips are the following:

- Take the first 30 minutes of every day to plan your day.
- Spend at least half your time engaged in the most important activities for your brand and mission.
- Be selective about accepting phone calls and returning messages. Some days it may seem that you spend all your time returning emails. And the emails you return often result in new responses. Establish one or two well-defined time slots each day to respond to messages. You may be amazed at how much time this opens up in your schedule.
- Hang a "do not disturb" sign on your office door when you need to focus on a project.

By the way, *Entrepreneur* concludes that "odds are good that 20 percent of your thoughts, conversations, and activities produce 80 percent of your results."[1]

Manage Your Money

If you've ever worked for yourself or owned a business, you know first-hand the challenges of managing your finances. You not only have to pay your own taxes, as well as taxes and operating fees for your business, but you also need to keep enough money coming in to cover your personal expenses. And what about retirement? Without an employer to subsidize health insurance or a retirement plan, this is your burden too.

If you don't hire a personal financial adviser (possibly another creative entrepreneur) or have the time and interest to learn basic finance yourself, you may never be able to retire. Worse still, you may not be able to recover from an unexpected setback, such as an accident, a health crisis, or a natural disaster. Because your future is less certain than the future of peers who work for others, your financial plan is more critical.

If you don't have an individual retirement plan (IRA), open one at your bank. Like a 401(k) or 403(b), an IRA allows you to set aside money, tax deferred, until you are old enough to retire (when, it is assumed, you'll be in a lower tax

FIGURE 11.3 Entrepreneurs need to do more than most to ensure a stable financial future.

Credit: Shutterstock ID#70550545

bracket, and you'll owe less in taxes). You're eligible to fund an IRA as long as your income is under a certain threshold. (If you're above that threshold, you probably don't need an IRA.) If you're under 50, each year you can put aside $5,500 or your total taxable compensation (whichever is smaller). You can add $1,000 to that number after you reach 50.

Even if you're still years from retirement, do more than simply fund an IRA. Talk to a financial advisor about your needs. Find a certified financial planner in your area at plannersearch.org, which is managed by the Financial Planning Association, the professional organization for certified financial planners.

As an entrepreneur, your needs will be different from others'. While people employed in more stable sectors (and there are fewer every year) such as the government may be able to plan for their future with some precision, entrepreneurs can expect to have good years and bad. In good years, it's essential to put away more money to cover shortfalls in bad years. A financial planner will discuss your financial goals, including current financial needs as well as retirement goals, and create a plan to help you achieve them.

Achieve Work-Life Balance and Avoid Burnout

After years of recommending proper work-life balance for every worker, from office staff to independent contractors, literature now suggests the work-life balance ideal we have long strived for is actually a myth.

The challenges you face in achieving work-life balance may differ somewhat from the traditional framing of the problem in the context of an office environment in which usually male workers negotiate with spouses and children to divide limited time among work and family responsibilities. As an independent contractor, your concerns may be more personal. You may, for instance, focus on finding ways to maximize your productivity without jeopardizing your physical or mental health, or curtailing your creativity and other factors that are key to your continued productivity.

According to *Forbes*, entrepreneurs are particularly susceptible to burnout. After all, no boss can push you as hard as you can push yourself. Entrepreneur Chris Myers shared a few tips for avoiding burnout as an entrepreneur in a 2016 *Forbes* column. The tips he shared included the following:[2]

- Change the scenery. Break your usual routines by moving to a new spot every so often. Get up from your desk and walk around the block. Stretch your legs. Grab a coffee. You will be more energized when you return.
- Be in the moment. Practice mindfulness. Maybe even try meditating, whether you formalize your mindfulness as transcendental meditation advocate and director David Lynch does or simply take time to breathe deeply, slow down and deliberately focus on what you are doing right now. Avoid the temptation to rush through your work.

According to a 2015 *Harvard Business Review* article, mindfulness "changes the brain . . . in ways that anyone working in today's complex business environment, and certainly every leader, should know about."[3]

Practicing mindfulness can help you stay focused and keep you from feeling overwhelmed. When you are working for yourself, keeping things in perspective can be difficult. With few or no other people in the immediate area to bounce ideas off of or to provide a reality check on your thoughts and fears, maintaining priorities can present a particular challenge.

Although these challenges are not the exclusive domain of entrepreneurs, like everyone else, entrepreneurs enjoy a higher quality life *and* produce better work when they are healthy, in good physical shape, and well rested. Although it may seem painfully obvious, keep in mind that overwork or abusing your body can have a negative impact on your work and reputation in both the short and long term. While the occasional late-night project or 80-hour workweek may be necessary, maintaining that kind of schedule can be destructive over time.

Get enough sleep (seven hours a night is good) and eat well (avoid highly processed foods and foods high in sugar, fats, and carbohydrates, as they may create a short-term spike in energy levels, then lead to lower energy levels and, ultimately, a crash). Also build time in your daily schedule for exercise. It doesn't need to be intense exercise, but try to at least a walk around the block. Remember that sitting at a desk for hours each day can not only lead to mental and

FIGURE 11.4 Entrepreneurs are particularly susceptible to burnout.

Credit: Shutterstock ID#383327554

emotional burnout, but it can lead to health issues. Use a Fitbit to remind yourself to get up every so often and get moving.

Make the Most of Your Time

Many creatives and professionals complain that they don't have time to read a book or read the paper, or to otherwise stay informed of world events. If this describes you, find ways to intelligently multitask. For instance, listen to National Public Radio (NPR) or BBC radio as you are getting dressed in the morning or commuting to work. Commute time is great for listening to audiobooks or The Great Courses.

Every day new apps are developed that can help you stay organized and do more in less time. Take advantage of them. Apps on your smartphone or tablet can make formerly dead time like that spent in line at the post office or the grocery store more productive. Use that time to catch up on news headlines, respond to e-mails, or check in on an online class.

Limiting the time you spend interfacing with technology or completing necessary but mindless administrative tasks will help free up time for more important or interesting pursuits. Keep in mind that often experiences with no clear connection to your work or meaning outside of themselves can bring new ideas or help you think through problems. If your mind is open and curious,

FIGURE 11.5 Make the most of your commute.

Credit: Shutterstock ID#279703610

you will find ideas and solutions everywhere, regardless of whether you are actively seeking them out. No good or new ideas come from burned out or closed minds.

Stay Engaged and Inspired

If you work in isolation or relative isolation, it can be tempting to fall into routines. These can prevent you from growing as a creative professional. The good news is the relative flexibility of an entrepreneurial lifestyle allows you to take an active role in managing your life. Not limited by a work schedule set by your employer, you make your own rules and can plan around your needs.

Absolutely have to do morning yoga or take a lunchtime run? Need to be home to keep an eye on the kids or care for an aging relative? As an entrepreneur, you can build your life and work around these needs and obligations. That doesn't necessarily mean you won't eventually fall into routines. We all do.

Routine is comfortable, and change is difficult. But as an entrepreneur, you are uniquely qualified to reassess and adapt. Those quick-change skills also apply to your personal life. Put them to work.

As an entrepreneur, you are used to putting your career needs first. This builds your skills and confidence, but taken too far, it can bring burnout. As a human being, you have physical needs (food, clothing, shelter among them). Meeting these needs keeps you going. And as a creative, you have mental needs. Just as

FIGURE 11.6 Build exercise into your schedule.

Credit: Shutterstock ID#136301591

FIGURE 11.7 Make time to visit a museum every so often.

Credit: Shutterstock ID#191409509

you go to the gym or run the trails to work out your body, you need to stimulate your brain. Without an active brain, the quality of your work will decline.

Engagement is key to creativity. This includes engaging internally, seeking out new stimuli, listening to music, reading books, watching movies, visiting museums, and finding ways to experience new things every day. It also means engaging externally, paying attention to the news and world events.

Not only will staying engaged make you a better informed citizen of the world, but it will bolster your brand's reputation for competence and intelligence. More important, it will make you a happier person. Let's not forget that despite having spent most of this book discussing how best to meet others' needs, none of this means anything if you're miserable.

Notes

1 Mathews, Joe, Don Debolt and Deb Percival. 2011. "How to Manage Time with 10 Tips that Work." *Entrepreneur*. Accessed September 28, 2016. https://www.entrepreneur.com/article/219553.

2 "Forbes Welcome." 2016. *Forbes.com*. Accessed September 28, 2016. http://www.forbes.com/sites/chrismyers/2016/03/17/3-ways-to-avoid-entrepreneurial-burnout/2/#40bb2abe18ea.

3 "Mindfulness Can Literally Change Your Brain." 2015. *Harvard Business Review*. Accessed September 28, 2016. https://hbr.org/2015/01/mindfulness-can-literally-change-your-brain.

RESOURCES

Legal Issues and Rights

A working knowledge of libel law is essential for anyone who plans to publish anything, anywhere, on any platform. This applies to websites, blogs, and potentially even social media sites. Whether you realize it or not, anything you publish or republish, regardless of whether you consider yourself a journalist, is subject to libel law. As any First Amendment attorney will tell you, anyone can sue at any time for any reason. Actually breaking the law—knowingly or not—is not necessarily a prerequisite to getting sued.

You could get sued for what you write or images you post, or for republishing other people's libelous material. Although it is less likely for you to face legal action for republishing a libel, keep in mind that it is technically illegal, and it could result in a lawsuit. Like with all prosecutions, ignorance of the law is not a defense.

Sear this into your brain: "Anyone can sue for any reason at any time." Despite this, you should make every effort to minimize your exposure to legal action. Knowing the law and adhering to it may not keep you out of court, but it can help ensure you win your case.

Libel Law in a Nutshell

In the United States, libel law ensures protections to journalists and publishers under the First Amendment. In the U.S., the burden of proof for a libel case is on the plaintiff (the party filing suit). It is the plaintiff's case to prove. The English system, on the other hand, puts the burden on the defendant. The journalist (or writer, blogger, or social media poster) must prove that he or she did not violate the law.

The basic components of a defamation (libel) claim are that:

- Information was published or disseminated.
- The information was false.
- The information was about the plaintiff.
- The information was harmful.

If the plaintiff is a public figure, he or she (or, more likely, their lawyer) must also prove actual malice. This means false information was published with reckless disregard for the truth. Actual malice is a higher bar than negligence or an error in fact-checking. That said, courts don't look favorably on negligence either.

Statute of Limitations

In the early days of social media, we heard many cautionary tales about old posts coming back to haunt people long after their subjects thought they were deleted. Although people are smarter now about what they post, it remains true that anything posted to the Internet (by you or by others) can never be erased completely. With the help of online archives and sites like The Internet Archive's Wayback Machine (https://archive.org/web/), content never really goes away. While there are statutes of limitation requiring plaintiffs to file their lawsuits within a specific period of time after publication, some states consider online publication "continuous." This means you could be sued at any time for content posted even years ago.[1] Similarly, jurisdiction remains a cloudy issue for online publication because the Internet is everywhere. This means that regardless of your own geography, you can, in theory, face a lawsuit from anywhere the post in question could have been accessed.

Pre-Publication Review

If you work full-time in a newsroom or for a company you do not own, you are most likely covered by your employer's insurance. This is a great luxury, considering First Amendment attorney fees are usually hundreds of dollars an hour. If someone else is willing to offer you legal protection, take advantage of it. If you plan to break news or publish an investigative report, accept your employer's offer of a pre-publication legal review. Keep in mind that if you wind up in court defending yourself against a libel suit, and it becomes known that you refused any offer or suggestion of pre-publication review, the court may see that as negligence. Negligence is tough to defend.

Opinion as a Defense

One element of libel law that is not so tough to defend is opinion. In the United States, statements of opinion are protected by the First Amendment. That does not, however, prevent journalists or other publishers of opinionated content from getting sued. The operative question for courts is whether the content in question is, in fact, opinion. Under libel law, if something can be proven either true or false, it is not an opinion. As First Amendment attorneys like to say, when it comes to libel, "Truth is the best defense."

For example, you can write that your boss is a disgrace to the company. That is, after all, an opinion. It is protected by the First Amendment. If you write that your boss takes bribes (a fact), and you prove it, that's good reporting. But if you write that your boss takes bribes and you can't prove it, you will likely get sued, and you will lose.

Copyright Violation

Copyright claims are among the most common online and across social media. Most veteran bloggers and publishers are now aware of the risks and what to look for. However, it is worth mentioning that independent publishers still face risk of lawsuit from posting images and audio they did not create and do not own the rights to. These days content that violates copyright laws, such as a video with a Beatles soundtrack or a Web page that features a professional photographer's photo, is quickly removed from sites like YouTube, Pinterest, or Google's image search. But those who routinely violate copyright law can still face prosecution.

According to the U.S. Copyright Office, "If a work is registered prior to infringement or within three months of publication, statutory damages will be available as an option for monetary relief, and the recovery for attorney's fees may be available."[2] But the work does not have to be registered for its owner to pursue an infringement case. Those who create content are always considered the owners of their work unless they sell the rights to someone else.

You may also find yourself on the other side of the issue, discovering that someone has published your content online without your permission. Specific sites and services (such as Google, YouTube, and Facebook) have their own policies for reporting copyright infringement. If you are not satisfied with how a particular company handles your complaint, you can elevate it to the Intellectual Property Unit of the Federal Bureau of Investigation (FBI) at https://www.fbi.gov/investigate/white-collar-crime/piracy-ip-theft.

Royalty-Free Material

Royalty-free material may cost you some money to use, but it is a lot less expensive than buying rights-managed work. The proliferation of blogs, independent websites, and online businesses has led to an explosion of available royalty-free images, video, music, and other material. One reliable source, Creative Commons (creativecommons.org), allows you to search for media across platforms including Google images, Flickr, Wikimedia Commons, YouTube, SoundCloud, and others. Keep in mind that Creative Commons is merely a search engine for these works. It neither owns the works themselves nor manages their rights.

Wikimedia Commons (commons.wikimedia.org), which is part of Wikipedia, offers a small but growing selection of images and, increasingly, video. They offer a decent selection of high-quality images from the U.S. government, including the military branches and the White House, that are in the public domain. Because these images were captured by U.S. government employees, they belong to the American people. That said, the U.S. government or foreign governments may limit publication outside the United States.

Video Blocks (videoblocks.com), Audio Blocks (audioblocks.com), and Graphic Stock (graphicstock.com) are a family of subscription services for creatives who need reliable royalty-free content on an ongoing basis. Subscribe for unlimited downloads of the content you want (although premium content requires an additional fee), and unlimited uses. Once you download a video, photo, or drawing, you can use it forever.

Liability Insurance

If you work for yourself, publishing a blog, running a website, or making videos, you may consider buying liability insurance. There are now several firms that sell liability insurance to individuals in all fields. AXIS PRO (http://www.axiscapital.com/en-us/insurance-site/us-site/professional-lines-site/axis-pro-site/Pages/multimedia.aspx) offers liability coverage to media professionals and others. You can get a group rate if you join a professional organization such as The Authors Guild (https://www.authorsguild.org/). Alternatively, if you are a homeowner, consider buying an umbrella insurance policy, which offers broad liability protections as an extension of your homeowner's insurance. Read more about these policies in Chapter 2. Or simply ask your insurance agent about them.

Do You Need an Attorney?

If you have no employees, and you are not facing litigation, you may want to wait before hiring an attorney. Once you do decide to hire employees, you are subject to labor laws, and it would be wise to consult a lawyer or keep one on retainer in case personnel issues arise. Employers are responsible for the safety and well-being of those who work for them while they are on the job. Yet if you follow current hiring trends, it is much more likely that those you hire will be independent contractors like yourself.

The Small Business Administration (SBA) suggests that individuals going into business for themselves can handle their own DBA filings, registrations for licenses or permits, taxes, and creation of an LLC or partnership. Unless you are forming a corporation, you should be able to file all the paperwork you need to start your business. While you can do both things yourself, you may want to hire an attorney if you are filing a patent or buying or selling a business.[3] Lawyers that specialize in these areas know the law better than you do. Hiring one can save you money and aggravation down the road.

For liability concerns, content publishers may be able to get free, *pro bono*, or inexpensive legal representation from the Online Media Legal Network at Harvard's Berkman Center for Internet and Society. The Online Media Legal Network (https://www.omln.org/) is a nonprofit that supports independent journalism. It calls itself a "referral service" for "qualifying online journalism ventures."[4] First Amendment lawyers volunteer their time and expertise because they believe in supporting a free press. This means you are more likely to qualify for their support if the work you do upholds journalism's charge to protect democratic ideals while exposing corruption and corporate, bureaucratic or political wrongs. You are less likely to win their support as a celebrity gossip blogger.

Notes

1 "Online Defamation Law." Electronic Frontier Foundation.
2 "U.S. Copyright Office—Stopping Copyright Infringement." *Copyright.Gov*. Accessed October 2, 2016. http://www.copyright.gov/help/faq/faq-infringement.html.
3 "When to Hire a Lawyer for Business Matters (and When to Do It Yourself)!" The U.S. Small Business Administration, *SBA.gov*.
4 "About Us: Overview," Online Media Legal Network. https://www.omln.org/aboutus

INDEX

Check out these other titles to help advance your career in broadcasting! Find these and more at Routledge.com.

The Entrepreneurial Journalist's Toolkit by Sara Kelly

The *Entrepreneurial Journalist's Toolkit* provides a solid foundation of multimedia journalism and also teaches readers to create solid business plans and develop funding proposals while maintaining high legal and ethical standards. This book details the process of pitching and working with clients, managing multi-platform communication campaigns to maximize reach, keeping the books, and filing taxes. It provides everything a new or experienced journalist needs to get started as a media entrepreneur.

Multimedia Foundations: Core Concepts for Digital Design, 2nd Edition, by Vic Costello

Understand the core concepts and skills of multimedia production and digital storytelling using text, graphics, photographs, sound, motion, and video. Then, put it all together using the skills that you have developed for effective project planning, collaboration, design, and production.

Presented in full color with hundreds of vibrant illustrations, *Multimedia Foundations*, Second Edition trains you in the principles and skill sets common to all forms of digital media production, enabling you to create successful, engaging content, no matter what tools you are using.

The second edition has been fully updated and features a new chapter on video production and new sections on user-centered design, digital cinema standards (2K, 4K, and 8K video), and DSLR and video camcorder recording formats and device settings.